The Fourteen Lives of Matt Perry

Word by word the book is made.

CHINESE PROVERB

authorHOUSE®

AuthorHouse™
1663 Liberty Drive, Suite 200
Bloomington, IN 47403
www.authorhouse.com
Phone: 1-800-839-8640

First published by AuthorHouse 01/02/2009

ISBN: 978-1-4389-4008-3 (hc)
ISBN: 978-1-4389-4007-6 (sc)

Printed in the United States of America
Bloomington, Indiana

This book is printed on acid-free paper.

All book proceeds will be divided equally among these nonprofit institutions:
Waynesburg University; Connecticut Rivers Council, Boy Scouts of America.; North
Carolina High School Studies Foundation; Rainbow Foundation SIHTASUTUS

This book is dedicated to all the women who touched my life in their special way: particularly my Mother Mary Pisacich who gave me my middle name Valentin, others include my sisters Anna and Katherine, sisters-in-law Judy and Eva, ex-wife Mary Ann---and most recently Nadezhda (Hope) in Estonia.

PREFACE

This book addresses the question, What was life really like for an American citizen born to parents from village Remetinec in Croatia?

More broadly, this is a family saga. About emigration and its aftermath.

Legal emigration but nevertheless the immigrant experience repeated millions of times since the founding of the United States of America. The secret of American strength.

And American vigor. Hybrid vigor.

And American resilience.

And modernity, USA-style.

The United States of America is an entity unlike any other.

Like honey, it attracts anything in the forest – especially bears.

Like a light, it attracts anything that flies – especially insects.

Like fish bait, it attracts anything that swims – especially fishes.

On a scale that has never been matched, anywhere in the world. Not in China. Not Russia. Not India. Not Australia. Not Great Britain. Not Germany. Not Brazil. Not Canada.

So how does this system, this juggernaut, actually work? Mate(Matt) Perry tells his version of the story from the inside out.

It is quite a story. Some of it is true.(That is for each reader to decide.)

Time to begin.

JOHN RIM

Who is John Rim?

That does not matter. Matt Perry does matter because he writes *his* story for you.(What he remembers.)

His recall is sufficient. He has prepared a read for you. Times thirteen.

This time , it's lucky.   JR

AUTHOR'S NOTE

My book began concurrently with the work of someone else: My brother Ed. Unknown to me, he was attempting a family genealogy.

He started with documents research and translation. Some family members were at first reluctant to get involved — for their own reasons. (There were a few skeletons in several closets, I suppose.)

Then came a family reunion in the summer of 2007 at Logan, Utah. Everything changed at once.

Immediately I began collecting data on the accomplishments of family members. The current generation had had been energized by my modest achievement — I had actually graduated from college, unlike any of my forbearers.

For reasons unknown, my image among close relatives was "the family detective." This was consistent with my fascination for research, strengthen by years in college.

In looking at my parents in retrospect, together with detailed self-examination, I found the seeds of a book which came to be called *Fourteen Lives*. The many lives of Matthew Valentin Perry interwoven with stories about brothers, sisters and other relatives and friends.

At last, help poured in.

My largest debt is to a friend, John Rim, who encouraged me throughout the project. He suggested research source materials, provided feedback to my questions, and edited the first draft. Quoting Franklin, "A father's treasure; a brother's a comfort; a friend is both."

Also: Annaliza Kelly for her typing and illustration assistances while a student at Wesleyan University.

Also: editorial assistances from Trish Patricia Comstock and Maggie Clancy, who provided many suggestions.

Also: Adam Eterovich for his exhaustive information and guidance on Croatian Heraldry, Croatian Heritage and Croatia History.

Also: Joel Blum and his wife Dorothy, and the Bates family, who believed in my approach.

Also: Harry Block and Raymond James who provided viewpoints and data.

Also Peter Perry (no relation) who gifted me with a genealogy program, computer expertise, and additional Croatian history.

Also: Tony Brancieri and Don Verchick for their continued computer expertise and guidance.

In the family, gratitude to sister Kate and brother Ed.

Also sister-in-law Judith and brother Bernard.

Also nephew Timothy and cousins Janet Czepiel, Fabijan and Krunoslev Pisacic and Robert Cindori.

Also Don Langenfeld and Phyllis Klaben.

All tried to echo that old Croatian slogan, "Work hard, play hard, and be merry!".

CONTENTS

INTRODUCTION

WOMEN

Even at early age, I, realized that women were treated as second-class citizens I constantly was on their side to gain full citizenship. I returned to the culture called *Old Europe* that was characterized by a dominance of a woman in our society because of their life-generating powers.

I felt that I was not a full citizen myself so I had empathy for them. I had a few disillusionments or disappointments with women – as I did with men – but always pushed for their corporate, political and social rights because I was motivated to fill that void that I felt I of not being bourgeois. They always became my best friends as you will see throughout the book.

PLANNING

Because of my analytical skills, some called me a visionary but said I failed to implement my many creative ideas. There could be a lesson in this sound assessment, but I failed to recognize this deficiency even though I had several chances. It could be that I was an observer rather than a leader.

LOYALTY

In some industries, client satification is very important. This is especially true in the financial industry. I always felt that my first loyality was to my clients which did not necessarily go well with some of my employers. They wanted commission dollars to offset their immediate expense rather than taking the Long -term perspective.I never wavered in my client-oriented philosophy.

I was loyal to other employers because they paid my salary and they placed their faith in my judgment but when a conflict of interest arose, I chose to leave the company rather than compromise my values. The loyalty to my company was steadfast because I knew that a satisfied client stayed with the company and that was good for business. Yet when a conflict of interest—greed—reared its ugly head, it was important for me to tell the truth even though it might not improve the bottom line.

GREED

In the financial industry I felt that there was too much greed---and because of that, some were not acting truthfully while I regarded truth as a value. Maximizing self interest is usually more prevalent in verbal discussions than in written dialog.

I always believed in stating the facts and views as best as I understood them to be . Of course, self deception is common place for the prospect of a financial killing. It is a lure that often colors judgment. Alan Greenspan noted in his Congressional testimony recently that he was "shocked" that markets did not work as anticipated. "I made a mistake in presuming that the self-interest of organizations, specifically banks and others, were such as that they were best capable of protecting their own shareholders and their equity in the firms." A very costly call.

HEALTH

I faced chronic stress and an overactive autonomic nervous system---influenced by constantly changing industries and-pressure.

Stress may have been aerobics for the mind, but the taxing challenges may have caused depression and some of the other health problems. This is, however, how I earned my living—less self destructive plus "self inflected" but endured for economic reasons. I might have been healthier if I had remained in my first career field---plastics---and practiced some of the stress management techniques in this book. Most people would have stay the course career wise and not change careers but I did not.

But then, I might not have written this book.

Like most authors, this book is written from my point of view and self interest. This allows me to live 14 times!. I apologize to any family member, friend, client, employer or foe that may differ from my perception. Hopefully our tale is a piece of family history to pass on knowledge and experience to future generations. This is the story behind Dad's family in America as the family knows it. It is easier to document a kingdom than a family. Some of it is based on hearsay. Memories are generally not perfect but there should be a core of truth. Mistakes happen even in the best of families.

I leave it to an upcoming writer in our next generation to fully trace and document our ancestry in Croatia. That which was bitter to endure may be sweet to remember. If we go back far enough, we may even find some noble blood in the family. That area of the world certainly is dynamic and full of history. The challenge is yours. This is the foundation.

Even in animals there exists the spirit of their sires. Latin proverb

This project started when my brother Ed was attempting to do a family genealogy. There was little family participation and cooperation. I was not aware of the amount of work he had put into the project until our family reunion in Logan, Utah, during the summer of 2007.

Granted our memory may have been at fault, but rarely our judgment.

Unaware that Ed had been working diligently to collect and translate official family documents that Dad and Mom saved, I started collecting data on accomplishment of the current generation of family members. I experienced some of the same difficulties as brother Ed. I had to live up to the reputation of family detective; i.e. if you wanted to find out something or find somebody, ask Matt. The lacunae also didn't stop me as I was accustomed to silent criticism when I tried to push my values, ideals, dreams and goals on other individuals. This is human nature.

I was most lucky to be the first to go to college in our family. Every family member after me received a college education. Most majored in science or engineering. Recently we had some graduate with some graduates with a liberal arts degree who are concerned for humanity rather than just a comfortable living. Future generations may also have enough compassion to help family members and neighbors here in the US as well as overseas. It is never too late to learn.

You are ushered in according to your dress; shown out according to your brains. Yiddish proverb

I apologize to any family member, friend, client, employer or foe that may differ from my perception. Hopefully our tale is a piece of family history to pass on knowledge and experience to future generations. This is a story behind Dad's family in America as the family knows it. It is easier to document a kingdom than a family. Some of it is based on hearsay. Memories are generally not perfect but there should be a core of truth. Mistakes happen even in the best of families.

Of course, there has been family strife (or-there have been family conflicts) but that proves that we're human. The important thing is not to hold a grudge. That is self defeating in the long run. I am very proud of being a Pisacich and how far the family has come. I'm sure we will continue to grow when we emphasize education, perseverance, integrity and humility over material things. We need to be good neighbors to all.

Great things cannot be bought for small sums. Latin proverb

My largest debt is to my friend, John Rim, who encouraged me throughout the project, suggested research sources, provided feedback on my questions and edited the first draft. Quoting Franklin... A father's a treasurer; a brother's a comfort; a friend is both. I am equally indebted to Trish Patricia Comstock who helped take my fragmented manuscript into the current form.

No road is long with good company. Turkish proverb

I am also indebted to Joel and Dorothy Blum and the Bates family who literally stayed with me as their financial advisor from the early 1980s even though I kept transferring firms. They believed in my approach to long-term equity investments and I believe we all gained by it. I don't think the brokerage firms liked it.

Harry Block gave me his positive viewpoints and insights on various financial service firms. Raymond James was helpful in providing performance data for me after I officially retired. Two are better than one.

On the technical side, I am indebted to my friend Peter Perry who wrote the Super 25 Program. He also maintained the program for a number of years and gifted me with a genealogy program. He later spent many hours entering and analyzing the data that went into the program and gave me Croatian history lessons from one CIA Fact Book. He, Tony Brancieri, and my bridge friend, Don Verchick, kept my computers running in spite of me and Microsoft.

I am very thankful for Brother Ed sharing his documents and interview tapes with me and for Sister Kate accepting my calls checking her memory. Nephew Timothy was gracious in sharing his European travel log with me. My cousin Janet Czepiel was more helpful than many relatives in collecting and editing the Tuk/Belinak Family data (I approached her late in the game.) She also had her son- in- law, Don Langenfeld translate some family documents. Don had his native -speaking friend check words in the older document that are no longer part of contemporary Croatian speech. Prior to 1991 independence, Serb expressions were common in the Zagreb area. — and German too.

I thank Phyllis Klaben, clients, my many bridge friends and relatives for understanding the absorption required for this work. I did try to play bridge when needed. I tried to echo the old Croatian slogan – work hard, play hard and be merry.

MATE(MATT) P.

CROATIA ALSO
KNOWN AS HORVATA

I was not able to track the Pisacic until around 1809 when Dad's grandfather was born. He was of peasant origin. Apparently the family name received two (2) coats of arms, one on September 28, 1628 from King Ferdinand II and the other one awarded by the Nobility Varazhdin Committee in 1760. The first one has a medieval pelican and then second one a goat. More discussion later.

"Pisac" in the Croatian language translates to "writer." Dad was a precise record- keeper, using a ledger. He recorded, filed and saved receipts for every expenditure he made from when he came to America till his untimely death in 1950. (The receipts were carefully filed in shoe boxes.) My initial business success may be attributed to writing even though I had a limited vocabulary and was a poor speller. Perseverance, analytical skills and excellent secretaries satisfied my supervisors, magazine publishers and professors in graduate school. Several in our next generation are competent writers.

Grandpa Pisacic and grandma Stujlan were born in Remetinec Village near the town of Varazdin, Croatia. The village of Remetinec has hills and more hills, reminiscent of San Francisco and the Bay peninsula in California. In addition to the local hills—suitable for growing grapes and making wine—this area has the occasional mountain, including Mount Zumberak, some wetlands and rivers, more than 200 waterfalls, and a sand dune, as well as oak forests and nesting storks and fish ponds.

The same tectonic force which created the Alps of Italy, Switzerland and France also gave Croatia its "little Alps," as I call them. These Dinaric Mountains separate much of the Dalmatian seashore from Zagreb and the rest of central Croatia – Rementic and Varazdin included.

The region around the village of Remetinec is known as *Hrvatsko Zagorje*. Nowadays "Hrvatsko" means "Croat." "Zagorje" means foothills. So Croat foothills (Sometimes translated Croat highlands.)

Varazdin is one of the most northern towns in Croatia, not far from Graz, Austria, and Budapest, Hungary. Prior to 1849, this "country" didn't mean much in Central Europe but during 1849-1867 it was part of the Austrian and Hungry Empire (not a nation state). Each had a "head of state" (the "Dual Monarchy") and enjoyed nearly complete internal autonomy. The two were linked into an "empire" by a complex web of intermarriages in and among the various branches of the Hapsburg dynasty. The borders between the states varied from time to time depending on who was married to whom at the moment. During most of the empire's existence, Austria was the dominant partner and the Austrian Emperor pretty much controlled external affairs.

1918—1929 Yugoslavia (Kingdom of the Serbs, Croats and Slovenes) After World War I, the "Kingdom of the Serbs, Croats and Slovenes" was formed "to unite all of the South Slavic people". This included Slovenia, Croatia, Bosnia and Herzegovina, Vojvodina and Dalmatia that had been on the losing side in the war, and Serbia, including Macedonia, and Montenegro that had not been on the losing side. Whether Montenegro "was brutally annexed" or "willingly joined" depends on who is telling the story. (1918-1929)

The idea of uniting all of the South Slavic people was one of those idealistic academic visions that completely ignored reality. The reality was that the Serbs and the Croats had been viciously brutalizing each other for centuries and both had been viciously brutalizing the various other ethnic minorities in the area— Slovenes, Muslins, Jews, etc.

From the start, this thing was dominated by Serbs who imposed a highly centralized government system controlled from Belgrade (Serbia) . This offended the Croats (and others) who had envisioned a decentralized federal system with a large degree of local autonomy.

1929-1941 Yugoslavia (Kingdom of Yugoslavia) This bumbled along until 1929 when the King, Alexander 1, seized power, abolished the government and established the Kingdom of Yugoslavia as an absolute monarchy. This was also dominated by Serbs. Alexander was assassinated in 1934. Peter 1 (age 3) succeeded to the throne. The regent was unable to sustain absolute power and things went downhill.

1941-1945 Croatia (Independent State of Croatia. An impending bloody break-up was averted in 1940-41 when the Nazis invaded forming an Independent State of Croatia (Nazi puppet state–Italian dominated to 1943, German thereafter). They established several "independent states" some dominated by Italy, some by Germany. Italy had already annexed much of the Adriatic coast in Slovenia and Dalmatia during the 1930's. The "legitimate" government of Yugoslavia including the King abdicated to London. They may still be there for all that anybody seems to know or care.

1945-1963 Yugoslavia (Federal Peoples Republic of Yugoslavia Marshall Tito in charge) .Communist partisans led by Josef Broz (Marshall Tito) harassed the occupiers throughout the war. When Italy was defeated in 1943, and Germany in 1945, Tito, supported by the Soviets, proclaimed and established the "Federal Peoples Republic of Yugoslavia". Although Tito was a Croat, and despite the name, this was a highly centralized, rigid dictatorship again based in Belgrade and dominated by Serbs.

Tito's break with Stalin in 1948 left him with a communist dictatorship but one not dominated by Soviet Russia. The result was substantial Western support. He made several major social improvements, especially in education and public health, and started a shift from the prevailing localized agrarian society to a European oriented industrial one. Underlying ethnic conflicts were controlled by violent repression.

1963-1991 Yugoslavia (Socialist Federal Republic of Yugoslavia) After Tito's death in 1980, he was replaced by an ineffectual committee that could not sustain power and things again went downhill. In 1990-91, Yugoslavia blew itself to pieces. Slovenia, Croatia, Bosnia and Herzogovina, and Macedonia declared their independence, leaving only Serbia and Montenegro. Open warfare and assorted atrocities ensued. All the new republics had substantial minority populations and "ethnic cleansing" became popular. Dead bodies and refuges proliferated. The UN (and USA) intervened and eventually got things more or less stabilized.

1991-present. Croatia (Republic of Croatia)—Serbia and Montenergo separated peacefully in 2006. Kosovo, a province of Serbia, has declared its independences but this is not recognized by Serbia. Responsibility for most of the high level villainy during the wars has been attributed to Serbia and several Serbian leaders have been or are being tried by international tribunals for "war crimes". Most of the republics are in the process of joining the European Economic Community.

Remetinec Village/Varazdin—The nearest city to Remetinec Village, a few miles to the north down is Varazdin, the economic and cultural center of the Zagorje and the Medimurje regions. This countryside city with its mountains is on the right bank of the Drava River and Varazdin Lake, and lies at the intersection of the main roads leading to the Slovenian and Hungarian borders, and railroad junctions Varazdin-Zagreb, Varazdin-Koprivnica, Varazdin-Cakovec. The town is 79 km (45 miles) north of Zagreb, the capital.

The chief occupations in the region of Varazdin include farming, viticulture and livestock breeding. There are numerous health spas in the area. A well known landmark is a linden tree more than 400 years old in the town of Gornja Stubica. This tree was the site of an assemblage, in the year 1573, to protest feudalism. The major manufacturing is textiles, artificial silk production, leather processing, wood and timber, metallurgy and the printing industry.

The 2001 census population for Remetinec was 1,539 and Varazdin, 41,434 . (Zagreb was 691,724.)The estimate for 2007 was the same for Remetinec and Varazdin but Zagreb increased to 702,000.

Several interesting things came from this area. A cavalry unit composed exclusively of Croats;. Called *Royal-Cravate*, it gave the world the name "cravate" in 1651. When you wear a tie, remember its Croatian origin.

There was also a noted Croatian engineer and inventor from this region: Slavoljub Eduard Penal (1871-1922). He is best known for his "automatic pencil" which was invented in 1906. His other 70 patents include the solid ink fountain pen (1907), first Croatian two-seated airplane (1909), hot water bottle, detergent, railcar brake, anode battery and a medical tonic called "Radium" to help cure rheumatism.

Lovro Pisacic, had five children by his wife: Janica (1884), Franjo (1887), twins (1888) Blaz and Pavao, Mato (1894), twins (1897) Franciska and Jurck. His wife Katrina Kuskadija died shortly after Mato (my Dad) was born, on September 18, 1894. Lovro never remarried, so Dad, being the youngest, was brought up without a mother's love. Lovro died in 1938.

Dad's brother Paul married into the Klara family. He had four children with his first wife, Anna: Lukas (1908), Matek, Mirko (1921) and Fabijan (1925). Lukas was a soldier in World War II. Nobody seems to know whether he died in combat or decided to stay in Germany. My Mom had an excellent relationship with Klara but quite strained with the second wife. At that time, when people died, they were not embalmed and they were buried that day or the next day. There was nobody to pronounce a person dead. Sister Katica always felt that Klara never died, but rather was buried alive -because Katica thought she heard Klara cry out when they were preparing her for burial.

The estrangement between my aunt and my Mom may have occurred when Dad was in the U.S. because Mom and her daughter Katica had separate sleeping quarters, traveled much, had fancy clothes and had a brick house built in the main part of the village that Mom rented out to a railroad man. This was done with the money that Dad sent to Mom when he immigrated to the U.S. in late 1923.

The maiden name of Grandma Stujlan is Katarina Puskadiza. Mom had one brother, Mirko, and two sisters by this Stujlan marriage. Mirko died in World War I. Her one sister's name was Jelon, (Helen). She married into the Cindori family. They had two children – a boy and a girl. The girl may have been named Katrina. Mom was born on October 15, 1898.

Grandpa Stujlan had two daughters, Frances and Madja, by his first marriage, so they were Mom's stepsisters.

Mom and Dad married in January of 1921 and lived in Grandpa Pisacic house until they left for the U.S. Weddings were always in January because they had to work the fields for food in the summer. The winters were generally snow-covered and harsh because of the high altitude, similar to the Austrian Alps.

Mom's mother didn't want Mom to marry Dad because he already had a girlfriend and he did not bring sufficient property to the family. The local custom was that the parents picked their daughter's husband with the determining factors being property and dowry. Mom overruled her mother's wishes, and married her mother's godchild (Mato Pisacic). Traditionally women played subservient roles in this country's mountainous regions. Mom was one of the first in her village and family to break down some traditional family patterns. She developed a more independent identity, which did not become general in Croatia until after World War II.

Dad and Mom had their own bedroom area on one side of Grandpa's house. The house was essentially a very large room with an eating table in the center. A large stone stove was on one side and sleeping bunks on the other two sides. The fourth side was the entrances to Mom's and Dad's quarters. Katica was born November 29, 1922.

After World War I, there was an epidemic of typhoid and rheumatic fever in this as there was all over Europe. Katica was treated in Varazdin for an infection of the ear. Mom took her there by cart hauled by the family cow. During this time, Mom was also sickly and was treated by physicians and health spas in Varazdin and

Zagreb. (Mom's cousin died at an early from typhoid fever.) Every care package that Dad sent Mom from the U.S. included hard candy for Sister Katica

The oldest women in the household cooked and watched the children while the other men and women worked the fields. The wives returned home to get cooked food for their men in the fields. Women would work their own fields by moonlight and rented their farm labor out for money to neighbors or church fields during the day. Clothes were washed on the river bank and banged against the rocks for thorough cleaning. Baskets of clothes were carried on heads to the river and back.

There was no outhouse.

The mattress was straw, and the covers (parani or feather tick) had duck or chicken feathers inside two sheets sewed together.

The family had a cow, pigs and chickens. Growing one's own food was the key to survival. The cow was not only used for milk and cheese, but also for plowing and transportation.

Grandpa also had a good-sized vineyard. This region is well known for its Varazdin wine. He would take Sister Katica to the vineyard to pick and eat the ripened grapes. They also had a pear tree but the household was forbidden to eat the pears because they were sold at the market for money. In West Mifflin, the family had a dwarf pear tree that produced extra large juicy pears.)

Mato Tuk, Dad's sponsor to the U.S., was more affluent and a more refined person who lived further up the hill from Dad, who was a cousin to Mato Tuk's wife, Ursula(Ann), who was a Pisacic before her marriage to Mato Tuk.

Mato Tuk had a white stallion. The area where Mato lived was called "the village of the Tuks." Wealth was judged by the number of animals owned and property size.

Mato Tuk sent for Ursula to come over to the U.S. four or five years after he arrived but the grandmother would not permit Mato and Ursula Tuk to bring their daughter, Katarina,(1916) to the U.S.

Ursula left for the US on the *Martha Washington* from Trieste on July 23, 1911 with three men friends and relatives from Remetinec. She was four feet, 11 inches tall, and had fair hair and eyes, according to the records at Ellis Island. She told them that she was going to meet her husband, Mato Tuk In Maynard, Ohio. Ursula gave birth to two daughters, Mary and Ann. She died of tuberculosis about one year after having her second child Ann at 30.

Mary Tuk Belinak, born January 23, 1913, and Ann Tuk Kaczmarek, born September 8, 1914, were daughters born in Belmont, Ohio to Mato and Ursula Tuk.

Mary had three children: June, born August 29, 1934, and died November 10 , 1960; Janet Catherine, born January 19, 1937; and Joseph Michael, born July 27, 1946.

Ann Tuk Kaczmarek had three children: Robert (1938), Richard (1942) and Edward (1948). Robert married Yvonne and they had Michael and Missy. Richard married Sharon and they had Andrew and Allison. Edward is not married.

A church is four walls and God within. French proverb

Life revolved around the church. At that time, the Roman Catholic Church was a highly organized religious community in Yugoslavia with multiple archbishoprics, bishoprics, parishes, monasteries, convents, theology schools, priests, monks and nuns. Mom, with no formal education was self-educated in finance and diplomacy while working in the local priest house by donating some of her time in lieu of tithe to the local parish.

Christmas and Easter were the two big holidays.

There were also church fairs and three-day pilgrim excursions to Ludbreg. When Dad was in the U.S., Mom and Katica would take the train rather than walk these excursions. This was a Eucharistic place of pilgrimage of the Sacred Blood of Christ and one of the few in the world which have been established by written document by the Pope, approving public veneration of the Holy Relic following the miraculous appearance of the Sacred Blood of Christ in the chapel of Bethany Castle in 1512.

Primary school for the boys was three to four years. There was no education for the women. Only the wealthy families sent their children to secondary schools. A 1958 Yugoslavia law lengthened the country's primary education sequence to eight years and made attendance compulsory for children from seven to fifteen years of age.

Dad left for America to better himself during the later part of 1923 on the ship *Antonia* and arrived in the US on January 15, 1924. His name was anglicized to Pisacich by the immigration authority. He was sponsored by Mato Tuk, a cousin, who came to the U.S. earlier to work in the coal mines in the Pittsburgh. area.

Dad briefly worked in the coal mines in Glen Robbins, OH but moved on to Duquesne PA to work at the new Carnegie steel mill.

On Christmas, they went to midnight mass. They would then have *struku* (cottage cheese strudel), blood putting, *laditina* (jellied pig feet and ear), rye bread, kielbasa and *zlevka* (traditional folk cake).

On November 29, Katica's seventh birthday, Mom and Katica left for France to immigrate to the U.S. on the *Berengaria*. The arrangements were made by a travel agency. Since it was winter time, the trip was rocky because of the many storms. Katica toured all decks of the ship, including first class, while Mom, as sick as she was, had to chaperone her. Because of existing U.S. laws, Katica, now anglicized to Katherine (Kate) ,was automatically a citizen and Mom entered the U.S. as her chaperone.

Both Mom and Kate were ecstatic with the size and beauty of Grand Central Station in New York where they embarked on a train for their new life in Duquesne PA. When Mom and Kate arrived in Duquesne, Dad was not there to meet them as he was cleaning the four- room apartment he had rented on Duquesne Avenue. The police tracked Dad down and delivered two exhausted travelers to their new home. They stayed in this four-room apartment for less than a year because of the high rent and no work. They moved across the track where other immigrants lived.

Quick Assimilation—some reasons why dad, his family and most croatians assimilated in America are:

They did not play Croatian politics. They were realistic and quickly worked into the American political system.

They believed that their ethinic retention could be maintained by their songs, food, sport history, culture and institutions.

They believed in the separation of the church and state.

THE BALKAN WARS AND WORLD WAR I AND AFTER (1914-1941)

Wars had dramatic consequences for the people in the area of Croatia where Dad and Mom were born. In the Balkan Wars, Serbia helped expel the Turks from Europe and regained lands lost in medieval times. By 1914 the alliances of Europe and the ethnic friction among the South Slavs had combined to make Bosnia the ignition point, and Serbia one of the main battlegrounds of World War I.

When Austria-Hungary collapsed after the war, the fear of expansionist Italy inspired Serbian, Croatian and Slovenian leaders to form a new federation, Yugoslavia. This new kingdom had to

1) repair war damage

2) repay debts

3) eradicate feudalism by passing land reform.

4) integrate differing custom areas, currencies, rail networks and banking systems.

5) make up for shortages of capital and skilled labor.

The agricultural sector, which employed over 75% of the Yugoslavia population, underwent radical reform that failed to relieve nagging rural poverty. The government did erase remnants of feudalism but the peasants received plots too small for efficient farming to support the rural population. Yields fell.

Poverty and ignorance dominated most of the peasantry. Mato Tuk and Dad decided to come to America. Mato Tuk did, however, plan to return to his homeland. World War I intervened.. He did not want to fight in the Austrian-Hungarian Army.

YUGOSLAVIA IN AND POST WORLD WAR II (1941-1991)

After the war many heroes present
themselves. Romanian proverb

The Axis invasion caused panic in Yugoslavia, as enemies apportioned this rugged mountainous country in which three mountainous regions accounted for about 60% of the territory. Bloody encounters involved both invading and domestic forces throughout the four years of war.

The Communist-led partisans (led by Josip Broz Tito,) using the formal name of People's Liberation Army and Partisan Detachments, rose from near oblivion to dominate the country's resistance movement against the Croatian fascist group *Ustasa*, supporter of the prewar government. The pro-Nazi practices of this fascist group caused animosities that lasted long after the war.

Mato Tuk knew Tito. He was a son of the village butcher who, as a boy, delivered his Dad's meat. Mato Tuk was quite surprised when Tito became head of Yugoslavia.

The Yugoslav communist, Tito, was faithful to orthodox Stalinism until the 1948 split with Moscow. The subsequent Moscow-led economic blockade compelled Yugoslavs to devise an economic system based on Socialist self-management.

After Tito's death in 1980, long standing differences again separated the communist parties of the country's republics and provinces. Economic turmoil and the re-emergence of an old conflict between the Serbs and an ethnic- Albania majority in Kosovo exacerbated these differences, fueled resurgences of nationalism, and paralyzed the country's political decision-making mechanism. Even the winner of a war suffers from lack of bread.

The Yugoslav government invested heavily in rebuilding the national education system. Agrarian reform appropriated church land, Catholic schools were closed. Formal religious instruction was discouraged. Between 1945 and 1952, many priests were shot or imprisoned in retribution for supposed wartime atrocities.

By education, people differ widely different. In 1953, 15% of the active nonagricultural population had not finished four grades of elementary school and 64% had not completed eight grades. The government built new schools, libraries and other facilities. The qualifications of the teaching cadres were enhanced. Bend the willow while it is young.

A 1958 education law lengthened the country's primary education sequence to eight years and made attendance compulsory for children from seven to fifteen years of age. Between 1945 and 1981, elementary school enrollment rose from 40 to 99% between ages seven and ten and 93% of those between eleven and fourteen were in school. Student-teacher ratios fell from 59:1 to 20:1.

By 1989, the majority of the teachers in primary and secondary schools held university degrees. The schools began employing a variety of teacher aides , librarians, media specialists, medical personnel, special-education instructors, vocational-training specialists and computer programmers.

It should be noted that in 1966 Yugoslavia and the Vatican signed a protocol in which Belgrade pledged to recognize freedom of conscience and Roman Catholic jurisdiction over ecclesiastical matters for Yugoslav Catholics. In return, the Vatican agreed to honor the separation of church and state in Yugoslavia, including prohibition of political activity by the clergy.

We are all born equal and distinguished
only by virtue. Latin proverb

Since World War II, women in Yugoslavia have won civil and political rights. They gained access to education, employment, social welfare programs, health care and political office. Although women became better educated and increasingly employed, they did not generally win full equality in the job market or advancement to high social and political positions.

After 1945, the Yugoslavia's Communist regime snuffed out any magnification of Croatian nationalism denouncing advocates of Croatian national interest. In the 1970s and 1980s, Croatia remained the second most prosperous Yugoslav republic. National aspirations reached a new peak in the early 1970s. The possibility of federation caused Tito to crack down on the Croat nationals in 1972.

In 1990 the victory of Franjo Tudjman's anti-communist Croatian Democratic Union in the parliamentary election brought a new rush of Croatian nationalism. They campaigned to distinguish themselves with a separate language and the language was reformed to a more exact, true Croatian. In every -day speech, especially in mixed and border areas, Serb expressions still find their way into the spoken language. German words and expressions are still in common use among natives of Zagreb. German has long been the second language of the country, and most people understand it quite well.

New Slavic-root words were introduced to replace words borrowed from foreign languages, Croatian national symbols reappeared. In October 1989, a statue of revolutionary patriot Josip Jelacic was restored to Zagreb's central square, 42 years after its removal by Communist authorities.

This small and oddly-shaped country looking somewhat like a boomerang or the crescent moon consists of six areas.

The north-east part of Croatia is the land of the Pannonia plains which were the floor of a huge inland sea 40 million years ago. Sedimentary and windblown deposits have created layers of fertile soil that are over 400 feet deep in some places. This is prime farm land.

The central part contains hills and a few mountains which separate the fertile plain from a narrow, rocky Adriatic coastline and the big bay and the massive mountain range to the south and Istria in the southwest.

15

The Varazdin region is the area where Dad and Mom were born. The first written reference to Varazdin was in 1181 when King Bela mentioned the nearby thermal springs. Among the most interesting examples of natural environment show-pieces are the protected forest-parks of Trakoscan and the Drava River. The caves at Donja Voka, Vindija and Mackova Spilja, are major sites of geological and anthropological interest.

Gaveznica-Kameni Vrh is a fossil volcano where semi-precious stone may be found. The Opeka Arboretum, a protected horticultural site, is one of the nature reserves in central Europe. The species inventory comprises approximately 14,000 plants of nearly 200 different species.

The River Drava includes artificial lakes, sandbanks and canals. A fisherman's paradise!

Ivanscica Mountain, with a summit at 1061 meters, topped with an iron pyramid, is a marvelous spot to view the hills of Zagorje, Sljeme, the Slovenian Alps in the distance, and the Pannonian Plains all the way to Hungary.

Along the convoluted shores of the Mediterranean with its many islands is one of the most beautiful bays in the Adriatic. From this coast, access to Zagreb is possible through four mountain passes.

> *Seldom are men blessed with good fortune and*
> *good sense at the same time.* Latin proverb

This Big Bay area of Croatia is the homeland of Marco Polo. The Marco Polo family lived in Korcula from the 13th century almost to this day.

Marko, his father Nicolo and Uncle Matteo set off from Venice, Italy and reached the capital of China, Khanbalik, in 1275 after a four-year journey. They traveled to different regions of China in the service of Kublai Khan.

On his return, Marko wrote about his encounter with this highly developed Chinese culture: the beauty of their towns, their customs and relations, about 'true wonders' and about religious tolerance. Marko introduced a new way of thinking and inspired future explorers. He had a tremendous influence on the course of new discoveries. His drawings are accompanied by his geographical, historical, economic, ethnological and personal comments.. *Travels of Marco Polo* was the impulse which led to the discovery of America, according to H.C. Wells' *History of the World.*

CROATIAN HERALDING

*You may suppress natural propensities by force,
but they will be certain to reappear.* Horace

BACKGROUND

Heraldry first appeared in the middle of the 12th century. It sprang from devices, boldly painted in bright colors, which the French knights bore on their shields to identify themselves in tournaments and battle. Later these arms were carved, painted or enameled as crests, on surcoats, tombs, windows, churches, houses or wherever the owner or patron desired decoration.

INHERITANCE of TITLE

An individual coat of arms belongs to one man only, being passed from him to his male-line descendants (No coat of arms for a surname.) If a person marries somebody with a title, they can utilize it but only under the married name.

The Old Croatian Hereditary Nobility titles were: Knezova—Princes, and Velikasa—High Nobility. There was a union of Hungary with the Twelve Croatian Clans (presumably descendants of the original tribes that had taken possession of the country in the sixth or seventh centuries). Croatia had no male heir so it was with the head families of these clans that the Hungarian king entered into discussions as to the terms on which he was to ascend the throne of the Trpimirovici. By 1102 all acquiesced, recognizing Koloman as their sovereign. The agreement was that the Croatian nation would retain full possession of Croatian territory and national property; more particularly the twelve noble families :Kacic, Svacic, Subic, Kukara, Gusic, Cudomiric, Mogoric, or (Muric), Karinjani-Lapcani, Polecic, Lacnicic, Jamometic or (Jamonstic), and Tugomiric or (Tudomiric).

During mid winter of 1249, the Mongols successfully rode across the frozen Danube River. The Hungarian king ennobled the entire community of Turopolje near Zagreb but had to flee for the coast. Zagreb was largely destroyed.

A certain number of plemina (clans) and bratsva (brother-hoods) remained free. They were free communities which operated under the general aegis of the lords of the surrounding territories. Sometimes these communities acquired titles of group nobility, Plemenite opcine. Often, too, they has serfs of their own. They were successful in conserving their privileges until 1848.

During the Habsburg-Austrian Period (1527-1740) the titles increased to five (5):

1. Knez—Prince; 2. Grof—Count; 3. Barun—Baron; 4. Vitez—Knight and 5. Plemic—Nobleman.

The Austrian emperor continued to grant titles for faithful and loyal services to him until the end of World War 1 when Croatia ceased to be under Austrian control.

From 1636 until 1753, Austrian Military (Nobilitationen) grants were issued bestowing certain rights of nobility in return for special military service such as thirty years of service or valor in the face of the enemy.

TRANSFER OF TITLE

An individual coat of arms belongs to one man only. There is no coat of arms for a surname. It is a legal possession, as hereditary as any other piece of property in accordance with certain laws of inheritance.

The sons in each generation inherit the paternal shield but alter it slightly in a tradition known as cadency with the addition of some mark which is perpetuated in their branch of the family. The eldest son maintains the original coat of arms upon his father's death.

When families merge through marriage, they also merge or combine (marshalling) their respective coat of arms.

Women have always been able to inherit arms from their father and to receive grants of coats of arms. However, they can only pass these inherited arms on to their children if they have no brothers. When married, a women could bear the shield of her husband upon which her arms are marshaled. It could not be extended to their prior name or other family members. Only holders of the actual name could carry or derive any benefit from the title— whatever that benefit might be , mostly prestige, which means a whole lot in semi-feudal/hierarchical societies. A title also offers access to contacts with higher social levels, great land-owners and church officials.

SYMBOLIC MEANING

It is generally impossible to accurately decipher the meaning of the symbolism on any personal coat of arms. If there was a specific meaning to the symbol to those that were issued hundreds of years ago, they are probably lost in history. Medieval men were fond of legends attributing peculiar behavior to animals and relating those examples of behavior to human virtues or vices. Much of the symbolic meanings were obtained from Marija Gimbutas book *The Language of the Goddess,* Thames and Hudson

Nevertheless, the following are generic symbolic meanings for the two coats of arms that were issued to our descendants. The first one, 9/28/1628 was issued by King Ferdinand of Austria to Peter Pisacic and also brothers Matthew and Stephen. They were from the Zagoria area (village outside of Zagreb).second coat of arms was awarded to Ivan John Pisacic by the Varazhdin Committee in 1760. A copy is in the Croatian archives in Varazhdin.

Boar: Bravery; fight to the death. Symbol of death and regeneration.

Claw: The biter bitten. Pars pro toto of the Goddess of Death and Regeneration.

Dragon: Valiant defender of treasure; valor and protection

Goat: Political ability. Stimulator of awakening nature, guardian of young life, portrayed flanking the life tree.

Lion: Dauntless courage; often represents a person or group of people

Pelican: Self-sacrifice and charitable nature (based on the myth that in times of famine a female pelican will nourish her young by piercing her breast having them feed on her blood. Waterfowl birds bring happiness, wealth, nourishment.

Ram: Authority. Magic, wealth-bringing animal, sacred to the Bird Goddess, associated with water fowl and the snake.

Rock: Safety and protection; refuge

Gold/Yellow (bezant): generosity and elevation of mind

White/silver: peace and sincerity. The color of bone, symbolic of death.

Green (vert): hope and joy

Blue (azure): loyalty and truth

Red (gules): martial fortitude and magnanimity. Color of life.

Purple (purpure): royalty and justice

Sword: Justice and military honor

I leave it to the younger generation of family members to determine if they are direct descendents of a reputable noble family.

CROATIAN AGRICULTURE IN WEST MIFFLIN

Be it ever so humble, there's no place like home. Payne

Dad purchased several lots of land in West Mifflin PA in 1936. The hilly topography was similar to Croatia's village of Remetinec. It was surrounded by towns that were once part of Mifflin Township: Duquesne, Munhall, Whitaker, Dravosburg, Jefferson Hills, Lincoln Place (Pittsburgh), Hays (Pittsburgh), Pleasant Hills and Baldwin Borough.

Father Mato had a two-family house built on this land in the middle of the Great Depression. Dad constantly put on additions so he could collect more rent during the housing shortage. He built a second house himself, adjacent to the big house. There was room for another house to be built on this U-shaped lot.

He raised a cow, later two; four pigs; a hundred plus chickens; twenty-five turkeys and ducks. Turkeys had to be raised on an elevated wire floor because they are prone to disease. Ducks waste had a bad smell as did pig waste. Animal husbandry was not easy.

To feed the animals, Dad cut and gathered the hay by hand. The hay was also used for animal flooring. Dad purchased commercial feed, and some hay when the winter was long.

Bernard, Ed and I watched our cows in the fields. Sometimes the cows would come home on their own when we were sidetracked by activities like swimming. The cows could be miles away but they would hear my mother call them to come home to be fed and milked.

The cows wanted to eat greens in people's gardens during the hot and dry summer. Dad would have to pay between $5 and $10 in garden-damage fines each time the cows wandered into a neighbor's garden. We believed the garden owner invited the cows in, to collect the fine. We were told by the "feed man" that Dad did not care about the economics of maintaining the animals but it kept Mom and the children busy.

Another memory is the hay stack of winter feed and flooring for animals. The stack was 30 feet in diameter and 25 feet high. All the sweat work from Dad, Mom and me – cutting, drying, gathering and delivery – went up in the air with the strike of a match. My next door neighbor, Eddie, who was four years my senior, wanted excitement so he decided to light a match to the hay and put it out immediately! He did it once with no adverse consequences but the second time there was a tremendous updraft. This created a fire that was visible for miles. It took hours for the volunteer firemen to put out the fire. Several firemen went on top of the stack to pitch- fork the hay so that the water would put out the fire.

Dad tried to in vain to get the father of Eddie Gross to compensate our family for the loss. Mr. Gross refused though he had a good position with U.S. Steel Corporation and was a church elder. We were "hunkies" and our animals polluted the air. After the fire, Dad built a huge storage bin for hay. The recycled steel came from US Steel.

After some fifteen years, I happened to be home with Mother when Eddie Gross rang our doorbell. He had moved, and was now a minister. The haystack episode bothered him greatly for years. So he decided to get it off his chest. Fate had it that the day he elected to travel 25 miles to apologize I was visiting Mom. He might have lied to his father that it bothered him so.

I raised and bred racing and fancy pigeons as well as rabbits as a hobby and small business. (My first challenge in trading and negotiation was interesting Dad.) The twelve rabbits I kept at a time were each in a 2'x2'x4' pen. The rabbits that I did not trade or sell were killed for meat. They reproduced rapidly.

I had a harder time to convincing Dad that I could raise pigeons. I started with a few, in a coop on top of the railroad tie poles that fenced in the chickens, turkeys and ducks. I built another coop on an adjacent pole and connected the two by a 3"x3"x3' wire walkway.

Dad used every bit of his property to produce food as he did in Varazdin. He was a Calvinist in action. Our front lawn consisted of garden patches of lettuce, carrot, parsley and tomato plants. The rear garden came up to the houses. Dad also liked to build cellars for food storage.

A thing of beauty is a joy forever. Keats

When Dad died, I wanted to change the landscape almost immediately. My brothers and I put a lawn in front of the house. We put in badminton and croquette courts and built a large outdoor grill in the back. This was hard work as we had to level the hill for the courts.

I was in college. I sent landscaping instructions and diagrams to my two younger brothers Bernie and Ed about what to plant and where. My goal was to have something in bloom or in color always, even in winter. First they had to pick up the plantings at the Railroad Express station in the next town (McKeesport) and carry them home on the bus. No wonder they never forgave me for this! I paid for the plants because Mom had two young sons and a slow daughter to care for.

We got rid of all the animals including the cow Sally which was like a pet. W e tore down the barn (that was built to last several life-times) and hay storage bin. And animal pens. The neighbors were happy. The borough was growing. Our hill was becoming populated. We now had immediate neighbors on both sides of our houses.

As for the big piece of real estate across the street from us, it was divided into small lots. As a result, one large stone house (originally built during the Revolutionary and expanded during the Civil war) ended on a very small plot of land. The house had a long history but now it stood alone.

Shortly thereafter, much of our back- yard-area was seriously damaged when the borough government put a sewer line across our property. The contractor agreed to pay for us but nothing happened. (The contractor went bankrupt.) Despite all the changes, the plantings continued to beautify the homes until sold years later.

Mom had a series of heart attacks and strokes. We then sold the large house, keeping only the back-yard property to reduce Mom's worry. We kept the small house. To reduce Sister Katherine's responsibility, the family elected to give the property away after Mom died in 1978. Sister Anna could not live in the house alone and we three sons expressed no interest in maintaining the family homestead.

Music is the best cure for a sorrowing mind. Latin proverb

MUSICIANSHIP AND PERFORMING ARTS

Father Mato very much enjoyed attending the various Slavic concerts and dances at Kennywood and West View Park. He enjoyed the guitars and banjos of the Pittsburgh Tamburitzans very much. My brothers and I listened to the Saturday afternoon opera when we were free from work. All of us enjoyed The Lux Radio Theatre programs. When we listened to programs like "The Lone Ranger" or "Jack Armstrong" we had our finger on the volume control, and we would turn the volume down so Dad would not hear the shooting.

About 1942, I convinced Father Mato to buy me a cornet from the Sears catalog for about $50. I took private lessons from the McKeesport band director. I didn't accomplish much with the horn but I did have a four- piece band in 8th grade.

Bernard started practicing with my cornet. Soon afterwards, I bought him a Martin orchestra trumpet for $200. Unfortunately his music teacher, Mr. Kale Lasoffy, thought that a heavy-duty Conn-brand marching-band trumpet was better so he had Bernie exchange the Martin for a heavy Conn. That killed the tone quality, my investment and Bernard's enthusiasm. After that, Bernie became more interested in sports instead.

Music does not fill the stomach. French proverb

Richard Gorscak, my nephew, started out with Bernard's trumpet, followed by a trombone and then the baritone. Mr. Lasoffy was also Richard's teacher. Later the instructor was Matthew Skiner at Duquesne University. Richard became a virtuoso with the baritone. He appeared on Ted Mack's amateur hour – unusual for a solo -brass instrument player. He didn't win because we did not know enough to have his friends, neighbors, and relatives' mail in cards to vote for him.

My nephew Donald, Richard's brother, also played the trumpet with Mr. Lasoffy as the instructor. He had his own dance band while at college. His younger brother Dennis and his sister played the clarinet for a while.

My nephew Kevin Pisacich (Bernard's son), played the trumpet and trombone. His sister Karen played the flute. One brother David, played the drums, and his other brother, Timothy, played the piano.

Jason Gorscak, son of my nephew Richard became the first accomplished piano player in the family.

My brother Ed's wife was interested in classical music at an early age.

With a few exceptions, instrument players seem to cluster toward the science and technology fields. It will be interesting to see what the next generation will produce.

MILITARY TRAINING & SERVICE

If the fence is secure the dogs will not enter. Chinese proverb

Mom's brother Fabijan was killed during the First World War while in the Austrian Army. Dad was also in that same Army.

Steve Gorscak, my brother-in-law, joined the US Navy on September 10, 1942, and returned to civilian life on December 31, 1945. He served as Fireman First Class on the *USS St Louis*. When his mother became very sick emotionally because she had four sons on the front line, Steve, her favorite son, was reassigned to the *Delta Queen* ferry in San Francisco.

I enlisted in the Navy Officer Candidate School (OCS) Program but was discharged for medical reasons.

Bernard served three months in the Navy Reserve for basic training. I believe he would have enjoyed the Service very much because he loved the discipline and physical training of military life. He enlisted under a law (enacted by Congress) during the Korean War that one could join the Navy Reserve, get three months of basic training, and be on call for a lifetime.

Stanley Czepiel was drafted into the US Army during the Korean War.

LEAVING THE NEST

Greater things are believed of those who are absent. Tacitus

Father Mato arrived in America on January 15, 1924, - leaving his father, wife and daughter three years after his wedding—on the *Astonia* sailing from France. He was 29 years old. Daughter Katica was less than two years old. He was sponsored by a Croatian neighbor and cousin, Matt Tuck (Mary Belinak's father). Father Mato spent ten months in Glen Robbins, Ohio, as a coal miner.

Dad upgraded the family to clean and rural living in 1936 by buying land from the Oliver Family in West Mifflin, PA – a mile-and –a- half from his new work- place. Dad had recovered some of the money he lost with Mellon National Bank in the Duquesne Bank closure.

As was the custom in Croatia, Mom joined the Pisacic family household when she married Dad on January 29, 1921. She left the Pisacic family in Croatia to join Dad in America on January 29, 1929. (Eight months before the Wall Street crash that triggered the Great Depression.)   .

Sister Kate and her husband Steve moved out of their small but comfortable but small apartment one year after they were married in (May, 1947) even though there was a housing shortage in West Mifflin and she was pregnant with Richard.

I left for NYC in 1954 after college and a brief stay in the Navy. I forfeited my college graduation gift of a new Pontiac because moved away from Pittsburgh.

I borrowed money from my sister's friend Johann — to buy a new Crestline Ford when I moved east from my sister's friend, Johann, and Frank Koncoli in NYC. I stayed with Frank Koncoli and wife (and children) several weeks until I got situated.

My career involved many moves.   Elizabeth, NJ; Rego Park, NY; Jackson Height, NY; Ardsley, NY; Bronxville, NY; Appleton, WI; Lancaster, PA;. Dayton, OH; Cleveland, OH; Des Plaines, IL;. West Mifflin, PA; Enfield, CT;. Beaver Falls, NY; New Haven, CT; New Canaan, CT; Mystic, CT; and Cromwell, CT.

Brother Bernard was not subsidized by Mom when leaving Pittsburgh to attend college in New Jersey and living with me. Bernie refused to take money in his last year of college when Mom offered it.   After graduation he took a job with Charles Pfizer Company in Brooklyn, NY. . After a few years in Brooklyn, he requested a transfer to Connecticut where he remained until retiring in 1997.

Brother Edward, the youngest sibling, stayed in Pittsburgh for college so he could take care of our Mom and sister. Mother's friends Jennie Budinak, Agnes Grasso, and Mrs. Schwartz from the Old Country had some sons who remained single and took take care of elderly parents and unmarried daughters.

Both Mom and Sister Anna would often speak of the Budinak-Grasso-Schwartz precedent. After Edward graduated from college, Mom was very upset that Edward did not take a job offer in Pittsburgh. He compromised with her by coming home most weekends even though he traveled much for GE's Aerospace Division. Mom and Sister Anna were again upset when he started dating a girl in Pittsfield MA. They did not want him to leave the nest. They were both home-makers and dreamed of taking care of three "boys" forever. They also wanted "social security." from the boys. They both sacrificed for the boys all their lives – this was their in-house retirement plan. This was normal and the customary in the Old Country.

Brother-in-law Steven Gorscak tried moving to NJ with me for a short time when work was scarce in the Pittsburgh area. He became homesick for the family, lacked self- confidence and returned to West Mifflin.

Steve's son Richard was a bit homesick during his first year at Wabash College in Indiana. He almost quit school. Uncle Ed happened to stop by at this critical time. Richard soon had additional experience living away from home, working at Bell & Howell in Chicago during the summer.

ENTREPENEURSHIP & FREE ENTERPRISE

*Drive thy business, let not that drive
thee.* Benjamin Franklin

FATHER MATO

Father Mato had his wife build a home in Croatia with the money he earned while working as a laborer in the US. Even though Mato lost most of his US savings during the 1929 crash, he hired an unemployed carpenter to build a two- family's home in West Mifflin PA. It was completed in 1936. He also rented the top half of the house to help pay the bills.

Even with a building material shortage during the war, Dad elected to build a smaller second house adjacent to the "big" house. He also made additions to the big house. (A good relationship with Levine Hardware helped him obtain scarce building materials.)

During the fall of 1950, father Mato fell and died while repairing a second- floor window in the big house.. I deliberately avoided helping him by exercising poor safety practices. To this day, I regret this decision but then I might not have learned my other skills.

MATT PERRY

I exhibited the same entrepreneurship at an   early age by selling newspapers, eggs and milk. Also trading, breeding and selling rabbits and racing pigeons,. Business makes men.

JAPANESE LICENSING AGREEMENT

God looks at the clean hands, not the full ones. Publius Syrus

In 1962, a group of commercial development specialists from Lucidol had an opportunity to obtain an exclusive licensing agreement from a Japanese plastic- additive manufacturer. The group dispersed because I wanted our research director, Dr. Jim Harrison, to join the group to balance the marketing expertise. Later the commercial development manager Richard Berry, and his boss, the Research Director both succeeded in starting their own separate business. My outside consultant, Hans Stauffer of Stauffer Chemical, told me that we should have done the Japanese deal regardless and sold our interest later. This would have been an excellent chance to do business with others people's money.

CONTEMPO COSMETICS, LTD

When two ride the same horse one must ride behind. English

Since we were doing a tremendous job for DeSoto Chemical Corporation and Sears Roebuck, a group of middle management employees from DeSoto formed a task force in 1966 to find a business for ourselves, suited to our background.

Initially we considered several industrial processes but finally picked cosmetics because of its high gross margin; and because my wife had sales and laboratory experience in that industry.

We were a week or so too late to purchase a local one- product perfumery.

I then made successful contacts with Mary Quant in England who had just introduced a new mini skirt line of products. I wanted my wife to run the firm. I acquired United States- and Canada -licensing agreement with an international cosmetic firm in England: Gala Cosmetics, Ltd.

I negotiated 120-day credit terms on imports so our need for capital was minimal, provided we air- freighted the cosmetics to the US and obtained a good turnover rate.

My initial plan was to act as a consultant to Contempo and stay employed with DeSoto Chemical Corporation, the Sears subsidiary. The other team members pulled out because they needed the many Sears benefits for their families.

The business went defunct in 1971 because of the economic recession that started in 1969. The department stores had no money to buy the merchandise so the highly- capitalized cosmetic firms were giving the stores six months credit and a 2% cash payment on top of that.

Never before was cosmetics sales hit by a recession. Sales increased because women wanted to look great to offset their depression. This tine, however, most women did not wear bras, wore colorful clothes, and had a disarming openness.

This phenomenon was called the feminist revolution.

The baby- boom generation of women no longer accepted my marketing cliché "use our cosmetics to look natural." This was a peak of rebellious times.

Women asked themselves "Why should we buy cosmetics to look natural?" They decided to practice frugality. Many cosmetics lines went under. (Zsa Zsa Gabor's was the first to go.)

We also had marital problems since I really could not cope with all that disarming sexual openness. Now sex wasn't just for reproduction but was also for meditation and ecstasy.

I was too under-capitalized to try to blister-pack our products for the changing shopping culture and lifestyle. We needed to be in discount stores (like Kmart, Walmart did not exists)) as well as the drug store chains where sales expenses were lower. At the end, I interested the Marshall Fields department store in a revolutionary marketing concept but it was too late.

I probably should have taken the six-figure unsecured loan that Northern Boulevard Bank was offering us when we first incorporated but I didn't want to pay interest on money until I needed it. When I needed it, the banks were not there.

Maybe I should also have cut our product line in half and concentrated on our unique products like:

1. Our mascara which was approved by the Eye Research Foundation for contact lens users

2. Our facial make-up which would not change colors on black women because of their ph and

3. Our nail hardener and polish which was by far the best. Before we came along, Revlon and Almay had the best nail products.

I finally decided to throw in the towel in 1970. Why?

1. No income for several years because we did not take a salary.

2. High living and clothing expense.

3. Our marriage was deteriorating.

I had free access to Sears' counsel as a courtesy for being an ex-employee. The counselor suggested we declare bankruptcy and pay ourselves back salary rather than the corporate debt. I refused to file for bankruptcy against the advice of this counsel. Now I feel that maybe he was right.

OTHER MATT PERRY VENTURES: POLYMERS, OIL, REAL ESTATE, ETC

Smooth talk covereth many faults. English proverb

THE CROSS- LINKED POLYMER PROJECT

Several other venture ideas crossed my desk during the early 70s but I lost much of my creative spark until I met Dr. Irving Muskat, chemistry professor and dean at the University of Miami. Dr. Muskat formed the C-J Corporation. He obtained a patent for cross-linking a thermoplastic polymer which could have wide application in the transportation industry.

He knew United States Attorney General John Newton Mitchell who had contacts with the US patent department chief a Mr. White. Nobody questioned the patent but it was similar to a Japanese patent issued six months earlier. The patent was signed by the patent chief himself.

Dr. Muskat had no pilot facility to produce the several million pound-orders I developed. I received orders not because ours was a superior product but because competitive products were priced to the moon. Why? Price manipulation of styrene.

Later, as a consultant for Debell & Richardson in CT, I did a pilot study for Gulf Oil Corporation about price manipulation of styrene.

Dr. Muskat was still trying to improve the products cross-linking capabilities at the time of his death.

OIL AND REAL ESTATE PARTNERSHIPS (1980-1981)

Between wrangling and disputing truth
is lost. American proverb

While at Shearson (New Haven) I was asked by the president of a fertilizer manufacturer to find a partner and write up a private partnership for him. (He asked again the following year.) Permission was granted by Shearson as long as they shared in the commissions. They did no due diligences on either project.

The first project was oil drilling in the Denver area. Everything was in place, including finance with a Canadian bank before the client's attorney and I flew to Denver for the signing a day after Christmas. At dinner and after a drink or so, my client wanted to re-open the negotiations. He thought he was in the driver's seat because everything had to be signed by December 31st to capture the 1980 tax benefits. Dinner was a failure. Each group went to their suite. I tried to act as messenger and mediator. Finally the general partner said that he would meet my client for breakfast. We did but they told us that they now had their own bank financing and they were going to do the total deal without limited partners. I returned empty- handed and lost time and money. My client was in luck as the bottom fell out of the oil market.

The next year I found a nice piece of real estate in Jersey City, New Jersey. The company president over negotiated again and the

General Partner did the deal by himself. The company president really lost on this one as real estate skyrocketed.

A few years later this tax attorney and this president were indicted and jailed for tax evasion.

> *We are slow to believe that which, if true, would grieve us.* Ovid

METAL INVESTMENTS PARTNERSHIP

Deeds not words are required. Latin proverb

In 1985, an investment partnership under the name of Metal Investments was formed between John Richards an ex -GE employee, Robert Breitbarth , retired president of a cable company: Howard Runda, an ex Baker McKenzie consultant and me. The objective was to set up a rod-and wire -mill for the production of specialty copper alloys such as beryllium copper. Using conventional or new processes such as a casting process under license from General Electric Corporation or a process developed by John Richards or a combination thereof.

We gave Richards 70% of the company for his expertise and labor. The partnership was terminated by Howard Runda and I when I found out that Richard had very bad credit problems with his family. Bob Breitbarth stayed with him for awhile but eventually pulled out. Richard was a tremendous sales person. He missed his calling.

EMBRYO FOR A FINANCIAL MANAGEMENT GROUP

Better be too credulous than too skeptical. Chinese proverb

I was surprised recently to find outline notes for the formation of a financial management group!

Among the people invited were:

- a graduate school professor who was founder of a successful money management group at Harvard. Earlier, he was treasurer of a small specialty paper company in West Springfield MA.

- a retired CEO of GE's venture capital group who was my client and friend.

- an international consultant for Boise Cascade.

- a Yale business professor who was founder and CEO of a specialty insurance company.

This turned out to be the meeting which never met!

> *An intelligent man needs but few words; a good drum doesn't require hard beating.* Chinese proverb

SUPER 18 AND SUPER 25 PROJECTS

In 1988, my friend and client T. E. McCleary and I developed the Super 18 Program for evaluating stocks utilizing Value Lines bases. We offered one portfolio to satisfy all conservative investment objectives.

The securities generally were large cap, more mature, defensive, with a history of increasing dividends and earnings. The selected securities paid at least 2% dividend and had positive earnings histories for the past 10 years. In years of poor markets, the combined appreciation and dividend components of return were always greater for lower price/earnings (P/E) groups. This operation was a tedious manual process but our clients profited greatly.

We used four reasonable and accepted premises:

1. Brokerage firm research used to predict earnings could be biased, showing below- average performance with high risk.   We relied on an independent data base (Value Line) which had an excellent track record in predicting earnings.

2. Stocks are an effective asset for outperforming inflation (which was prevalent at that time) with relatively low risk. The fundamental objective is to preserve and increase the clients' wealth.

3. The best indicator for superior future performance is sustained superior past performance.

4. The time to buy a stock is when it is undervalued in the market. The time to sell a stock is when it is overvalued in the market

In 1992 my client Peter Perry, (no relation) and I developed the Super 25 Quantitative Model Portfolio using the four premises.

OUR SIX-POINT APPROACH

Point 1. *Bottom-up security selection.* We focus on securities that were undervalued by at least 14% discount from computed value, and had above-average fundamentals and earning predictability. We use Value Line's earning estimates because a study by the Wharton School of Business indicated that they were the most consistent.

Point 2. *Use a spread- sheet.* Decisions were made more quickly by our quantitative model. We expanded from one to five portfolios.

This development avoided our overpaying for small and mid cap EPS growth in those dynamic times. Cyclical securities were excluded from this program because they lacked earnings consistency.

Point 3. *Evaluate the merit of specific securities.* Not the relative merit of major markets

Point 4. *Concentrate on a few stocks.* Identify outstanding investment opportunities while minimizing market risk. Portfolio would contain 25 securities when fully invested vs. the initial 18. We also expanded the universe from large caps to mid and small caps.

Point 5. *Focus on securities with high return.* Our initial screen reduces 3,000 stocks to a universe of 775 stocks with consistent and sustained growth, and represents 99 industry groups. To be accepted, the security has to have a total return higher than industry average. We use a 13% return for each year for 10, 7 or 4 years.

Point 6. *Sell when the stock reaches rational value.* The stock is sold unless this is prevented by tax consideration or other account restrictions.

In 1994, we expanded our portfolios to ultra conservative, conservative, moderately aggressive and aggressive. In 1995 we added an emerging growth portfolio.

The securities in the Moderately Aggressive portfolio were generally less mature and pay little (or no) dividend, i.e. a yield of 0-2%. They used cash to expand the business.

The Aggressive portfolio was smaller cap, i.e., market value under $ 1.5 billion. They are. well- established or relatively new firms with five years of positive earnings history. They may have paid substantial (or no) dividends.

The securities in the Emerging Growth portfolio were generally newer or spin- offs from large companies with a minimum 20% growth rate for four years. This growth rate is nearly three times the 7.5% Standard & Poor (S&P) 500.

Securities in this Emerging Growth portfolio were both smaller and larger cap. Normally they paid little or no dividend.

(Please refer to the Appendix, page   for the performance data and the analytical approach for these portfolios.)

We had to enter the data manually every week. This frightened small brokerage firms.   They didn't want any responsibility. They were scared of being sued. Like most brokerage firms, they liked things to be verbal; i.e., not in writing. "One can, within reason, quote any numbers or ideas one wants as long as it is not in writing. "

Value Line was not interested in supplying us data- base format at that time *at a reasonable price* because they had their own asset management group.

Finally Zack's made some of the data available in the data base format but it still took us days to transfer data from their five disks of Research Wizard each month.

Transferring the data was very location—sensitive. We had to get short- term and long- term technical analysis rating from Value Line and any earnings estimate changes during the time interval.

I should have sold the program to an asset manager or a large discount broker with a large data base. Today, Zack's and several other asset managers appear to have similar stock evaluation programs.

BRIAN PISACICH, MY NEPHEW— THE ACTOR

Beauty and wisdom are here conjoined. Petronius

Actor. 30- Second commercial for *Scott's Turf Builder,* The Scott's/ Miracle-Gro Company. Marysville OH 43017

Brian and his family became actor and actress for Scott's fertilizer thirty- second commercial on February 27, 2007. The commercial had a big national schedule on the networks and cable on programs such as 60 Minutes, NBA Playoff, NASCAR, NLB, Sharks, Criminal Minds, Crime Time and Ghost Whisperer. He and the family had to join the Screen Actors Guild to produce the commercial.

The history of this accidental career is that Brian was asked to participate in a focus group on January 27, 2007 about lawn fertilizer. Since Brian loves to cut grass, he agreed. The interviews were taped.

Brian was among many to be called for a second interview which was sent to Scott's ad agency on Madison Ave in NYC. Then they asked Brian and his family (and 15 other families) to come down for a third interview.

Initially, another family was chosen to go to Los Angles. Scott's did not like the way that commercial turned out. Brian and his family were chosen to do a re- shoot.

They were in LA, Hollywood and Universal City. The morning of the Oscar Awards, they were near the Kodak Theater in Hollywood for wardrobe fitting.

The next day, there were a total of 45 people and tons of equipment on the set. Brian and his family had their own trailer and makeup artist. They were filmed at a private home in Pasadena from 9 until 6 followed by more voice work outside (in the dark) until

7. They were amazed at the time and effort that went into a 30-second commercial.

RICHARD GORSCAK'S PROFESSIONAL SOFTWARE CONSORTIUM

Authority issuing from one is strong,
issuing from two is weak. Chinese

Richard Gorscak successfully formed Professional Software Consortium, Incorporated in 1981. His first year was tough on him, his employees, his family (two young children) and his marriage. This privately- held company specialized in travel-reimbursement financial systems and payroll, accounting, and disbursing interfaces. Their products were used in every branch of the armed services and were deployed at over 750 sites around the world. Civilian agencies also rely on their system's unique support of Permanent– Change- of– Station (PCS) trips for civilian travelers.

KEVIN PISACICH'S TECHTRONIC

By labor, fire is got out of a stone. Dutch proverb

While a student at the University of Rhode Island, Kevin Pisacich owned and operated Techtronic, a mobile and office communication sales- and-repair- firm. Clients included Fleet Bank and the State of Rhode Island. Kevin learned quickly that small trades lead to great profits. He ceased operations when he left the university.

LOU ALBANO'S AND ROSEMARIE GORSCAK'S ANIMAL EMPIRE

Eloquence enough, but little wisdom. Sallust

Lou and Rosemarie Gorscak introduced, owned and operated their new plush (stuffed) animal gift- service, called Animal Empire, in 1999. Their marketing strategy was to sell the customer's loved ones a realistic version of their favorite animal instead of flowers or the usual Teddy Bear. They marketed on- line. They closed the operation in December 2005 for lack of sales. They sold their rights to a person in California. They had the opportunity to sell the company when internet companies were hot -- better to sell with regret than to keep with regret.

By trying, the Greeks got into Troy. Theocritus

LOU ALBANO PAINT & PAPER- HANGING CO

Lou took over his Father's interior and paper- hanging business after his Dad's retirement. Clients include home owners and some business buildings.

CHLOE CZEPIEL LANGENFELD NIGLIO

After taking a course at Allegheny Community College for a year, she started her own business. As C.E.O. of CCabstracts, she delivers vital information to both buyers, sellers and people financing home sales. She is a mom of three daughters, housewife and in her spare time, she sells real estate.

ANTONIO GENCO

He is C.E.O. of his own company X1 Systems. They install custom home cinema, multi-room audio/video and home automation in private homes.

ACADEMIC BRAIN POWER

*By eating, we overcome hunger; by
study, ignorance.* Chinese proverb

MATTHEW PERRY

I was laboratory instructor at Waynesburg College during my senior year. I was offered teaching fellowships at Michigan State and Penn State but at the last minute chose to go with industry.

At Brooklyn Polytechnic University I co- published, with Engineering Professor, Dr. Paul Bruins, a series of articles on plastic additives.

At NYU Business School, I received token payments for term papers from several industries.

In June 1959, I joined the Paper Institute as research administrator in Appleton WI after turning down a position as economist at the Midwest Institute in Kansas City. I was in charge of commercial development for uses of sulphite liquor. I also acted as liaison to academic and industrial research groups and subcontracted some projects to universities.

At DeSoto Incorporated, I was a participant in writing a book on costs for the National Paint, Varnish and Lacquer Association.

I gave marketing research seminars at the American Management Association in NYC and attended a Commercial Development

Association decision- making simulation workshop at Stanford University. One of the attendees was the future president of General Electric Company, Jack Welsh.

At Contempo Cosmetics, I published "New Look in Eye Make Up" and "Outdoor Girl Facial Fitness Program."

In the financial service industry, I published and gave seminars on financial planning subjects.

BRIAN PISACICH

President, Boston College Investment Club. Served on Student Judicial Board and Academic Peer Achievement Board.

DAVID PISACICH

David was recommended in his freshman college year for their math assistant program. He assisted professors in tutoring students and evaluation of homework assignments in advanced algebra and calculus.

David was accepted into Cornell's two-year MBA program in Ithaca, NY beginning fall 2008. His wife Sarah just completed her Masters Degree in accounting degree at Bentley College in 2008.

JASON J.GORSCAK

Research assistant at Johns Hopkins School of Medicine 1/98-1/2000;

Research Coordinator at Becton Dickinson, Franklin Lakes, NJ 6/98-8/98

Research Assistant to Ingrid U. Scott MD, MPH Dept of Ophthalmology, Bosom Palmer Eye Institute beginning 8/2001.

SPORTSMAN

*Skill will enable us to succeed in that which sheer
force could not accomplish.* Latin proverb

I was not athletic: I missed out in sportsmanship practices of fair
play, take loss or defeats without complaints or victory without
gloating and gracefully accept results of my actions. I did, however
learn the "High Fives" to Sportsmanship through hard knocks.

Brother Bernard was the first in the family to express an interest
in sports. He was quite active in track but could not play football
because of schedule conflict between working a night shift and
night practice. His engineering school did not have an athletic
program. His wife, Judy was active in high school basketball.

Bernard's son Brian excelled in track at Saint Bernard High School
and was All- American Connecticut State Champion. He was
recipient of a four- year Indoor/Outdoor Track scholarship at
Boston College. "Most Improved Athlete "was awarded to him
for returning to varsity level after overcoming injury in 1985.

He continued his interest in track by participating in various
triathlons. His golf is above average. His ex-wife, Debbie, is also
a runner.

Bernard's son Kevin became interested in triathlons when he was
in his 30s. He also is a golfer.

Karen, Bernard's daughter, was a softball player in high school and college where she obtained a softball scholarship. Post college she also continued her track interest, winning many triathlons.

Their other two sons, David and Timothy also excelled in track and golf.

PUBLICATIONS

*Either write things worth reading, or do
things worth writing.* Franklin

Jason Gorscak's publications will be listed in up coming Family
Book. Mine will also be listed there.

TIMOTHY PISACICH

BA Providence College 5/2007 Political Science/Writing

Tim was one of the first in the family to study abroad while doing
his undergraduate work. He exhibited his independent nature
which is a requirement for a successful writer. The following is
Tim's summary of his adventure.

"Towards the end of my sophomore year, I made a quick decision
to study abroad first semester, junior year. Although I knew I
would miss my friends and the great professors at Providence
College, I thought the experience of studying in a place such as
Scotland would be educational and provide a unique opportunity
to spend a significant amount of time abroad.

After surprisingly limited research, I flew into Gatwick, London,
on August 24[th,] 2005. I spent my first week seeing the sights in
London. The start of the trip wasn't easy: I vividly remember

getting into London, carrying a semester's worth of luggage and having no idea how to get to my hostel. It wasn't until I followed numerous vague, often incorrect directions (this involved me getting on and off crowded buses with luggage) that I finally found the run-down building that housed my hostel.

I began my week in Scotland with two pre-session courses before term officially began. Afterwards, most of the local students arrived and full-time classes began. I took General Politics, which re-sparked my interest in political science, particularly political theory. My Scottish Literature class also reaffirmed my lack of interest in my current English major, causing me to change majors while abroad! I also took a photography class which was a great opportunity to learn more about photography and capture some of the city of Glasgow on film.

With a lighter workload that Providence College, I was able to enjoy visitors, life in Glasgow, and weekend traveling. Some of my best memories in Glasgow are from the two-week period two of my brothers, Dave and Kevin came to visit. Kevin and I also made a trip out to the Isle of Arran where we drove a rented car throughout the "mini-Scotland" island to see standing stones, castles, a brewery, a beautiful sunset. I enjoyed spending time with my flatmates, including the local Scottish freshmen and American students. At the university Claplaincy, I got to know more "uni" students, as well as Fr. John and Sr. Bridget. Every week-day the Chaplaincy had wonderful home made free lunches after daily mass. I helped out as an RCIA (Right of Christian Initiation for Adults) leader at the Chaplaincy. The University had a great gym and library – two places where I spent time during the week..

However, the weekend trips are what made my semester in Glasgow exceptional. I traveled to the Highlands, to places such as Glencoe, the Isle of Iona, or the Isle of Skye. I never fell in love with Glasgow as I did with the Highlands. One weekend some friends and I walked about thirty miles from Fort William to Loch Ness. I also took weekend trips to Paris and Dublin since Ryan Air offers such affordable flights. Some of these trips were with a group of friends, but I also traveled alone, especially when my flatmates were interested in hitting up the bars in Glasgow again, and again, and again.

When the semester ended and most American students went home for the Holidays, I took off for Ireland where I had a relaxing few days in the town of Lahinch where I was able to see the Cliffs of Moher.

After Ireland, I traveled throughout Italy for Winter Break. I got into Rome just in time to turn 21 in front of the Vatican and stayed through Christmas. After Christmas, Eric Powell, a friend from P.C., came to Italy and we traveled to Florence, Venice, Verona, and Milan. I was very glad to see a familiar face since I was beginning to feel homesick.

Back in Connecticut, I unpacked and packed for the upcoming semester at P.C. during the two and a half days I was home. I learned and saw much during my semester abroad, but I think the greatest lesson I learned was to live in the present. It would have been such a shame if I didn't *live* the experience of meeting new people, traveling to Paris, going to mass in St. Peter's, etc. In other words, I could have gone to see these great places, taken a picture, and left without experiencing the place for myself. I could have worried about things of the past, or been too excited about future trips to enjoy what I was doing in the present.

COMMUNITY AFFAIRS

WAYNESBURG COLLEGE

Either win the horse or lose the saddle. English proverb

Being in a Presbyterian College and town, and a member of *Alpha Phi Omega* National Service Fraternity, I elected to teach Sunday school at the local Catholic Mission Church. At that time, there was religious prejudice among the various sects of Protestantism. Catholics and Blacks were considered lower in social status. Jews were a minority but were successful in business, and tolerated.

I was a Unitarian without knowing it because I was allowed to teach that all religions were equally good as far as God was concerned. I reinforced the inherent worth and dignity of every person and the wisdom of the entire world's religions. The priest was a cast- off from the diocese of Pittsburgh. Since his family had money, we made the church basement a community center for children of all faiths. This recreation center with ping pong and electronic games became a tremendous hit with the children. This helped break the anti-Catholic sentiment in the community at least among the young. Two of the boys in my class went on to seminary.

CHILDREN'S VILLAGE --- DOBBS FERRY, NEW YORK

One ripe fruit between two green. French proverb

The Youth Group of The Dutch Reformed Church in Bronxville sponsored a cottage in Children's Village. My friend Pat Stauffer was active in this group. The Village was across the highway where I worked. I became active with the children. They wanted to wash and wax my big fire-engine-red DeSoto, a car with large fins.

Children's Village is a private, non-profit corporation formed in NYC during 1851. Known as The New York City Juvenile Asylum, it addressed the enormous problem of homeless immigrant children. It moved to Dobbs Ferry in 1901 to a 277-acre farm and changed the name to The Children's Village. This campus won the 1906 World's Fair Award for architecture. The Village evolved into a sophisticated treatment center for emotionally-scarred children whose conduct was self-destructive, dangerous and beyond the control of parents –and who are victimized by abuse or chronic neglect.

One resident attracted my attention. The house parents claimed he was incorrigible. When he told me that both his parents were artistic, I encouraged him to paint. I purchased the necessary supplies and said I would buy his paintings. He would make money, and it would be easier than washing and waxing my car. His self-destructive attitude completely reversed.

He produced some good paintings. I left for a new position in Appleton WI so I lost touch. I understand that he became the pride and joy of the staff. He became a PR success.

All Children's Village records were destroyed in a 1994 fire. I still have his first dreary, cold painting.

REPUBLICAN PARTY POLITICS: LANCASTER PA; DES PLAINES IL; PITTSBURGH PA.

Man is a political animal. Aristotle

When I was Republican precinct captain during the 1960 presidential election, the Republicans and Democrats worked together to get 100% of the registered voters to show. We were two votes shy of reaching that goal. (Two voters were out of town.)

My wife and I were active volunteers with the Republican Party from 1968 to 1970 in Des Plaines IL. I tried in Pittsburgh but was not trusted by the higher party echelon. Several high- ranking members were indicted in a campaign- contribution scandal. I registered Independent. I just could not take any more of Nixon.

PITTSBURGH'S SINGLES INTERMEDIATE BRIDGE AND SOCIAL CLUB

He that is at sea must either sail or sink. Danish proverb

I decided to form a club for a singles social bridge group in Pittsburgh. This club was an instant success because it truly was social bridge, i.e., good food, beer, wine and approximately 50/50 ratio of men to women.

The men were mostly professionals who attracted professional women. One excellent player who bullied the women had to be warned.

Three couples married during the first year of operation. The club was fortunate to have excellent leaders and workers throughout its history.

The club still exists but the game became more serious with the "party crowd" leaving. The current membership is mostly women.

NEW HAVEN'S SINGLES INTERMEDIATE BRIDGE CLUB

Society is no comfort / to one not sociable. Shakespeare

In 1980, I met Carl Yohans, Betty Miller and Muriel Chapman at a Westport Unitarian Singles Club dance. We decided to form a bridge satellite for the Westport CT group in New Haven. During the formation, we met to play bridge, write by-laws and develop strategy. We duplicated much of what was done in Pittsburgh.

We selected the Unitarian Universals Church in New Haven as our home base. It had a kitchen.

We met on the first and third Friday of every month. To attract men, women members brought pleasures for the palate in accord with the Spanish proverb "Not with whom you are bred, but with whom you are fed."

The club was an immediate success. New Haven CT broke away from the Westport group. We then moved to larger quarters at the Spring Glen Congregational Church where we still reside.

The club's social activities include holiday picnics at the home of Carl Yohans, St Patrick Day Celebration at a Country or Graduate Club, Christmas luncheon and gifts for tots, Super Bowl party and bridge, tail gate party at Yale Games, bridge tournament with buffet dinner, Metropolitan Opera in New York, art exhibits of two members (Jinny Goggin and Mary Cameron), and trips to Mohegan Sun Casino, steam train and river boat excursions and Thimble Island cruise.

The club is very fortunate to have a reserve of willing and serious leaders for various responsibilities. The club also has a dedicated historian, Jo Farricielli, who documents our activities with photos. As we get older, it will be harder to attract younger people. Many of the men died or moved to a warmer climate so now the membership is about 85% women.

The membership adhered to the by-laws and kept bridge games social, even though there are many Life Master Members.

HARTFORD'S SINGLES BRIDGE CLUB

Among thorns grow the roses. Italian proverb

In 1993, I was asked by the new president of Meeting House Singles in West Hartford CT to form a singles bridge group for them similar in structure to Pittsburgh PA and New Haven CT. Initially the group met at my place and then in my clubhouse in Cromwell CT.

They could not afford the rental fee for the clubhouse so they began meeting in people's homes. They also dropped their affiliation with The Meeting House Singles Group in Hartford. This club never took off as did the other two social clubs. A few players influenced the club members to change the by-laws to more serious playing even though there were many American Contract Bridge League games in the area.

My friend Phyllis Klaben became interested in bridge lessons. I usually joined these lessons for recruitment. Phyllis became a good hostess and public- relations person for the club but was intimidated by some players. Currently the games have a pre-game social and mid-game dessert.

Matthew Perry

GREATER HARTFORD LEADERSHIP GROUP (GHLG) APRIL 2002

In calm weather, everyone is captain. Maltin

Hartford is a neighborhood of different ethnic groups, races and immigrant people. This metropolitan area was one of the nation's producers of well- known luminaries in various fields: arts, architecture ,education, entrepreneurship, literature, government, military service, publishing, investing, religion and sports. I decided to join the GHLG. Quoting Horace, *My own safety is at stake when my neighbor's wall is ablaze.*

I joined Class 3 of the Third Age Initiative in April 2002 at the urging of Phyllis Klaben. Phyllis Klaben The organization had a mission to develop a diverse array of community-minded leaders, near retirement, to address key issues facing Greater Hartford. The president of the group was Ted Carroll.   Doe Hentschel was Program Director. Originally our project group consisted of eleven women and seven men. Later some people left our group but other people joined.

We had creative people. We formed committees to consider projects:

- Theme school for Hartford, or

- Mortgage foreclosures, or

- Credit rating, or

- Elite colleges tutoring program for low-income youth, or

- Refurbishing Lozada Park in Clay Hill. (This project was chosen. It had a poignant history.)

The group had difficulty in getting consensus and implementing the plan to transform a large, vacant lot with little use into a center for the neighborhood to gather safely, for children to play and for the community to take root. This project received approval including the State Legislature with the help of State Senator John Fonfara. . In 2006, the project was turned over to The Society of Latin- American Firefighters for implementation after funding was promised by the state of Connecticut. On May 30, 2008, legislation passed to provide $350,000 for the transformation of Lozada Park. The project will be managed by the City of Hartford with the Latino Firefighters serving as the key organization overseeing the project.

For the Greater Hartford Group I did a pilot study with volunteers who tutored high- school students to help students enter top-notch colleges, focusing on applications for admission, scholarships and financial aid. Hopefully this project will be reactivated by a future Greater Hartford Leadership Group.

HARTFORD/CROMWELL HIGH SCHOOLS

Education is an ornament in prosperity and refuge in adversity. Greek proverb

In conjunction with John Rim, I spoke with the Hartford and Cromwell school systems to consider funding from the Bill and Melinda Gates Foundation for school improvement.

FAMILY SERVING IN COMMUNITY AFFAIRS CONNECTICUIT JUVENILE JUSTICE ALLIANCE. BRIDGEPORT CT

Judges should have two ears – both alike. German proverb

After college graduation, my nephew, Timothy Pisacich, was the first in the family to volunteer a year of full-time service to an organization. He joined the Connecticut Juvenile Justice Alliance (CTJJA) in the inner city of Bridgeport CT.

It was launched in November 2001 as a collaborative effort of the Center for Children's Advocacy, Connecticut Voices for Children, and the Tow Foundation. Its mission is to promote a safe, effective and equitable system of services designed to meet the needs of children and adolescents at-risk for becoming involved in the juvenile system of justice.

The alliance is primarily an advocacy group working to improve the juvenile justice system throughout CT

TOWN TREASURER. WATERFORD CT

Brother Bernard was elected town Treasurer for six years (three terms) even though he is an independent.

GROWING-UP

*Take the first advice of women and not
the second.* Latin proverb

The Women in My Life had an impact on me. Each of them was interesting in their own way.

I interacted well with women from an early age. I listen, praise and take their advice. I have their characteristic of being changeable and not rigid in my views.

Faithfulness is ingrained in the family culture. Grandpa Pisacic never remarried after his wife died. He chose to raise Dad and his other children by himself.

Dad was faithful to Mom when he was alone in Duquesne for five years. He didn't squander his money on women or booze like his fellow workers but sent money and care packages to Mom and Kate, and put money in the bank here in the US. He practiced what he later preached to Kate "It does not matter what you earned. What matters is what you saved."

I had a complete relationship with my wife, Mary Ann. Nobody else.

AT OUR FARM IN WEST MIFFLIN

*He that tilleth the land shall be satisfied
with bread.* Bible proverb

I was brought up on a small farm so I saw that various animals copulated and ejaculated. I don't think I related it to human sexuality. Some memorable positions and actions included the rabbits doing a back flip after copulation; the pigeons flapping their wings to make sure they impregnated the mate sufficiently; and me holding the cow's tail to the side to make sure the bull did his assignment. When Sally or Fannie went into heat, it was my job to walk her several miles to the nearest bull.

One hot summer day, when I was about 8 years old, my older female and male neighbors were bored. Suddenly the nice- looking blonde who lived next to us said "Lets f---." I wasn't exactly sure what that meant. I did know, however, that only adults did it. It was disillusionment as one of the older girls said I was too young so I was excluded. I don't know what they did as they went to another hill. The girls may have known how and what they were doing but I doubt the guys did. I think I knew how because I watched various animals.

A few years later when friends from Ohio (neighbors in the old country) visited Dad and Mom, they brought their 20- year- old son with them. He wanted to visit the red light district on the South Side of Pittsburgh. He looked all over for a prostitute with no success. He returned to my parent's home "full" and dejected because he heard Pittsburgh had quality.

A few years later, I decided to try this on my own. The prostitute was an attractive 20- year- old. I could not get an erection no matter how hard I focused on the task. Don't know why. I was very apologetic. She did not want to take my money but I insisted. That was my first and last time in a red- light district.

AGE 5: OLIVER ELEMENTARY SCHOOL

I have not yet begun to fight. John Paul Jones

At Oliver Elementary School playground I was beaten up for making a proclamation that when it rains, it does not rain all over the world at the same time. My sisters Kate, Anna and I were walking down Grant Street and observed that on one side of the street it was raining and the other side it was not. Kate, like the other children, thought it rained all over the world at the same time. She remembers this episode.

ACROSS THE TRACK IN DUQUESNE

In June, 1941, US Steel, with government assistance, wiped out a 38 acres section of Duquesne to expand America's steel production. It was a $10 million defense plant expansion.

The mills had been idle since the 30s and the country was gearing up for war. My dad, mother, two sisters and I had lived in this section of town five years earlier. Most of the 200 displaced families relocated into public housing in Duquesne and West Mifflin.

The apartments in this section of Duquesne were generally two or three rooms (kitchen and bedrooms) sharing a common toilet in the basement. The nationalities of the families living here were: Croatian 25%, Serbian 25%, Hungarian 20%, Polish 15% and Blacks 10%. Some entrepreneurial women owned homes which became boarding houses.

Slovak families lived in a cluster on the other side of the tracks, First Street. Dad moved us to Second Street, to a larger apartment with a laundry area, for a short while but had to move back to Linden Street - because of cash- flow problems when work slowed.

The neighbors took care of and watched out for one another. They spoke with pride of one another. With the exception of Dad and Mom everyone worshipped and attended church faithfully. Mom did not attend services until after Dad's death. Dad went to church only during the High Holiday.

Water washes everything. Portuguese proverb

THE GREAT ST PATRICK'S DAY FLOOD IN PITTSBURGH PA. MARCH 1936

Right after we moved to West Mifflin; there was the great Pittsburgh flood of March 1936. (Later called "The Great St Patrick's Day Flood" or a "500-year" flood). Mom took Anna and me to witness the destruction that the Monongahela River did to the area where we used to live.

The cause of the flood was warmer- than- normal temperatures which led to the melting of snow and ice on the upper Allegheny and Monongahela rivers. On March 17, the waters reached flood stage at 25 feet. Heavy rains overnight caused the waters to rise quickly, and on March 18, the water peaked at 46 feet, 21 feet above flood stage.

The water finally receded to 24 feet, five days later. The steel workers were out of work because of the damage that the mills suffered.

Ice and flooding in the Pittsburgh Region is a phenomenon dating back 20,000 years. That was when the Kansan and Wisconsin glaciers invaded the district and advanced southward. Prior to the glaciers, the pre-historic Monongahela and Ohio rivers flowed northward into Lake Erie.

They were three streams that over time merged to become the Allegheny River. After the glaciers advanced into the region, the southern shores of Lake Erie became icebound. The streams and rivers flowing into the lake were forced to find other outlets.

Gradually, huge pools formed at the stream mouths, causing back- flooding. The Monongahela River always flowed north, but because of flooding in the Lake Erie area it began to drop its suspended silt into its lower reaches. When the ice cap began to melt and retreat northward, the Allegheny Basin filled with deposits of glacial outwash left by the ice sheet.

These glacial deposits contributed to the present problems of flooding. In some areas, deposits are 150 feet deep. The land reacted when the glacial pressure eased, elevating up to 350 feet in the unglaciated areas. This upheaval formed the divide just south of Lake Erie. Ever since, drainage has- flowed southward towards Pittsburgh.

The development of flood controls on the rivers helped alleviate the worst flooding problems. Its effectiveness was proven in 2004 when Hurricane Francis dumped four inches of rain, followed a few weeks later by Ivan with a whopping six inches on an already saturated- region. The rivers crested at 31 feet. Although the flooding was bad, it could have been worse than the Great Flood of 1936.

> *Who robs a scholar, robs twenty men, (because much of what a scholar possesses is borrowed.)* English proverb

AGE 8: EMERSON ELEMENTARY SCHOOL

In third grade, I and my male friends were infatuated with select females in our classroom. My first choice was Donna Davis because she was well developed for her age. She was interested in my neighbor, Arthur Tusay, who played the guitar and sang country- Western music beautifully. Dona never married. She became an executive secretary with US Steel.

In third grade, Mrs. Eleanor Roosevelt visited for a school dedication. It was the first local public school built since the Great Depression. Prior to her coming, there were arguments, debates and sometimes fights about Roosevelt's domestic policies. We all echoed what we heard at home. We all cheered her and waved flags that were given to us on her arrival.

I became attracted to Carol Dorman because she seemed to like me. She took me to the movie and paid for the milkshake on our first group date. Carol and I remained friends through junior high school. Her parents elected where she would go to high school. At the time, our township did not have any high school so we could go to any schools within a 10- mile radius. But the family was responsible for bus travel cost. That definitely was not in our family budget so I attended the one that was less than a mile away – Duquesne High School.

The town of Duquesne was settled in 1885 and incorporated in 1891. Peak population was 20,693 in 1940. The original portrait of the first settler, Benjamin Tate, hangs in City Hall. It was done by the first African American child born in Duquesne.

Duquesne is about 12 miles south- east of Pittsburgh and is nestled along the Monongahela River. British general Edward Braddock and American colonel George Washington marched through the area but were defeated by the French in 1755. Duquesne was later named in honor of the French governor-general of Canada, Marquis of Duquesne. He was appointed by King Louis XV of France.

This small village began to flourish in the 1880s when the Duquesne Steel Company was formed and started to produce rails. The Howard Glass Works and the Duquesne Tube Works were also started. The township was incorporated as Borough of Duquesne in 1891. The Carnegie Steel Company purchased Duquesne Steel in 1899 and renamed it Duquesne Works.

It is never too late to give up our prejudices. Thoreau

Nothing is achieved without toil. Horace

Afro/Americans migrated to the Pittsburgh area from the South as early as the 1890s as replacement workers for the strikers and later to replace whites who were drafted into the armed forces during the two World Wars. Levi Claggett was the first black to graduate what is now Carnegie Mellon University and to become a famous artist. Harmony between the various nationalities and races led to inter-ethnic and inter- religious marriages. Interracial marriages also occurred later.

A continuous- process and quality- oriented steel mill was the heart and soul of Duquesne during its brightest moments. The mill employed proud workers from all over the world, including immigrants from nearly every country in Western Europe who had come to America to join the growing industrial labor force. During the war, it employed more than 10,000 men and women who contributed to the production of steel used in the manufacture of bullets, artillery shells and armor.

The mill was a city in itself. It was a self-supported operation. All the facilities it needed to function were located on site. (More than 325 acres). These included water treatment and power plants, four boiler houses, chemistry and metallurgical lab, small hospital, carpentry shop, coal dock, own security force and a railroad. The transportation system consisted of 25 miles of track for men, materials and machinery, using six locomotives and 20 donkey engines. They also owned and operated the Union Railroad which was used to transport coal, coke, pig-iron and other materials to the steel- making operations in Duquesne, Homestead and Braddock.

Andrew Carnegie was in the forefront in improving working conditions for workers. Safety became a major concern. As early as the 1920s, he introduced a Safety- First Program. Danger signs throughout the plant were in five different languages to help protect the diversity of immigrants.

 Seven- day workweeks were reduced to six days. Shifts were reduced from 12 hours to 8 ½. In the 1920s, he also offered health and accident insurance, pension plans and housing assistance as well as the opportunity to purchase stock options.

Carnegie also believed that training employees helped the company perform better and boosted production. He offered classes in English, drafting, drawing and mathematics.

CHURCHES AND THE CARNEGE LIBARY

*He who is near the church is often far
from God.* French proverb

Dad attended St. Mary's Croatian Roman Catholic Church in Rankin once or twice a year. It is one of the oldest and largest Croatian parishes in the United States. It was erected in 1896 and merged into a larger parish group in 1994.. He also sporadically attended Croatian Sacred Heart in McKeesport which closed in December 2006.   It consolidated with two other parishes: St. Mary and Holy Trinity.

 Sister Kate started attending Holy Name Church which had a seating capacity of 800. This church, completed in 1899, was considered the finest in its day. Andrew Carnegie donated a magnificent pipe organ to the church in February 1901.

Recently John Rim and I visited Saints Cyril and Methodius and Saint Raphael's Croatian Catholic Parish on 41st Street, New York City. The New York church is a mirror image (except Holy Name lost part of their church tower in a lighting storm) of the Holy Name Church. Both churches were initially Irish parishes.

As a youngster, I was religious. I enjoyed attending the Novena services at Holy Name Church that were performed by a visiting priests or missionaries. I always prayed to the Blessed Mother for the betterment of our family so that we would not work so hard and have more leisure and study time. I wanted to enter a monastery as a monk but family discouraged it

All the other children attended the church and Sunday school at Holy Name but switched to St. Joseph's Church that was founded by two prominent German Catholics. We had to be members to purchase lots in the older section of the cemetery when Dad died.

When Sister Kate and I attended the Duquesne public school system, it was considered one of the best in the state but the municipality (including the school system) started to deteriorate in the 50s. Petty crimes perpetrated by small-time hoodlums became common. It became the worst- performing school in Pennsylvania even though the Commonwealth Pennsylvania and the Federal Government plowed large sums of money into the system.

The crown jewel of the city was the Carnegie Library of Duquesne. It was constructed in 1901. Over 2,500 libraries built by Andrew Carnegie were "free to the people." It was the community's meeting place. It was where you learned to not only read, but to swim, listen to concerts, play an instrument or gather with friends to play billiards or to celebrate Christmas.

It had a beautiful spiral stairway to the second floor. A 90 foot flagpole stood for nearly 90 years before it was torn down in 1968 to make way for a school annex which never materialized. Houses now occupy the site where this beautiful structure once stood.

As the building was demolished, many of its beautiful assets were scattered to the wind. This architectural wealth included hand-made wrought iron scroll work and brass fixtures manufactured by European craftsmen, and great slabs of imported Italian marble used to assemble the grand staircases. Only a chosen few know the location of the many parts that made up this magnificent building.

The exception is the 90 foot flagpole which was cut. Half of that pole was re-erected outside the Duquesne Annex Fire Department in West Mifflin, PA.

The recent per capita income for Duquesne was $12,067. About 31.3% of families and 34.7% of the population were below the poverty line including 52.9% of those under age 18 and 19.7% of those ages 65 or over.

There was a Commonwealth proposal to dissolve Duquesne High School on June 5, 2007. The students would be sent to other public high schools on a tuition basis. The district would continue to provide classes for grades K-8. The irony is that back in 1946, West Mifflin high school students were funneled to various regional schools with Duquesne taking a major share of the students. Now West Mifflin will reluctantly be taking a major share of Duquesne students. It is a sad day to see the demise of what was once one of the better high schools in the country.

I saw less of Carol Dorman during high school because she attended a different school in nearby Munhall and because of my work schedule after school. Her high school was a beautiful white, Greek structure building opened in 1904 just after Munhall was incorporated as a borough in 1901. This building was demolished when Munhall, Homestead and West Homestead merged as the Steel Valley School District.

Apparently Carol's father insisted that Carol attend an all girl's college – Pennsylvania College for Women (PCW). Carol was bright but she flunked out of PCW. I was a prude, and was not there when she needed me.

She met a nice man and was married. They had one child. She was devastated when her husband died of cancer after 12 years of marriage. She became totally dedicated to getting her son to graduate from medical school. (He did.) I tried several times to contact Carol. Nobody seemed to know what happened to her.

AGE 11: EDISON JUNIOR HIGH SCHOOL

The bully bags a lion from a distance but runs when
a mule starts kicking. American proverb

While attending Edison Junior High School. I was bullied by this big kid, Charles, from the "project." I finally said "Lets fight after school" despite the fact that I would receive a licking when I came home. (My folks were anti-violence).

The news spread quickly all over this small school as Charles was bulling other boys as well. He claimed to be the toughest kid in our junior high school of about 125 boys. We met on the softball field – on one side were the girls and boys who favored me and on the other side were a few friends of Charles from the "government housing project." These kids were considered incorrigible because they came from across the tracks adjacent to the steel mills.

I won the fight and was proclaimed the "King." I don't think I abused that title except once. In seventh grade the students had the opportunity to either take shop or home economics. I chose the latter. This class was followed by music appreciation. The teacher was new, dedicated, hyper and was determined to push classical music onto us. We should love it as much as she did even though we were restless 7th graders and we just would not dare admit to our peers that we did indeed appreciate some of the classical music –especially opera music.—To show that I was with the boys, I suggested they take a bag full of rivets from the shop so we could throw one at a time at the teacher from different parts of the classroom when she had her back to us and was writing on the blackboard.

 She lost control, cried and went to the principal's office. He came back with her and asked who did the throwing. Since nobody answered, he told us that we would remain in that room until somebody confessed. Since nobody else stood up, I did. He thought I was making fun of him. I told him I instigated the idea but he still did not believe me.

He told me I was expelled until I brought my mother to his office. The principal knew me and my mother since 3rd grade at Emerson Elementary School. My mother always backed the principal and his teachers on everything. This was the only time I got in trouble in school.

Unfortunately this dedicated music teacher left our school shortly thereafter – not a very good joke. I had to live with that for quite awhile.

Since the principal knew the financial situation of our family, he started giving me working papers when I was 12 years old. His secretary helped out by leaving an age card on her desk and leaving the room. This made it easier for them and me as I just had to complete the card to say I was 16 years of age. Luckily for me, I easily passed for 16.

The political tone in West Mifflin was Republican. Politics was never discussed with the family. Dad joined the Democratic Party during the war.

When I was in third grade, West Mifflin had the first school built since the Depression. This was to accommodate the students who moved into public housing from across the track in Duquesne. Even in third grade, the students were very active politically at that time. There were debates and fights, pro-Roosevelt and against Roosevelt. Some of the newcomers (including my Dad) were pro-Roosevelt while the natives were against.

This public housing project still exists, many converted into condos which are in excellent shape. The school just recently closed. It was an excellent school and a very nice building to the end.

KENNWOOD AMUSEMENT PARK WEST MIFFLIN PA

An army of stags led by a lion would be more formidable than one of lions led by a stag. Latin proverb

This is one company where every member of the Mato (and my sister's family) worked at one time or another. Just about every high school student in the West Mifflin area worked there. My sister Katherine also started there in 1949, then again in 1953, followed by a long run from 1961 to 1998 when she retired at the age of 79. She loved working and keeping up with the young people.

On our side of the family, Bernard and Edward both became managers of the bigger stands. Edward did not return the second year because of his A&P position.

In my sister's family, Donald was manager of the Tower but requested a transfer to ice boy because it paid more, and he worked more hours. Richard only worked in the stands for one year while his sister Rose was a stand manager for three years.

I started with the refreshment company but soon transferred to the amusement group because they paid more and I worked longer hours.

Since Kennywood was so important in our lives, some of its history is in order. It was founded in 1898 as a small trolley recreational park. The park was designated a national historic landmark in 1987. It was begun by the Monongahela Street Railway Company, which was controlled by Andrew Mellon. The carousel pavilion and the restaurant (originally the casino) are the last two major buildings in existence today, dating back to 1898.

Kennywood survived tremendous competition from a dozen parks during the turn of the 18th century. In 1906, Pittsburgh Railway Company assigned its lease to A.S. McSwigan and Frederick W. Henninger.

During the early 1910s, the park built two large roller coasters, The Racer and the Speed-O-Plane. They were replaced in the 20s by Jack Rabbit (1920), Pippin (1924) and a new Racer (1927). The park added a large swimming pool in 1925.

The Great Depression from 1930 to 1935 was especially hard on the park. Dances helped keep the park alive as great dance bands played from 1930 to 1950. Racial problems caused the closing of the dance pavilion and the pool in the 50s. The former became a dark ride and the latter, space for large spectacular rides.

The park prospered in the second half of the 30s and new rides including Noah's Ark (1936) were added. During the Second World War they were not permitted to add new rides but they purchased a used Ferris wheel and a miniature train which are still in use. Many new rides were added to Kiddeland in the 50s because school picnics grew enormously. During the 60s and the 70s the park again had competition. This time the competition was from Disneyland and other theme parks.

The management team decided to spend money to be competitive. The turnpike was built in 1966; Pippin was redesigned into the Thunderbolt thus making Kennywood "The Roller Coaster Capital of the World." The ravine portion of this coaster and the tunnel were retained while a new super- structure was added. In 1991, one of the most popular additions to the park was introduced: The Steel Phantom, 3,000 feet long, four- looping coaster with top speed of 80MPH and longest drop of 225 feet. This beat any coaster in the world for speed and drop. Its conception was by Harry W. Henninger (I worked for Carl Henninger back in the 40s) and it was built by Kennywood Park employees. Since the park had no expansion land, the park took advantage of the same hillside property navigated by the Thunderbolt. They did this by placing the biggest drop of the Steel Phantom at right angles to the Thunderbolt, and literally went off the cliff. It was necessary to go over and under the Thunderbolt in the ravine.

This park was important to the children of our family and many families in the West Mifflin metropolitan area because it was source of income for college students. It also is something that we in West Mifflin and the Pittsburgh area are proud. Its well-run family management team keeps a balance of change and preservation of tradition. A good combination!

On Thursday, December 13, 2007 the President of Kennywood Entertainment Inc, Peter McAneny announced for the hundred families that owned Kennywood, "it's a good time to sell. It's getting to be a bigger and bigger group of owners." Active owners wanted to plow some of the profits back into the business while others looked for higher dividends. The company sold to Madrid-based Parques Reunidos (backed by British investors) which owns 61 amusement parks, water parks, animal parks and family entertainment centers throughout Europe and the United States. With the addition of Kennywood, their total annual visitors will top 22 million and revenues exceed $570 million. Kennywood's revenue is reportedly in the range of $80 million and $120 million a year.

The loss of this family-owned business will have a tremendous effect on the people of West Mifflin and Pittsburgh even though the new owners gave assurances the park would remain locally controlled and shared in Kennywood's vision and philosophy. What may disappear is the intense family devotion and personal sacrifice but in return bring an international reputation.

Our family will always remember this first class operation – it was a place where the middle aged felt young working long side the youth who got help with their college tuition.

This 105-year ownership, the Henninger and McSwigan families will go into the history books because very few family-owned business last more than a few generations. Forty percent make it to the second generation, 12% of those to the third and three percent make it to the fourth. Kennywood Entertainment, Inc is in its fourth and fifth generations of ownership. Of the family-owned business that survived, even fewer are owned by two unrelated families.

> *He, who neglects to study diligently in youth,*
> *will, white-headed, repent that he put it off*
> *until too late.* Chinese proverb

AGE 14: DUQUESNE HIGH SCHOOL

The girls in my high school did not seem to have an interest in me – maybe because I became shy. I was busy working. I did, however, do a good deed for the new Social Studies teacher, Dorothy Surgent. I thought she knew her subject matter but could not keep order in her class so I told the students to "cool it" whenever they got rowdy. The following year she decided to take a vocational guidance position at the high school.

Donna Davis did attend Duquesne High School but we interacted very little as she was in the commercial group. She was popular with the athletes.

BALSAMO'S FOOD MARKET

A man never surfeits of too much honesty. English proverb

While working at Balsamo's Food store meat department on Friday night and Saturday I was asked to supervise some 12 counter clerks on Friday night because they trusted me more than other clerks. I was disappointed once when I caught a bright part- time college student in a stealing partnership with a young cashier. Their Friday night scheme was ringing up only a portion of the customer's meat orders and pocketing the rest of the money. I talked to him but did not report him. He quit shortly thereafter.

This is exactly what the manager did on Saturday with no accomplice. One had to be very careful that the cash in the register matched the amount rung up because any discrepancy would raise a flag. Later my department manager was caught and fired for stealing huge amounts of cash and drop- shipping meat to other locations. Enough to buy a food chain in Cleveland, Ohio. The cash swindle was done the same way as the Carnegie Tech college student did on Friday night. No criminal charges were filed against the manager as he had enough minor "dirt" against the owner to jail him.

This was the biggest grocery store in the country at that time. They had a railroad siding for delivery of bananas, hind-quarters of beef, hams, poultry and canned groceries. The store also had a very big bakery, making all kinds of fresh bread and pastries, and a restaurant. Most of the fish they carried was frozen. No pharmacy.

The owner had a good thing going for him because his father, James Balsamo, had tremendous marketing and merchandising skills. He was a wholesale grocer in the 1920s. When a chain of markets went bankrupt, he agreed to accept (as partial payment) on the debt one of the chain's stores. Originally, they offered him a market in West Newton, a tiny coal mining town in Westmoreland County, but Balsamo fought and coaxed until they let him have their McKeesport store.

This location was Mr. Balsamo's best decision regarding real estate. The store abutted the Baltimore and Ohio tracks through the middle of McKeesport. These tracks were a public nuisance that the town fathers would fight for the next five decades. Back in 1854, when the plans for the B&O were restructured, McKeesport offered $150,000 as an "inducement" (kickback) to take the longer route across the outskirts of the city. When the city paid off the reduced kickback of $104,000 in 1906, the town had grown and the train became a smelly, noisy, dangerous, traffic-disrupting pain in the neck. After several bribes, an agreement was made to remove the track and the last train pulled out of downtown McKeesport on May 6th, 1970. Its removal left 24 streets free of grade crossings and cleared land through the center of town for development.

This location became a godsend. The crowded, congested, noisy station was a focal point in McKeesport. The National Tube mill's Locust Street gate was one block away and the area surrounding the store on Fifth Avenue was full of bars, coffee shops, and all-night restaurants.

The wholesale grocer had built a failed food market into a grocery empire on Fifth Avenue. Even in the 1930s customers were welcomed to taste deli cheese or vegetables for freshness, or to browse through bins of produce.

> *They are both thieves alike, the receiver and*
> *the man who steals.* Greek proverb

When I worked at the store during 1946, Mr. Balsamo's son was running the business. His father quietly worked in the produce department. The son's greed caused him to cheat the customers on weights and measure. The effect was that his employees stole money and meat from the store. To cover up lost revenue, the managers sold lower grade meats. It apparently worked for quite a long time.

Various meat department managers, some clerks and the butchers stole him blind. It is a wonder that nobody got sick from the bad ground meat. It was a mixture of fat gristle mixed with animal organs like kidneys and liver and ground several times with some chuck to produce a red color hamburger. This was done to offset the meat delivered to other locations as well as the pocketed monies at the cashier. The owner couldn't prosecute as they could turn State evidence against him on his minor offenses. To protect against employees giving away merchandise free to customers or pocketing monies, the store went high tech. The store had two-way mirrors, passageways and rooms everywhere so the owner could secretly view the employees.

The weight and measure man was leaving the store with bags of meat, groceries and bakery items. The family reputation was tarnished when he converted the store to checkout system. As the store grew, Mr. Balsamo's interest in customers shifted to horses and women.

The final blow was when the town decided to capitalize on new land available with a series of public –works projects designed to keep shoppers from heading to suburban malls. This was a total disaster even to this day. The business closed in 1974.

Beauty may have fair leaves, yet bitter fruit. English proverb

I dated Sue Oscheski, a bakery clerk who worked adjacent to our department. She was an attractive 18-year old Polish blonde who recently graduated from high school. About five or six years older than I. I had a supervisory post on Friday nights, she thought I was going to college.

I asked Sue for a date to go to the quality movie house, the John P. Harris Memorial Theater in McKeesport. It was the last show so we got out hardly in time to have a soda at Isaly's and catch a streetcar to take her home in Glassport. I believe that was about a 45 minute ride on the old 99 line.

I had to leave quickly with only a kiss to get the last streetcar back to McKeesport and transfer to the 68 line for Duquesne. From there, I had to walk 1 ½ miles uphill to my house. I got home about 3 AM. Mother was waiting for me. I got an earful for just one kiss because my mother was convinced that her 13-year-old son (me) was a lady- killer.

We didn't have a phone so all our calls went to the neighbor. The next time Sue called, she got an earful. She was told that she was old enough to be my mother and that she was robbing the cradle. I was so embarrassed that I never asked her out again.

She lived too far away for a person without a car to date. In this case, my mother may have been right.

Sue was at least 18 and attractive. She had a small window of opportunity so she wanted to get married as soon as possible and a college student would be ideal. It was an excellent opportunity for her to move up. The only way I could keep this part- time job after summer employment was because I told them that my mother was forcing me to go to college.

During my junior and senior year, I did date a young lady that worked with me at Kennywood Park. I remember going fishing with her dad several times and was bored. We ceased seeing each other when I went to college.

AGE 17: WAYNESBURG COLLEGE

Nothing is worth more than a mind well instructed. American proverb

Nobody in my immediate family graduated from high school. Sister Kate had all the qualifications and aptitude but in those times, it was unthinkable, especially for agrarian emigrant families.

I knew the senior members of the Shigo family since I was seven. I sold them newspapers and eggs from our farm. They were good tippers. They lived in Polish Hill – a hill directly below us and above Duquesne. Elmer told me how the kids of Polish Hill were sent up to Morganca Juvenile Correction Facility during the Depression for stealing from railroad-- cars coal for fuel and pig iron, to be sold for food money.

The Shigo family had three sons. The older Elmer (1/1/1928) became the first Eagle Scout for Troop 3, Homestead PA and Alex (5/8/1930) was more my age and a first clarinet player in the Duquesne High School orchestra and band. He also played the saxophone.

Elmer did not attend Duquesne High because he wanted to be a wood pattern maker so he attended McKeesport Vocational High School. He was offered an apprenticeship by Westinghouse but declined because his English instructor, a graduate of Waynesburg College, sold him on the idea of being the very first in his family to go to college. He received a work program for tuition, room and board.

I remember the large apple cooler he built for Prexie's apples to be used by the dining room at Walton Hall. It was built with two rows of cement blocks filled with cork. Walton Hall served a variety of apple dishes and desserts all year round.

Alex joined his brother at Waynesburg College. He in turn sold me on the school. The college offered me work to help defray costs. Alex tried to entice me to learn how to play the bagpipes but was more successful in developing my botany interest.

Elmer graduated after my freshmen year. He was immediately drafted into the Korean conflict in 1950. Alex was afraid of being drafted so his uncle Eugene Scilogye (a clarinetist in the regular Navy band) arranged for a Washington DC interview with the Air Force Band Director. Alex got the clarinet chair, delayed his schooling and was entertaining diplomats all over the world. He met his wife- to- be Marilyn at the Canadian Exposition in Toronto when she was 17.

I enjoyed botany but disliked memorizing everything in anatomy class. I also disliked dissecting animals. I became totally turned off when I saw cadavers hanging with hooks into their ears and students cutting up dead human bodies. This killed my aspiration for premed.

I chose chemistry even though I liked botany very much – probably because of the instructor, Charles Bryner. "No nonsense" Mr. Bryner was extremely well respected and liked by most of the serious students. He was a Navy veteran of the Second World War and started teaching in 1945. I received my bachelor's degree in chemistry in 1953.

After his four year tour with the US Air Force Band, Alex returned to Waynesburg College for his BS degree and graduated in 1956. He continued for his masters in biology in 1958 and a PhD in pathology at University of West Virginia at the suggestion of his mentor, Dr. Bryner. Dr. Shigo became known internationally in tree science. He has written and published 200 papers, journals and books as Shigo and Trees Associates. He also assembled 5,000 slides from his works during his 40-plus years onto a CD. Many of his theories were revolutionary. He died of heart failure on October 6, 2006 in Durham, New Hampshire. A series of quotations by Alex are permanently displayed at the National Arts Club in New York City.

More details about his life and works may be found on his web cite Shigo and Trees Associates LLC.

Elmer Shigo spent his life working for US Steel. He worked his way up to Superintendent of the Blast Furnaces. When most of the mills in Pittsburgh closed, he did a great deal on international consulting for US Steel.

Waynesburg College was a small private school. There was a friendly and caring relationship between the college president and the professors, and the professors with the students. The college was founded in 1849 by the Cumberland Presbyterian Church. The only religious requirement at that time was taking a course in the Old and New Testament.

Some of the specific professors that I became attached to:

Religion & President – Dr. Paul R. Stewart

Chemistry Department – Dr. Thomas Myers and Dr. William Gasser

Biology Department – Charles Bryner and Dr. Lee Henderson

English – Dr. Dawn Logan

Physics – Cecil Riggs

German – Gertrude Smith

Mathematics – Wilbur Blum

Art-Stanley Wyatt

Dr Logan's required readings of "In Walden Pond" and the other world's best literature had much more effect on me than I ever realized. It was new to me. I did very little reading before college because of my work schedule. The professor opened my inner frontier of self discovery. Thoreau gave me a guide to living the classical ideals of the good life.

Some Thoreau's quotes that had a lasting effect on me included:

"Beware of all enterprises that require new clothes."

"A man is rich in proportion to the number of things which he can afford to let alone."

"It is never to late to give up your prejudices.".

"However mean your life is, meet it and live it, do not shut it and call it hard names."

"Rather than love, than money, than fame, give me truth."

"Simplify, simplify" also "Simplicity, simplicity, simplicity"

I received my board at Walton Hall by sweeping the dining room, mopping the kitchen daily and mopping and waxing the dining room once a week. I received an assistant when I complained about my time constraint and was told to find a helper. I chose Charles Gaush. We alternated doing the daily chores, and accomplished the weekly job in about two hours. A freebee was the accessibility of the leftovers in the cooler as long as we didn't take advantage of the situation. I was also a laboratory assistant in my junior and senior year reducing my tuition fee. During my freshman and sophomore years, I worked at Roth's Men Shop as a clerk.

Some of my college extra-curricular activities included:

Sunday school teacher at Saint Anne's Catholic Church

President of Alpha Phi Omega National Service Fraternity

Delta Phi Mu Honorary Mathematics Society

American Chemical Society

After my father died at the beginning of my sophomore year, I had the Department of Art Professor, Stanley Wyatt, paint an oil portrait of my Father from a photograph. Shortly thereafter he painted my Mother's portrait.

My sister damaged Dad's portrait about 15 years later and Mom's shortly thereafter.

After Dad's death, I used to hitch- hike home. In my senior year, Mom purchased a 1953 Pontiac as a graduation gift providing I stayed in Pittsburgh. I found out that she meant it. She sold the car to my brother in-law when I left for the Navy.

Some of my close friends at college included Charles Gaush, who became my assistant in cleaning the dining room and kitchen floors at Walton Hall. He was an excellent school photographer and laboratory assistant. He could not get into medical school. He earned his PhD in Biology and taught at a medical school.

Melvin Soles, a neighbor from McKeesport PA, was a close friend for two years. He transferred to an Optometry School in Philadelphia. On graduation, he joined the Air Force.

Bob Dille, a Waynesburg resident, was in many of my chemistry classes. He graduated one year earlier, went on to medical school, and then to the Air Force making a career there.

Jean Bucher was a special event- school photographer, member of the College Octet Music Group, Delta Ph Mu Honorary Mathematic Society and Alpha Phi Omega Service Fraternity. Jean was a math major who had an interest in electronics.

My Mother wanted to keep her two younger sons around after Dad died so she elected to be one of the first on the hill to purchase a TV. The one TV station was about 12 aerial miles away so Jean purchased a large rotary outdoor antenna for me and installed it on the apex of our very pointed roof. The high winds never blew the antenna away; staying in place until there was no more need for the rotary device. Jean also helped the family with other electronic devices including a radio cabinet. He filled in when need be in cleaning the floors at Walton Hall with me and Charles Gaush. After graduation, Jean joined RCA as an electronic engineer.

The graduating class of 1953 and 1954 did not produce a year- book. Ninety- seven students graduated in our college class of 1953. Two hundred eleven matriculated in our class of 1949. Forty percent graduated. Twenty earned a Bachelor of Science degree. Another 26 earned the Bachelor's degree in Science and a second degree, Bachelor of Arts. The college became an University 8/22/2007.

FAMILY COLLEGE LIFE

Education leads to an immortal life. Latin proverb

My brother Bernard was given an opportunity to attend Wabash University in Lafayette IN because of his academic and sport abilities. Since his interest was chemical engineering, it was a five- year joint program they had with Purdue University. Brother Ed was a few years behind him so I suggested that he try finding a good four- year program at a good university. It was further suggested that he might attend a good state school where I was living, with lower tuition fees.

He reluctantly accepted, and attended Newark College of Engineering and lived with me for several years in New Jersey. He received his bachelors in Chemical Engineering in 1958.

Maybe Ed could have gone to a New York engineering school. I was living and working in New York by that time. He earned his Bachelor's degree in electrical engineering from University of Pittsburgh in 1961.

My nephew Richard did go to Wabash on an academic and music scholarship. He majored in physics and immediately entered a PhD program at Purdue University. Because of the high unemployment rate of physicists in the 70s, he dropped out of the doctoral program and earned a Master's Degree in Physics and Master of Science in Industrial Administration in 1971 and 1972 respectively.

Richard's Brother Donald stayed in Pittsburgh and earned his bachelor's degree in mechanical engineering in 1971. His younger brother Dennis received his BS in biology at Indiana University in 1976. Their sister Rosemarie also stayed in Pittsburgh and earned her bachelors in chemistry from University of Pittsburgh in 1980.

Bernard's oldest son Brian earned his BS at Boston College's School of Management in 1986.He had an athletic scholarship. His second son, Kevin, wanted to attend engineering school at University of Vermont because he loved skiing but was persuaded to attend University of Rhode Island where he did everything but study. He was a somewhat successful entrepreneur on campus but eventually left this campus site. He recently received his BS in business management at Albertus Magnus in 2003.

Bernard's daughter Karen received her BS in computer science at Fairfield University on 1990 with an athletic scholarship. Her husband Tom went to Clarkson and graduated in 1983. Her brother David earned his BS in Finance, summa cum laude in 2004 from Bentley College. He also had an athletic scholarship. David's wife, Sarah, also earned her degree from Bentley College in 2004 but in economics-finance and graduated magna cum laude. Bernard's youngest son Timothy recently earned his BA in political science/writing in 2007.

 Richard Gorscak's son Jason earned his BS from Johns Hopkins University in biomedical engineering on May, 2000 and his MD from University of Miami in 2004. His sister Melissa earned her BA in education from University of Miami in 2003 and currently completely her MA ay University of Central Florida.

Don's daughter Katie Leah earned her BA in communications from University of Dayton in 2002. Her brother Ryan Thomas earned his bachelors in architecture from Virginia Polytechnic Institute in 2005, summa cum laude.

Stephen Czepiel earned his BS in finance-economics, magnum com laude, at Duquesne University. He was accepted and began the Masters program at Carnegie Tech but left the program when Kidder Peabody transferred him to Philadelphia.

Alicia Langenfeld Genco earned her BS in Physical Therapy for handicapped children.

James Marsula earned his Civil Engineering degree from University of Pittsburgh

It appears that, in a given field, more elite colleges were chosen for undergraduate studies. Also science was the most popular study concentration but liberal arts studies are becoming a bit more popular because the fields of studies are being picked not only for income and job safety but job satisfaction as well. Graduate work studies are evenly divided. The science interest were: Computer related (2), Industrial Hygienist (2), Safety (1), MD (1), Chemical Engineering (1), Physicist (1). The non-science areas of interest include: MBA (2), Investments (2), Marketing (1), Accounting (1), Public Communications (1) and Counseling (1).

CHEMICAL ENGINEERING

Business before pleasure. French proverb

Don't mix business with pleasure. American proverb

*How happy the life unembarrassed by the
cares of business.* Latin proverb

NUODEX PRODUCTS, RESEARCH
CENTER, 1954-1955 AGE 22

*A drop of fortune (or luck) is better than
a cask of wisdom.* Latin proverb

I obtained this position through the auspices of Alfred Drucker.
I was employed by International Printing Company in Elizabeth,
N.J. as a junior chemist and was bored with the routine nature of
the job and the plant secrecy. I met Alfred Drucker as a resident at
the Elizabeth, N.J. YMCA. He just joined Reichhold Chemical as
a chemist from Brazil, S.A. I told Alfred about my dissatisfaction
so he contacted his friend Dr. Irving Skeen at Nuodex. I was
interviewed on a Saturday and joined the firm immediately.
Alfred soon brought his wife and maids to the USA and I became
close friends with them.

As section supervisor for this Specialty Chemical Manufacturer, I evaluated various vinyl stabilizers, fungicides, plasticizers, antioxidants and chelators. The evaluation results were published in *Plastics Technology.*

At Nuodex, the chemist, technicians and secretaries worked and played hard. Apparently their Christmas parties were quite wild. Good food, abundance of alcohol and love. I was told that at least one female got pregnant at these parties. There was no pill at that time. I did not, attend the party in 1954.

I was persuaded to change my name to a simpler name. Perry was chosen because it began with a P. The name change was official September 27, 1954.

About ten years after I left the firm, I received a precious letter from my mentor and research director, Dr. Irving Skeen. Apparently Dr Skeen did not get along with his son because he did not meet his expectation; He adopted me. I was the son he wanted to mold.

NIEMAND BROS 1955-1957 AGE 23

*Fortune truly helps those who are of
good judgment.* Euripides

I obtained this chemist position through my engineering professor at Brooklyn Polytechnic Institute. Dr. Paul Bruins was hired as a technical consultant to Niemand Bros.

My responsibilities were to act as full time technical advisor to the two Niemand Brothers (owners), plant superintendent Herman Kappler and the purchasing agent. One of the brother's sons had just graduated from Cornell and was entering the business. The firm wanted to diversify from just being a tubular paper converter to a combination of paper/plastics or plastics tubular products.

Increasing production speed was also important. The firm had excellent German machinists.

Some accomplishments included: manufacturing our own volume dextrin and vinyl adhesives, shrinkable Mylar tubular products for the electronic industry, changing some of the letterpresses to flexographic printing, extrusion and injection molding.

My sexual interest reappeared again in 1955. I invited a blonde, Dorothy Schumacher, to my one-bedroom Jersey City apartment. I shared this apartment with my brother Bernard who was attending the Newark College of Engineering School. As we were just ready to start foreplay, we heard somebody opening the front door. Being nude, we didn't have time to cover or escape to the bathroom so poor Dorothy received the dirty look of a lifetime from Bernie. Don't know whether it was because she was on his side of the bed or he was against premarital sex.

GEIGY CORPORATION 1957-1959 AGE 25

*The nearer you can associate yourself with
the good, the better.* Plautus

As a result of my publications in *Plastics Technology*, the division president, Mr. Hal Zussman (division president) offered me a position to create and administer a plastics department in Geigy Chemical Corporation to evaluate ultraviolet light absorbers, optical brighteners and other specialty chemicals for incorporation into various thermoplastic and thermosetting plastic products. Responsibilities included: sales development, technical service, development, market research, advisor to R&D efforts, technical bulletin writing and training of salesman.

When I took the job with Geigy Corporation I met Miss Lenny Rosenboom in the cafeteria. I was heading up the newly formed-plastics section of the Industrial Division and she was in the newly- formed Pharmaceutical Division. We hit it off quite well and met her parents several times but since we both were career-driven, we ceased dating. It was against the Swiss company's corporate policy to date somebody in the company so she and her parents introduced me to their friend Miss Pat Stauffer in Bronxville, N.Y. We also hit it off quite well. She suggested that I move to Bronxville from Ardsley and helped me obtain an apartment in the town's only apartment building. She also persuaded me to become active with Brown Cottage Children's Village in Derby, N.Y.

We had access to box seats at the Metropolitan Opera when her parents were not using them. Pat wanted to bring culture to this "Midwestern" man and I enjoyed it. At cocktail parties, some of her friends seemed to think anything west of Philadelphia was the end of civilization. Fortunately I had little problem mixing with the cocktail crowd because I was successful in my career and I quickly learned the dozen or so clichés words describing pop paintings.

One evening in 1957 Pat and I became passionate in love- making. When Pat told her mother about this episode, that was the end of our relationship. She was told that I only had a sex interest in her and that sex was just for reproduction and after marriage. (The sexual revolution didn't start until the 60s) Her mother sent Pat to a psychiatrist to expedite our breaking up.

That was the end of our relationship even though I maintained friendship with her father Hans who was president and majority stockholder of Stauffer Chemical Company. I believe that Pat's mother might have been a bit stuffy with Hans as well. He loved relaxation and his flower garden. We kept in touch. He was an advisor to me when I was contemplating setting up a specialty chemical firm as a Japanese licensee.

For years, I kept in contact with several family friends including Jan van Lear who worked for Stauffer Chemical company. I was also told by someone that I did not meet the expectations of Mrs. Stauffer. Pat eventually married an interior designer, Mr. Benson. When Mrs. Stauffer died, Hans remarried a next- door widower and enjoyed his flower garden.

There was a power play at Stauffer Chemical between the west and east coast operations. The West Coast won and Mr. Stauffer's son was fired as VP of Planning. During an unwanted merger with Cheseborough Ponds in 1985, son John sold all his shares to Cheseborough Ponds and convinced Pat to do the same consummating the deal over the objection of their father. Hans Stauffer was very proud of what he did for the firm. His family was successful in the vineyard business in Germany but Hans wanted to make it on his own. (He came to the US as a stowaway.) When he got to NYC, he hitchhiked to San Francisco and dropped in unannounced at his uncle's who owned a small inorganic chemical /fertilizer/ company. With Hans' leadership, they broadened their product mix and by the 70s they were the largest PVC manufacturer in the USA, exceeding Union Carbide in pounds and dollars. Much of my early plastics experience was with PVC. Later, during the oil crisis of the 70's, as a consultant for Springborn Laboratories, I studied the feasibility of replacing "C" (organic) with "P" (inorganic).

When I joined Geigy, I reported directly to the division president, Hal Zussman. To appease the people in Switzerland, he hired a PhD, Dr Bruce Garner, to head two departments. When I joined the firm, Basel headquarters wanted me to visit Switzerland for six months but I was eager to get the job done in Ardsley. I was also afraid of having an elliptic seizure there. That was a mistake.

I spent $2 million on equipment for Geigy before I set one foot in the door. Dr Garner was a very nice person who was a professor and research associate at Stanford but because my ego was hurt, I treated him poorly. I did not support him effectively. I would keep him waiting outside my office 10 or 15 minutes by staying on the phone. I should have tried to win his gratitude by keeping the projects in my department running by supplying him with good ideas.

I then probably would have gotten more money, perks from the division and corporate presidents because everybody wanted a PhD as Department Head. My ego caused the division president not to trust me. He could have provided opportunities that have changed my life as he wanted to look good to compliment his goal to be corporate president. Instead I chose to polish my resume. Perhaps I wanted to self destruct because of the break-up in my love life.

He was a far bigger person than I. He left to go back to the University about a year after I left. He told everybody, including the president, that my two -year work plan ran out and he was inept in that area. We could have been a tremendous team that Basel would have loved. Zussman, although brilliant, was constantly getting in hot water with the corporate people here in the USA as well as in Switzerland. Mr. Zussman never attained the presidency of the US operation.

At this time, I was attending New York University Graduate School of Business on Wall Street. I drove from Ardsley. NY to Wall Street in a very powerful fire- red DeSoto. I had to brake the car to go under 30 miles per hour. I received three speeding tickets and was arrested for going through a stop sign, and was about to lose driver's license. I panicked. Instead of hiring an attorney, I decided to leave town.

I had three job offers: Midwest Research Institute as Senior Economist, Paper Institute as Research Administrator and

Armstrong Cork (as production chemist for one year and then a transfer to their marketing department.) Initially I took the Midwest Research position when the director flew to New York and met me at my apartment for the interview. The job was offered pending approval by his staff in Kansas City. They approved but I switched to the Paper Institute when Averill Wiley pressured me to reconsider.

I may have been a bit scared to tackle a senior economist position at that time. These were troubling times for me.

At this stage of my life, I successfully moved from simple background to interacting and socializing with the rich and famous. I was becoming a successful young business man.

According to John Perkins, in his book *Confessions of an Economic Hit Man* we became one of the most powerful countries in the world through padded economic forecasts for the less developed countries and the manipulation of their corrupt leaders. John Perkins was hired as an economist for one of those engineering companies aligned with this plan. His role was to create forecasts designed to convince developing "third world" countries to take out billion- dollar loans from the World Bank to build infrastructures that would bury these countries in debt which they would never be able to realistically repay so that they would forever be indebted to their creditors.

I wonder if the Senior Economist position at The Midwest Research Institute was a training ground for Economic Hit Men. If it was, I don't think my conscience would have permitted me.

Fortune, good or bad, does not last forever. Arabic proverb

PAPER INSTITUTE 1959- 1960 AGE 27

Better that the world should know you as a sinner than
God knows you as a hypocrite. Danish proverb

After turning down the Assistant Director for planning position at the Paper Institute, I accepted. I was to be in charge of commercial development for sulphite liquor as briqueting of iron ore power, adhesives, fertilizers and household products.

Before leaving for Appleton Wisconsin I met Jean Bascom of Scarsdale who wanted to donate an official pool table to Children's Village where I was doing volunteer work. It didn't dawn on me at the time that she was getting a divorce. She called me when I was in Appleton and wanted me to move back to Westchester County. By the time I was ready to leave Appleton, she had found somebody else to her liking. During this period of time, divorced women married quickly—especially if the ex-husband remarried right after divorce.

While in Appleton, I also received a call from a person I had met while in NY. She claimed that she couldn't take NYC anymore and asked if I could come to Madison WI and visit with her. I said yes even though I had a blind date scheduled with a student at Lawrence College for that Saturday. I found out later that the student was the Dean's daughter. It was a big mistake to cancel that date. After I renewed my friendship with her, I returned home to Appleton.

Early Sunday morning, my boss, Averill Wiley knocks on my door. I was half asleep; he points his index finger at me and says "You lied. You are a divorced". I asked Averill what he was drinking. (I knew he didn't drink.)

I had a house- warming cocktail party a few weeks earlier for our staff members. Being devilish, I supersaturated some of the hors d'oeuvres with brandy. He told me that he never tasted anything as good my appetizers and kept coming into the kitchen for more.

Averill told me that he heard from the dean of Lawrence College (they were in the process of adopting The Paper Institute) that I lied. I told him that isn't so. I reminded him that you literally begged me to join you. Averill was stone -deaf and had to read lips to communicate.

I suggested that Averill check the facts and we could have a meeting Monday morning. He did, and said that I was right. "But I'm still on probation as I'm setting a bad example for the school having a drink at dinner and taking various college girls to dinner."

I told him he could have his job. I also told him that I was popular with the college girls because I treated them as equal. It was a local custom not to take a girl friend to dinner until she was ready to marry or at least be engaged

There was only one good restaurant that served liquor in Appleton. Compared to NY, restaurant tabs were extremely low. Two could eat cheaper than one in NYC. So why not have a companion?

A few years later, Averill thanked me for the learning experience. He was losing touch with his son but this experience got him back on track in time. He and other staff members, like Dr. Lawrence A. Boggs and his wife Mary Bugbee, communicated with me every Christmas, informing me in detail on what the Institute was doing and accomplishing.

Larry died 8/7/1993 at the age of 83. He was born and raised in Spokane, Washington and attended Washington State University. He received his BS in Sugar Technology and his M.S. in Chemistry at the University of Hawaii, Honolulu. He was at Pearl Harbor at the time of the bombing. He served as a Japanese language specialist with the U.S. Occupational Forces in Okinawa and Tokyo under General Douglas MacArthur until 1947. He retired in the Army Reserve as Lieutenant Colonel. Larry earned his PhD in agricultural biochemistry at the University of Minnesota in 1951. He moved to Appleton where he accepted a position as research chemist. His many interests included love of languages, music, travel and growing roses. He was fluent in Japanese, Spanish, German, Italian and French and was acquainted with Portuguese, Russian, Hebrew, Arabic, Chinese and Esperanto. He was professionally recognized in *Who's Who among American Men of Science* and in numerous scientific papers.

ARMSTRONG CORK COMPANY 1960- 1961 AGE 28

When you're in ill luck, a snake can bite you
even with its tail. Martinique Creole

I took the job with Armstrong Cork because that job was still available six months after I joined the Paper Institute. This was a production job but I was promised a transfer to the Marketing Department in one year if I managed their rotogravure printing start-up. I reported to Milton Ford, Plant Manager and Art Williams, Rotogravure Products Manager. I had the printing operation started within three months and then worked on the coating team for the next nine months. I believe I was successful because I listened to the people on line. I tried out their suggestions and never said that something was impossible. Many times their suggestions would work. I learned this back in 1953 when a lithographic ink chemist reluctantly listened to me, a junior chemist about a possible solution to a problem.

I wrote a company booklet for *In Process Control* about their clear- coat and paint- making line of products. My new testing methods reduced or eliminated the need for a supervisory chemist observing the complete operation which could take up to 36 hours. I also did an economic analysis concerning rotogravure inks. This study resulted in a fixed cost. After one year, I asked for the transfer I was promised but now was told that they do not transfer from one division to another, so I quit.

While in Lancaster, my friends and associates from Geigy Corporation either visited me or I came back to Westchester County. They introduced me to Liz Dinger, a bright, shy music major (cello) at Drew University at Madison N.J who worked at Geigy during the summer. When Liz visited me at her house, my Mother didn't understand her shyness and thought she was a bit aloof. Mother did not approve of marriage for my brothers or for me. She wanted a retirement payoff. She had invested heavily into sons and worked very hard for us to succeed.

On one weekend trip, my friend, Dick Fairfield, was to pick up Liz at school in Madison and drive her to Lancaster, PA. On the way, Dick had an accident. Liz got a big gash and permanent scar on her beautiful knees. All my friends in the car suggested that she sue Dick's insurance company to help mend her leg. Her parents and she initially rejected the idea. However, I pursued it by finding a low- key attorney in Bronxville to represent them. They interviewed my low- profile attorney but then Liz parent's neighbors suggested she get a NYC attorney who promised an instant million. They hired him and this   attorney filed a suit three times the amount that Dick was insured for. Dick, a close friend, who introduced us and was an up- and- coming executive, was very scared. When I approached Liz, she just said they probably would settle for the insured amount. I asked her about Dick's anxiety. I finally told her it was her choice to lower the amount of the claim or I would have to drop her. It was a very stupid ultimatum.

I met Liz in NYC a year or so later to tell her that I was getting married to somebody who looked like her. I got a message three months later that she was marrying her classmate. They live in Minneapolis and have several children. She is a cellist and he, a theater director.

I remember that in 1954 my sister's friend, Johanna Koncoli, lent me several thousand dollars to purchase a new Ford automobile, I decided to do the same. I lent Jack McHugh several thousand dollars to purchase a car although we hardly knew each other. Later, I also interceded in his mixed-marriage situation. They are still married. We still are in contact with each other.

LUCIDOL CORPORATION 1961–1962 AGE 29

Who can put trust in the strength of the body
or in the stability of fortune? Cicero

I was hired by two people, Dr. Visser't Hooft and Richard Berry, to find new ventures in areas other than peroxide-based products. My supervisor, Richard Berry and his superior, Dr. Harrison gave me the opportunity to take risks in doing my job more effectively and helping reach company goals. Later I prepared technical bulletins, assisted in advertising and promotional activities, searched for and did preliminary screening for technical personnel to do service work. I also designed the new plastics application laboratory and was advisor in the R&D effort.

"Doc" Visser't Hooft was forced to retire in a corporate power play which nobody recognized until the coup was completed and sent "Andy" Andrews to Buffalo as Executive Vice President. Andy knew nothing about the operation and Dr. Harrison was designated to teach him what was going on. Andrews seemed fated to make all the wrong moves. He hired Dick Schwab as Sales Manager, replacing Ken Ditzel, for no logical reason. The corporate people seemed to feel that Dr. Harrison knew too much about everything and they wanted to take control of Lucidol. In actuality, Andrews was used by a vice-president who lusted after the corporate presidency.

As so often happens, the nincompoops take over, ruin a perfectly good and profitable group and eventually leave two competitors in place.

At Lucidol Corporation,, I traveled all over the country from Buffalo as a commercial development specialist. On one flight to Syracuse, I met Marge Shoemaker who was working on her PhD in cancer research. Since there was not much to do socially in Buffalo, our section had a very close social network of our own including vice president of research & development, Dr. James Harrison; planning and marketing director/Richard Berry, advertising director /Tony Nasa, research coordinator/Derek Huibers. marketing director, commercial development specialists-Matthew Perry (non-peroxide products) and Kenneth Wylegala (peroxide products).

We had a party almost every weekend at someone's home. I usually brought Marge Shoemaker. . Many of the men, particularly the married ones, were always around Marge. She was brilliant and attractive. One weekend, John Bliss (our Texas salesperson) was visiting Buffalo. At the weekend party he asked Marge for a date. She asked for my opinion. I told her he was married. She did go out with him. I was fired soon thereafter because I was looking for another position.

I was very upset with John Bliss. He was later promoted to national sales manager when Dick Schwab was made president. The Peter Principle.

In my travels, I met Mary Ann Yanosek who became my wife. Our salesmen preferred to fix me up with a woman when I was in their territory— so that they could sleep at home. (Otherwise a salesman would stay at the same motel that I did, and we would meet after dinner.) Mary Ann was a pharmacist at University Hospital in Cleveland. She expressed herself well, and was assertive. Mary Ann resembled my old flame, (Liz Dinger) and she was quite intelligent and always looking for excitement.

Lucidol was a manufacturer of peroxide- type catalysts for polymerization of monomers. These catalysts are very dangerous and explosive. The plant blew up a number of years before I joined, killing 35 people. One of my tasks was to search for less explosive chemicals. I did patent and literature searches. The azo compounds were a good candidate. One such chemical in that group was a clean catalyst, non-explosive but very toxic. (It was used by the Germans in gas warfare during World War I.) However we found other azo compounds that could be used as blowing agents to expand polyvinyl chloride, polyethylene and polypropylene to give better electrical properties as well as reduce cost. This was an industry in its infancy.

The French had such a compound but its performance was unpredictable because of impurities. Their batch manufacturing process did not yield a uniform particle size. The Japanese, (Otsuka Chemical Company) made the perfect product: clean, with uniform particle size, resulting in a uniform -cell structure product. Later we had our brilliant process engineer, Dr. Huibers, start work on a continuous manufacturing process but Lucidol appeared to be dragging. They didn't want to take the risk for our bold strategy plan so I approached Otsuka Chemical to ask whether they would consider licensing their technology to a group of entrepreneurs. They agreed.

The importer who was buying the French compound agreed to negotiate with the Japanese firm for an agreement and capital. The importer (trading as U.S. and Foreign Chemical Company in NYC), was also going to put some of his capital and expertise into the firm.

During the third trip to NYC from Buffalo our group had arguments in the car. Should we include our research director, Dr Harrison, in our new venture? Personally I thought we had too many marketers in our group and Dr Harrison would give us balance in administration and research.

Dick Berry, my immediate boss, thought I was trying to usurp him. Previously he was never afraid of any of our team members having the spotlight. Our arguments continued throughout the negotiation sessions and because of this schism, our percent of the equity continued to decline. My friend Hans Stauffer told me later that we should have done the deal regardless of the equity position and sold it once we got it going. Everything was in our favor—the application where the product was to be used was in the embryo stage and we were dealing with a large, highly competent and ethical company to license the technology. Before Hans' retirement, Stauffer Chemical Corporation became the largest PVC manufacturer in the USA, ahead even of Union Carbide.

Before I left Lucidol, I convinced Dr. Ralph Hanson of Bell Laboratories (NJ) to join Lucidol in Buffalo. He was only mildly interested so I spoke with his wife. I wanted him on board because of his many technical papers and articles on PVC. He was also going to join our venture involving blowing agents and azo catalysts.

When we all left Lucidol, Dr Hanson decided to remain at Bell Labs but went to Stanford University for a short time. He retired at Bell Labs.

Dr Harrison left Lucidol and formed another peroxide manufacturer in Elyria OH, Aztec Chemical Corporation. Ken

Ditzel joined Jim and then moved to Houston as sales manager, taking Jim's secretary and his wife along as secretary at Aztec.

Dick Berry left Lucidol and formed an industrial engineering firm in Tennessee. Dr Huber received a patent on his continuous manufacturing process for making ADA (azodicarbonate) and was made manager of manufacturing. Lucidol did nothing with the compound so he left the firm for a large Dutch chemical manufacturer, Akzo.

The exodus at Lucidol started because I suggested to a senior research associate that he unfortunately did not have a chance to be research director because he was Jewish. He left shortly thereafter. I was next to leave because a head hunter erroneously sent my resume to Lucidol's president. The others in our clique left too, but not before we blackballed the company in the professional job market. We belonged to various professional associations like the Commercial Development Association. There was a shortage of chemical engineers and chemists that year, so applicants were selective in their job commitment. They would call some association member at Lucidol about the firm. We networked, giving plusses and negatives. Lucidol could not fill any of the open positions for a year or so! Finally Lucidol was able to hire a marketer. This broke the cycle.

It was not until January 14, 2008, that I learned about Dick Berry participating in the second In chon Landing in Korea in the bitter winter of January 1951. (It was the only time US forces had to be evacuated while gaining a foothold.) After 15 days, Dick was the only officer left in his mortar company. They lost 100 recruits out of a total of 160. He still has nightmares occasionally over this experience. He traveled all over the world but refused any return to Korea even when his granddaughter showed interest.

Dick's commented in a letter of January 6, 2008: "Lucidol was fun and my best friends were you and Ken Wylegala. In addition to getting things a done, we were a center of merriment among too serious people."

Leaving Lucidol, Dick joined Lundy Electronics in Glen Cove, N.Y. The owner was an inventor who had a patent on chaff used by the Air Force, and another patent on a bank sorting system which automatically over-writes checks when the bottom number is mutilated. The firm just received a government contract to design and build a shipboard wastewater purification system to produce less contaminant dumping. Their manager, Jim White, was looking for a project manager so Dick joined the firm. A prototype was developed at the King's Point Merchant Marine Academy and installed on a 180 -foot- long Coast Guard cutter.

Lundy Electronics was less successful in making polyester-fiber glass swimming pools, bath tubs and showers. They picked up another government contract from NASA to design and build a prototype for a zero-gravity toilet (zgt).Dick's boss returned to Boeing but the zgt project was a big success. It was installed on the Mercury shuttle, went with Neill Armstrong to the moon, and is still the prototype for the present sophisticated toilets and showers.

At NASA Dick caught up with a fellow classmate at Michigan Tech, Donald (" Deke")

Slayton. They both failed organic chemistry and had to repeat the course. Deke went on to earn a Master's degree at Purdue, went to the USAF demonstration team, and eventually joined NASA. He was sidelined with a heart murmur and became an astronaut trainer, a brigadier general. Later he flew anyway after NASA found that eight others had the same malady!

Dick then got into the environmental and civil engineering business. Carborundum Corporation bought Penetryn Corporation, a sewer sealing company. Carborundum was purchased by Sohio Corporation which became British Petroleum Corporation. Here Dick hired his manager, Jim White, who had been at Lundy Electronics (Boeing) to work for him. They incorporated Rembco in 1982. The initial geotechnical service was strengthening low-density and water-soaked soils by compacting them with grout. Shortly thereafter they initiated the use of compaction piles as supports for foundations that were settling. Then the foundations could be lifted.

During the next two years, they led the grouting industry in compaction pile technology. In 1985 chemical grouting was added to their list of services. In 1992, Dick's son-in-law joined the company to refine existing services and expand them by adding drilled micropile and minipile foundations. Revenue doubled in short order.

Dick was always an excellent scientist and engineer. For example, in 1995, while at Stanford University, he attended a lecture by Nobel Prize winner Richard Feynman California Institute of Technology. He was going to explain quantum electric dynamics (QED) in simple language. He was the 29- year -old assistant of Niels Henrik David Bohr who made the atomic bomb.

Retired, Dick still submits papers to the American Society of Civil Engineers. For example, he has a paper about why the Minneapolis Bridge collapsed. His prediction: Left on its own, the engineering community will build it back at great expense only to have it fail in another 25 years .He has a long term interest in more rational energy- alternative technologies. He is actively speaking and writing about ethanol, saying that it is a disaster and bad economics.

Currently Dick is working with Dr. Stephen Levy, Distinguished Professor at Tennessee Technological University (Crossville TN) who is also adjunct professor at the University of Tennessee (Knoxville). Levy is also a consultant to UT/Bechtel on e-glass for solar panels. Tennessee, Russia, Australia and China have large quantities of the right kind of sand (low iron content) that will transmit the ultra-violet (UV) sunlight to generate electricity. "One cent a watt" is their motto. Levy predicts it will be practical within ten years. The main problems are with controls and the antiquated grid, not with the glass. But Levy wrote that solar panels are not a panacea.

Dick published several non-technical papers. One was about Korea in the *Atlantic Monthly* Magazine. The other was a Christmas story, published by the Writer's Guild. It was about his experience near Valles, Mexico in 1934, when he was five years old.

NATIONAL CASH REGISTER (NCR) 1962 - 1962

A good leader produces good soldiers. Latin proverb

I got this position through a headhunter who told me that NCR was trying to transform more into an entrepreneurial firm and out of the Ivy League mode. My prime responsibility was: market research, selling research and licensing agreements for micro encapsulation in all areas other than NCR paper.

The IBM founder, Mr. Thomas Watson, was almost fired at NCR for smoking. The NCR president once made an unannounced visit to Thomas Watson's office. Fortunately Watson put the cigarette out in time. Watson had developed the electric typewriter but NCR was not interested in the product – they were in the cash register business. This was one of many errors made by NCR because of their conservatism.

At NCR, my contribution included revamping their current and future encapsulation licensing process to reduce possible antitrust action. I did not recognize the potential risks of asserting myself on this matter with my supervisor. NCR had a permanent injunction against them for many years. I made the firm aware of an IBM threat from an international patent search I did. IBM came up with a polymer process of encapsulating vs. NCR's gelatin process for sustained drug release.

Since I was the second person to leave this department within a year, Personnel asked me to come for an exit interview and tests. They concluded that I was an ideal NCR employee and asked if I would join their newly formed computer operation. I declined because the damage was done. I made plans to leave because my wife and her allergies could not stand the Ohio Valley pollution. My supervisor was promoted out of this department to head the NCR "No Carbon Required" paper operation in Appleton. He was much more qualified to handle this operation rather than licensing new technology.

Don Wilkinson had been at NCR for a while before I became his replacement. I had complimented Don Wilkinson's reports every time my boss criticized them by saying that I found the reports to be to the point, meaningful and very actionable. Being Jewish and from New York was not the only thing against him. I had been told he could be obnoxious and my one telephone conversation with him confirmed this impression.

A few years later, I read that IBM and NCR exchanged patents so NCR had a near monopoly on this expensive process. Sustained release became "big" in the drug industry.

I had been a very successful Republican precinct captain in Lancaster PA. I started to be active in politics in the suburbs of Dayton OH. Mary Ann was even more active.

THE SHERWIN WILLIAMS CO 1962 - 1964

*The superior man is easy to serve and
difficult to please.* Confucius

I prepared market surveys and acquisition studies on various consumer and industrial products as well as various patent searches and analyses. I reported directly to Dr. John Weaver, Research Administrator but also to Art Holton, Research Director and Harold Spitzer, Development Director. I became a task leader to establish a computerized retrieval system. The objective was to help the company look up formulas and make calculations more quickly without reinventing the wheel again. The universe was 4,000 raw materials and 16,000 finished products. Nobody else wanted to do it and I was new.

When the IBM 360 was purchased, the accounting people were up tight because they all thought they were going to lose their jobs. They sabotaged the computer at every opportunity. Little did they know that more jobs were to be created because more inputs were needed for the various new reports!

More people were also needed to interpret the many reports that were produced.

I had no computer knowledge but I was fortunate to have an excellent programmer and statistician on the team to reduce the numerical or logical operations by a properly instructed program. IBM said that our new 360 was not capable of completing the task. We accomplished our mission. I wanted to publish the study but could not receive a release. Mead Paper in Ohio developed two well known retrieval systems; one was in the field of Law.

On the day President Kennedy was shot, I happened to be in the office of Dr. Weaver, my supervisor. He hated President Kennedy so much that he was very happy about the assassination. I was

115

a Republican but lost all respect for this brilliant supervisor and started contacting headhunters. I could not look into his eyes anymore. Exposed to a dose of consumer marketing at Sherwin Williams, I was fascinated by its so- called science. Most headhunters were not interested in me because they felt consumer marketing was too sophisticated and quantitative for me to handle. One headhunter, however, had a client that was a subsidiary of Sears near Chicago which manufactured both consumer and industrial products. I interviewed them and was offered a job.

Mary Ann and I both loved Cleveland. I was going to Case Reserve continuing my MBA education. We had many friends and acquaintances at NASA. Our neighbors were interesting. NASA certainly influenced my nephew Richard Gorscak when he entered college. I acted surprised when Richard returned from the set-up tour and said that he was going to drop music as a major and replace it with physics. Joanne Temple, Public Relations Director at NASA, and I made an unbeatable bridge pair. We were always partners until Mary Ann came home once and found me playing bridge with three women. That ended my bridge playing for awhile since Mary Ann and I acted like typical married couple players. I decided to refrain from bridge playing.

During this time spell, I saw a complete transformation of a dedicated physicist from a quiet scientist to an extroverted bureaucrat in a matter of 120 days – 120 day wonder program. As true scientists, Bill Brunk thought marketing lacked "truth" and was basically "BS". He became a changed person when he was promoted to NASA headquarters in Washington. He filed for divorce, seriously started dating his secretary and was the life of the party given to him on his return visit to Cleveland.

While in Cleveland, I became very close friends with Ed and his wife Charlene Peattie. Previously he was a corrosion engineer for Armco (Arabian American Oil Company).Charlene taught English and art at the Armco schools. When Ed was forced to retire because of age, he taught corrosion engineering at University of Petroleum and Minerals in Dhahran, Saudi Arabia. Five editions of his book *Pipeline Corrosion and Cathode Protection* were issued.

I met up with Ed and Charlene when he joined Standard Oil of Ohio as an engineer

.Mary Ann and I always enjoyed seeing many slide presentations about their life in the desert. .He even had pictures of the king's Hiram which he could have resulted in his hands being cut off if caught. Apparently Ed had access to the King's and Crown Princes palaces. Ed wrote a book - *Green Desert* about his wonderful life in Saudi Arabia.

At the time Ed and Charlene were there, Armco was owned by four oil companies: Standard of California 30%, Standard of New Jersey 30%, Texas Oil Company 30%, and Socony Vacuum 10%.

1950, with the threat of nationalization, Armco agreed to share its profits on oil sales 50/50.It should be noted that the American government granted US Armco member companies a tax break known as the Golden gimmick equivalent to the profits lost in sharing oil profits with the King.

In 1950, the Trans-Arabian Pipe Line was completed linking Eastern Providence Oil fields to Lebanon and the Mediterranean.

Ed semi-retired to Sun City East, Florida where consulted to the US Navy and was active with MENSA. Charlene was active in the arts. They wanted me to retire in Sun City East but I was not ready. Ed passed away in his 90s, a few years after his wife - a beautiful one flesh couple.

My wife also liked her job as chemist for Bonnie Bell. She got help from a friend I knew from Brooklyn Polytechnic College and NYU whenever I couldn't give her a satisfying answer.

I took the Chicago position. When I called my wife from Chicago, she hung up the phone on me. Mary Ann delayed coming to Chicago but changed her mind when Bonnie Bell offered her a sales position in Chicago and I promised to help her be successful in this new career.

DESOTO INC (1964 - 1968

He's a fool who cannot conceal his wisdom. Franklin

At DeSoto, Inc. I became market research department manager and economist. I supervised 240 market research, economic, financial, new venture and acquisition analysis projects. I made a name for myself at Sears when I coordinated a merchandising study which increased their sales 40% from a $25 million base with commensurate profit increase. This project might have led to my being fired had it not been for our president, Mr. Greenberg at DeSoto. Paint sales at Sears were going down substantially so the buyer called me for consultation. Remembering my first meeting with the president at Geigy, I came prepared. He wanted another market study done but I told him that would not give him sufficient info to implement. It would just give him a bunch of statistics with no actionable solutions. I asked him how helpful last year's study was.

After I left, he called Mr. Greenberg and told him: "Who does Matt Perry think he is? He does not know what he is doing" Suppliers to Sears were very accommodating. Mr. Greenberg calmed him down by saying that I was an egghead and that "he really wants to help you. If you don't want his help, you could go to Sears' planning group for far less cost." Sales were still declining so the paint buyer called me for another meeting. At his request, we set up certain guide lines like "no surprises" and keep him abreast on anything he could implement without much capital expenditure so only the expensive implementation recommendations would be presented in the final report.

I hired the Institute for Motivational Research, (Croton- on-Hudson), NY for the project at a very reasonable price because they wanted to say that Sears was a client.

Sears was, by far, the biggest name in retail at that time. Dr. Dichter did not know that I would require original interviews and focus studies. I monitored their progress every step of the way. On completion, I paid Dr. Dichter an extra $2,000 to make the presentation. This was one of the best decisions I ever made.

Merchandising managers and buyers came to the presentation in Desoto's auditorium. Initially there was bickering about why certain things could not be done so Dr. Dichter finally said that they could be wasting the $2,000 bringing him in and $30,000 for the study, "so please sit back and listen to the report before saying what could and could not be done." Sales increased because of the implementation. We all got the credit. The merchandising manager, R.R. Thompson, of the Paint Department was promoted to head all Sear's operations in Spain. The buyer was promoted to merchandising manager in Chicago; Dr. Dichter was hired for a large study to predict Sears store operations in the year 2000. I became special project consultant for Sears at Whirlpool, HON Furniture, and Magic Chef.

I became an active participant in diversification activities in furniture, lamps, lighting fixtures, detergent and recreational products.

In 1966 we ventured into economic forecasting. I was happy with my staff willing to work six or seven days a week, ten hours a day for six weeks on this project. Because it was done in the summer, economic data were not available. We had no computer access to make charts or analyze data. All charts were done by hand. Our 1966 economic forecast was extremely accurate. Milton Freeman was impressed as was a Wall Street firm that wanted to sell it as a multi- client economic forecast report. Sears and DeSoto would not release it.

I tried to add another economist to our group. I was turned down because they claimed that my empire was already too large. They agreed to move up next year's planning meeting by several months so data from the National Association of Business Economists and Wall Street would begin to trickle out. We still did not have access to a computer to make and interpret hundreds of charts. It was too much work for our division to do. It would have been more appropriate for the Sears planning group.

Later, when I set up Contempo Cosmetics DeSoto permitted me to work only 50 % of the time on their projects until I was very sure I was going to leave. When I left, they sold a one- year- old $5,000 Impala to me for $1,000.

When Contempo got into financial difficulty, Sears offered me their best bankruptcy attorney free of charge. They treated me just fine. Leaving DeSoto hurt me financially and emotionally. Their profit sharing plan had been just super: the first five years they gave me 1.24 dollars for every dollar I invested in DeSoto stock. In the next five years the ratio was 2.48 followed by 3.72 and 5.04. Unlike today, the wealth and profits of a company were distributed to the workers and middle management personnel rather than just a few on top.

When Sam Greenberg retired as president, there was a series of successors. Bernie Malm was promoted. Other executives and middle management almost always told him that "Sam would not have done it that way." He resigned. George Nichols, the research director, succeeded him. I always showed Mr. Nichols a lot of respect while others did the opposite because they did not think he was a candidate for the president's job. He did not repeat Bernie Malm's mistakes.

When George Nichols retired a few years after I left, Sears made the former Sears-Desoto coordinator, Glenn Workman, president of DeSoto Inc. Sears was beginning to divest their interest in manufacturing.

George Karl, marketing director at DeSoto, was in the dog house with DeSoto management and was made general manager of the Wallpaper Division which our department had brought back to life with new products. I had been quite involved with this division. Karl, a very creative person, apparently did poorly in a line function and faded away.

Executive vice president Jean Balassie left and became president of Valspar Corporation in Minneapolis.

Two other industrial product planning people left shortly after I did. The advertising manager, John Rutledge, left the firm when they divested the Sonneborn Building Products Division to BASF. Allen George and Truman Dahlberg took the unwanted distribution portion of Sonneborn to Florida. This was the first in a series of divestures when Sears sold its interest in the firm and Sutton Holding was trying to take over the company.

Truman Dahlberg died from a heart attack in December 1992 and his partner Allen George in September 2006. Allen's wife Pat is now running the business.

There was litigation between DeSoto and Sutton for control of DeSoto followed by liquidation of about 80 percent of DeSoto, including the paint operation which was sold piece- meal. The first partial liquidation was selling the consumer paint business to the Sherwin Williams Company of Cleveland for $80 million. They then sold the industrial coatings and solvent business (including their aerospace products) for about $200 million. The final divesture was detergents.

My friend Pierre Matthews said he tried my style of management but with little success. He left DeSoto, Inc for the marketing research manager position with a valve company in Chicago. He then purchased, operated and managed a trailer camp and an orange grove near Orlando.

Wayne Hanson stayed with the firm until it was divested. He survived the infighting by not taking sides. He never would have been hired but my candidate was turned down by my supervisor, George Karl. I thought I had found an ideal candidate who had just earned his MBA. I thought he had everything to meet the demands of our company and Sears– intellect, drive, and creativity and communication skills. He was good and he knew it so he wanted a commensurate salary. It did not bother me that his salary would almost equal mine. George Karl said that he would not ever pay that salary for an inexperienced applicant. We hired Wayne with a lot of experience and good personality but little or no accomplishment because he was afraid to make decisions. He was a body who had to be retrained.

I always thought that secretaries make or break the boss. When I arrived here, I shared a secretary with another associate. She was good, able to read my handwriting, fast and gave me more than 50% of her time. When I asked the executive-row secretaries to help type some of my reports, I quickly obtained a young secretary who was not only a good typist but could take 160 words per minute dictation. Later I was also able to find a stenographer who typed over 120 words per minute.

I got in trouble with my personal secretary when I agreed to meddle in her social life. She asked me to evaluate her boyfriend for her. I agreed to a restaurant dinner where her boyfriend lived. He certainly was nice- looking but I thought that he was not ready for marriage. He wanted to buy a plane so he could learn to fly .She was quite upset with me and threatened to leave. She had an offer to be secretary to the president of Sarah Lee. She did not take that position but stayed with me until I left. She then left to get married and moved to Joliet IL. The whole department liked her very much; I loved her as a daughter and had high expectations for her. Luckily she stayed with us until they were married.

The stenographer came to my office early one morning to ask for my advice. Her boyfriend wanted her to leave that morning for Arkansas to get married. I told her that anything done in such haste would not work out. She agreed but by 10AM she had disappeared. The other staff members advised me that her boyfriend had picked her up and they left for Arkansas. The marriage lasted less than 30 days. She was too embarrassed to come back to Chicago so she went to Washington DC for a job. I was not surprised that she received a job offer with the CIA.

At DeSoto, I tried to be caring, motivating, and flexible about the way goals were achieved. I let my staff members know that they mattered to other associates and executives. I shared the laurels. I learned early that I gain more recognition and gain a stronger team if I give more credit to others.

I finally accepted the idea from the new division president, Mr. Malm, to shorten my reports. I guess I was more secure but I did add an appendix with back-up info for those who wanted it.

CONTEMPO COSMETICS LTD. 1968 - 1971

This above all, to thine own self be true, and
it must follow, as the night the day.

Thou canst not be false to any man. Shakespeare

One day at lunch some of George Karl's group at DeSoto sat around bragging how good we all were. Those attending were: Wally Brown, planning manager - industrial products; Ken McClain, advertising specialist building and industrial products; Pierre Matthews-associate analyst and economist- consumer and some industrial products. It was decided that we should form our own task force to investigate a business in which we would not have to invest much money but give our talent to the organization.

Building a large specialty chemical plant in Puerto Rico was rejected because of our lack of capitalization and lack of experience in that industry. I happened to see a small ad in the *Chicago Tribune* for a small Chicago- based Perfume Company for sale. The group suggested we get more info. My wife and I visited the seller. The owner signed a letter of intent. She thought we would have done well for her one- product perfume line in memory of her late husband. The product needed good marketing and merchandising expertise. Word got around in Chicago that my wife was offering her Bonnie Bell cosmetic clients good marketing and merchandising help. They suggested we pursue cosmetics.

About this time, Mary Quant, a British dress designer, received a great deal of press with her introduction of the mini-skirt and her new cosmetics line. I made phone reservations to place a call to her early one morning. She apparently liked my initial presentation and suggested that I call Mr. Stanley Picker, of Gala Cosmetics, Ltd. He had owned a cosmetic firm in the US in the 1920s but sold the company to American Home Products. He was able to move his operations to England, Australia, Africa and Europe. Research indicated they would be our best bet for sourcing product technologies as well as giving us a competitive price advantage because of the strength of the dollar—and their lower manufacturing , packaging and liability- insurance costs.

At the same time, I began negotiating with the oldest cosmetic company in the world. It might have been a much better venture for us. They wanted very limited and exclusive distribution. I do not remember if Bonwitt Teller or Saks Fifth Avenue was on their approved customer list but Neiman Marcus definitely was on their approved list.

D.G. Plant was assigned as liaison because Mr. Picker did not like the food in Chicago. I remember once in our negotiations there was a standstill on credit terms to our firm. Mr. Plant said that the solicitors would not approve it. I asked: "Who is running your company — you or the solicitors?" That was the best thing I could have said and negotiations thereafter went smoothly by giving an impression that he was under pressure.

Included in the contract were:

> 120 days credit terms on imports
>
> Manufacturing royalty rate half of the industry average.
>
> Exclusive U.S. and Canadian licensing agreement for Outdoor Girl, Gala and Minor Cosmetics.

We finally convinced Mr. Picker to come visit us in Chicago. His aunt owned the Barbizon Plaza in NYC so when he visited, he used the top suite and we the next best at nominal cost.

During the test marketing phase, our apartment was the office and warehouse. I didn't quit my day job at DeSoto. I leveraged my time after work. I had two secretary desks in our living room. The owner of our complex happened to live in our building and floor so he knew first hand what was going on. At times, we held the elevator back 15 minutes or more loading the sea -worthy crates into the apt.

We were successful in leveraging the money.   We developed a unique letterhead, stationary, brochure and public relations program. I "Patton-size" my management style and stayed quite positive. I did not accept the word no and accepted the challenges of the big inequities of Revlon, Max Factor, Coty (Division of Charles Pfizer). I dealt with doubt by finding the facts. My market research experience banished fear of the unknown. Knowledge gave me the ability to make realistic plans. However nobody has a crystal ball. History told us that cosmetics sales never experienced a bust in any recession. In fact, they increased. The specifics of my dreams and goals and how to reach them were written down in our business plan. Somebody other than me should also have measured performance for a given responsibility regardless of relationship.   Measurements should have included everything, from gross and net sales per person, per account, core accounts vs. new accounts, advertising, and promotion allowance. Small expense frugality must apply to all facets of business finance.

Mary Ann was quite successful as a cosmetic salesperson to drug stores by giving these small retailers innovative merchandising tools to help them compete with drug store chains. She was acting as a marketing consultant.—- outstanding customer service However, she was in another league when dealing with department store merchandising managers and buyers. I should have done whatever it took to bring in a capable sales manager and have Mary Ann work with him. We had the right product and the right profit margin but needed an innovative person to implement the mix we had designed.

 Considering our capitalization, we also should have stayed small a bit longer and worked the Midwest only rather than the whole

US and Canada. We were not Sears, ZsaZsa Gabor or Coty. . We retrenched but only after time and money was spent.

 Only later did I lose some confidence and trust with negative team members. Dr. Rimberg was the only person with whom I could discuss sticky situations. My physical and emotional capacity dried up. .Some may have discouraged me from making the decisions necessary to achieve our goals. Leadership training such as I received at Desoto may have helped. I should have worked even harder. I did not prepare for some of the daily disaster situations like marriage difficulties, dead-weight attitude and mostly the economic recession that began in 1969. I should have responded more quickly in my "Patton" style of management and communicated the need to make decisions, and that no decision is a decision.

 We were the leaders. Brainstorming for innovative ways to reach our customer, delivering better service at lesser cost and seizing market share from less innovative competitors was my specialty. I was running a bit thin when I was also getting involved in sales. A military type sales person who loved the business, was trained to make decisions and committed to the mission and use good judgment certainly would have made this company a resounding success. I should have spent more time looking for that person. After all, I had an excellent track record in attracting high quality people with a passion for the business. I did not meet the challenge of a top leader.

We built momentum with the department stores. (The small local drug stores were a distraction. They were, however, useful for test marketing) We successfully backed up every claim we made and believe we answered the question why they should buy an unknown line of products from a small firm like Contempo Cosmetics. Since our advertising budget was very limited, we built the brand name by PR releases to various women's magazines, fashion journals like *Women Wear Daily, local* newspapers, talk shows. and fashion shows. We were also successful in converting clients into references. We also did not have a cost problem at that time. We were sourcing from a low cost English supplier which had lower labor and liability insurance costs. We did not, however, surround ourselves with smart people to help run the business who were, at least, willing to learn the business on their own. They stopped learning. Perhaps attending seminars or classes might have helped.

My secretary Pat was the exception. Pat was fired several times for telling some of the board members that they had a dead-weight attitude. We always hire her back because we could not find talent and smarts equal to hers no matter how much we offered to pay. Fortunately she stayed loyal to us till the very end.

We were fortunate to find an excellent service oriented printing operation startup in our area. It was a husband and wife team— Leonard and Ann Thomas. They grew with us and in short order, they were able to produce high quality brochures, booklets and other printing materials for us at a reasonable fee. Later, the two partners split into two companies.

My other accomplishments included:

-Convinced Baker McKenzie, a top international firm, to be our legal counsel.

-Persuaded Arthur Young, a top five international accounting firm to work with us on a speculative basis.

-Negotiated with Northern Boulevard Bank to give us a six figure loan.

I made the mistake of not taking the cash Northern Blvd Bank was offering us. They liked our budgeting, forecasting and projections.

My naïve logic was "why pay interest on funds we do not need?" Frugality to the extreme.

The first investors were Pierre Matthews and me. Pierre's family owned a large communication complex in Belgium. Unbeknown to me, his family had me investigated prior to Pierre's involvement. Other investors included my old Lucidol boss, Dr Jim Harrison, a chemist;; his secretary, Dolores Bromley and the chemical engineer who developed the continuous process for manufacturing ADM (azodicarbonate), Dr Derek Huibers; my brother Ed Pisacich, an electrical engineer; Ed Peattie ,a chemical engineer whom I met in Cleveland and author of a book about his oil experiences in Saudi Arabia ; John Rimberg – the project director at Institute for Motivational Research; Willard M, a cosmetician and her friend, Bill H ,who wanted to operate the warehouse.

The company failed primarily because of:

1) under capitalization for the goals and objectives that we set;

2) the bad business climate from 1969-1971 making it more difficult for banks to extend credit to healthy business and consumers to spend; and

3) excessive costs after the test marketing period.

We didn't take advantage of the downturn opportunities that was presented to us because we were cash-strapped. W e had many advantages relative to our peers. We did not capitalize on our creativity nor did we have the necessary assets to make the business rise. Perhaps we also should have been more judicious with timely divestment of products to lower our inventory and concentrate on products with greater growth potential. We could not afford to have a full line cosmetic like Revlon or Estee Lauder. Frugality!

Sears merchandiser wanted only to promote his brand and I took him literally, especially when I made a good contact with Montgomery Wards Board Chairman. My contact with him was in response to his excellent youth article. This opened doors wide for me. However going from Board Chairman to Executive Vice-President to the buyer didn't help make points with the buyer. He felt forced to implement a thankless decision. If the product succeeds, he does not receive the credit for the find; conversely, if it fails, he is responsible.

The general business climate delayed Montgomery Ward's opening of their new Monroeville, PA store featuring cosmetics. By the time they finally opened this store, we had closed shop.

For cost containment marketing, we did a successful test market at Osco's Home Shopping Service. The male van drivers were quite successful in selling cosmetics with their coffee, tea and other sundries. The merchandizing manager came down with cancer so had to leave his position. It took time for his replacement to get up to speed and plan a new product line introduction. Timing is important.

Because my past associates and friends invested in me, I refused help from Sears' legal dept to file for bankruptcy. Approximately 90% of our corporate debt was paid prior to going out of business by selling most of our inventory to Marshall Fields at a very favorable price for us. It may have been one of the best negotiations I pulled off. Our treasurer, Pierre Matthews almost had a heart attack when I called their bluff. They made money. All is well that ends well.

Some mistakes I made with this venture include:

I sent Mary Ann to England to learn the products. England was fine but she spent dollars visiting France and then wanted to go to Russia until I ordered her home. This was excitement, a fantasy for her.

My brother Ed Pisacich, an aerospace engineer in California, was hired by Hughes Aircraft personnel from GE's Aerospace Division. I thought he might make a good operational person so I asked that he join Contempo. After all, I made the transition to consumer products. The successful president of Saks Fifth Avenue was an engineer. It was a hard business and perhaps family adjustment for him. Ed left us for a computer engineering position in Phoenix. I may have pushed him a little to join us. He certainly had the brains and a straight shooter but obviously lacked the passion and motivation to be tight-fisted for the operational responsibilities of a small business with family members.

We hired a West Coast company to represent us to cut down travel expense. Mary Ann was to train them. That was a disaster. To her credit, she admitted her folly. I had received several calls from the Federated Stores in Oregon to make a presentation. When the distributor never followed-up, I canceled their contract. They were just feeding on the upfront fees that we were paying them.

Mary Ann always loved clothes and fashion. It was hard for her to think that she was not Mrs. Revson and Mrs. Lauder. . When in a department store, she would charge large amounts on clothing and shoes at each store she opened. This was tough on us since neither of us took a salary. Because of the economic implication, it was the time to be frugal with the large store advertising allowances and sales clerk PM (push money) allowances. Mary Ann left me in September, 1969. She took a pharmacist position at University Hospital in Ann Arbor, Michigan. .

I tendered my resignation as director and president on December 6[th,] based on the conversation with Mary Ann and the other directors. I finally decided to cut my losses. I stayed in the Chicago area until December 22nd closing up as much of the company business as was possible. Several factors hindered the sale of the company:

- economic climate,

- pending divorce of principals,

- dropping the top notch law and accounting firms to save pennies

  In a nutshell, Contempo Cosmetics was a good idea but I failed to lead our team, our stockholders and our vendors to implement its potential. Nevertheless, we all tried our best.

In 2008, I talked to a few of the old directors for their input on why the failure. Surprisingly the consensus was the lack of dedication and passion. It was a little cost learning curve to be used to further them in the future. Perhaps true but thin leadership may have been the key.

Mary Ann returned to Connecticut after I settled in New Haven. She wanted to buy a franchise pharmacy so I and my friend Peter Perry did a feasibility-and-business plan for her. She was warned not to pay more than x dollars for the franchised store but she went against our advice because she felt she could lose the deal. I don't know where and how she got the money. She then sold the franchise store when a dispute occurred, and opened an independent store. She claims that she got into deep trouble with the State of Connecticut selling off-brand AIDS drugs at full price. Supposedly an employee was paid cash to lie about these transactions and reported her to the State. She lost her Connecticut pharmacy license.

She moved to Saint Augustine. Then she moved to Westchester County NY and got a job as a receptionist with a private- plane airport. I was very happy that she returned my two wallpaper lamps that I had purchased at Bloomingdales in the 1950s. In retrospect, I must have really loved her and her many skills including

1) public speaking

2) dealing with the public with tact and courtesy,

3) expressing herself well, and

4) being convincing. She was the best in many of those areas.

Pierre stayed in marketing research with a valve manufacturer, Anchor Coupling Inc in Libertyville IL. He then owned and operated a mobile home park and a large orange grove near Orlando. He returned to Chicago after his wife fell ill with the Alzheimer disease. She was a corporate attorney with Universal Oil Products in Des Plaines. Pierre was taking care of her full-time the last five or so years.

He has written a book about his grandparents and their publishing firm. He is now beginning to write a book about his wife Greta, her parents and himself.

Dr. Jim Harrison set up and successfully sold a specialty chemical plant manufacturing peroxides in Ohio and purchased a plastic fabricator in Brooklyn, NY. The second business operation was not as successful.

Dr. Derek Huibers worked for a Dutch firm, Akzo, in the US but we lost track of him and his family. Derek got "in the doghouse when she accidentally found out from another stockholder that he invested and lost his investment in Contempo. They were the third couple consisting of a Catholic women and a Protestant man where I was asked to counsel them, to save the relationship.

Ed Pisacich got a position with GE's computer division which was sold to Honeywell and then a French company. He became Manager, Manufacturing Engineering. His plant operations closed when the French company purchased the firm. He wanted to stay in Arizona so he retired at a very early age. He was offered a position with Compaq but did not want to move to Houston. GE in Princeton would have taken Ed back but Ed lost in the negotiations and decided to retire permanently when he lost faith in his fellow engineers.

Ed Peattie, this brilliant chemical engineer who wrote *The Green Desert* stayed active in his profession, Mensa, Community and the arts until he was 90+. He died shortly after his artist wife died.

John Rimberg changed his name when he entered politics in April of 1997. He had been professor of sociology at the University of North Carolina. As John Rim, he became registered agent and lobbyist for North Carolina High School of Social Studies Foundation (and later Rainbow Foundation as well).. He is actively interested in planning secondary schools.. Recently John took on the additional task of studying the future of his high school – The Bronx High School of Science. This high school has the distinction that seven graduates are Nobel Prize winners in physics.

CONTEMPO – THE AFTERMATH

Fortune truly helps those who are of good judgment. Euripides

The job market was terrible in 1971. I was fortunate to make the short list for a Planning Director position at Brunswick Corporation. I passed all the office interviews and personnel screening so a formal welcome aboard luncheon was arranged at a French restaurant. I had started smoking excessively about two years earlier (three packs a day). I did a no-no here. I was smoking excessively while drinking the very best French wine. Smoking and drinking good wine do not mix well as one's taste buds are dead. The luncheon was a disaster. The job offer was retracted.

The job market worsened so I decided to move to Pittsburgh with my Mother, who was dying from cancer. I was depressed from the bankruptcy, divorce and now, my mother's cancer. I was interviewed for a product manager's position with Avon Products. Personnel thought I was the ideal candidate. Avon chose another candidate, someone younger. Can you believe that there was discrimination at a young age of 40 in the 70s? When I heard that the personnel director was fired, I filed my Age discrimination suit with the government. Avon settled quickly out of court.

TRANSITION TO ANOTHER WORLD

CONSULTANT 1972 -1977

*Good fortune and bad are necessary to man
to make him capable.* French proverb

As a consultant, I was able to adapt quickly to new technologies, new processes as well as time pressure. Some studies included inorganic polymers, shrink/cross-linked polymer films, ablative water sprinkler systems, fluorescent lighting, cross-linked resin compounds, injection molding, styrene monomer pricing, vinyl dispersion resins, waste paper utilizations, ultra high molecular weight polyethylene. I subcontracted to firms to multiple companies including: Market Facts, C-J Corporation, Springborn Labs and U.S. Dept of Labor.

135

One of the most interesting projects at Springborn Labs was to find out, for a Japanese chemical company client, more about the "P" phosphorus technology that they read about in *Chemical Abstracts*. This was during the first oil crisis of the 70's and they were looking to replace the expensive "C" carbon from petrochemicals with "P" which is readily available in the world. They were looking for a product that could make a difference on a big issue that was destabilizing the world at that time.

I traveled with the Research Director, Engineer and Business Manager to various US facilities to negotiate possible licensing agreements. I noticed that they loved to exchange business cards. It was their custom to hand them out with both hands. They never placed them on a table. Trust was created holding breakfast and or dinner review meetings each day at the hotel and playing poker with the engineer on some of the flights. During licensing discussions they avoided giving the impression of deep interest so that it could not be turned to their disadvantage during negotiations should that come to pass.

The trip ended in a fancy Sushi Restaurant in NYC. They invited me and my wife (if I got married again) to Japan. They apparently did not think too much of our technology so they put a large task force of some fifty PhD chemist of the project to develop polymers from phosphorous. The oil crisis ended a few years later.

The quickest and shortest jobs at Springborn Labs were when I was hired by Spencer Chemical to do a preliminary study on styrene monomer pricing practices. Spencer Chemical had purchased much of Gulf Oil's operations. In short order, a pattern of price fixing was established. Spencer did not want a copy of the report nor did they want a more thorough study. I wondered why the Federal government could not prove price fixing when the monomer price moved from $.10 a pound to over $2.00. We never were asked to testify in Washington even though I subcontracted with one of the leading plastic consulting firm at that time.

On January 12, 1977, while working at this consulting firm, Springborn Labs, I had a severe episode of vertigo which lasted 1 ½ days. I was hospitalized at Johnson Memorial Hospital in Southeastern Connecticut. I did not notice any hearing loss at that time but it became very apparent to me by 1978. On 5/19/1980, a left acoustic neuroma was noted by Temple Radiology in New Haven.

I also met Beatrix (Trix) Jones of Wilbraham Mass at a singles' social function. Supposedly she eyed me from across the room and said to herself, I'm going to marry that guy. Trix's ex husband, an insurance executive in Hartford was getting married again and moving to a lower level sales management job in Colorado because he hated the cut-throat politics in Hartford. I was not psychologically ready for marriage because I was financially insecure. Apparently money was not important to her as she sold her large home, married a missionary and moved to the Philippines with him

I also met Natalie Grow whom I knew previously from a Chicago MENSA group. She married someone from Cambridge, MA, moved there and was working with the Putman Funds. It is nice to be young and full of energy. I stayed acquainted with Natalie for quite awhile.

UNITED STATES DEPARTMENT OF LABOR – 1972

The one person with courage is a majority. Thomas Jefferson

Because of my political activity with the Republican Party, it was suggested that I apply for a regional director post with the Environmental Protection Agency in Chicago. Because of pending problems, they wanted an outsider as director. I told a fellow MENSA member that I was being considered. He then asked the agency to post the job so he could apply for the position. This GS-16 job was given to another. The agency ran into a great deal of legal problems.

After that, I received an appointment as industrial hygienist with the newly formed OSHA under the Dept of Labor in Pittsburgh, PA. I liked the work but I made the mistake of receiving commendations from labor unions as well as corporate executives. The DOL bureaucracy in Philadelphia could not comprehend that both the labor union and management could be happy with the results of given survey as long as it was done in a professional manner, i.e. no agenda.

I was surprised to experience some politics benefiting corporations. Once I was called to take a statement from an injured man at the hospital on Neville Island in Pittsburgh. The nurse would not permit me to see the patient even though he was not in a life threatening condition. I had to go in the back way to obtain a report about the accident. Apparently this was not the first accident at the chemical plant. A previous operator died of lung disease in a similar accident. The chemical company was a large donor to the hospital. OSHA had some internal politics as to who had jurisdiction on this case – OSHA said NIOSH and NIOSH said OSHA. They both were excellent in passing the buck and surprisingly, nobody seemed to care about the worker who could die. I do not know what happened to the operator and who got jurisdiction on the case as I left OSHA.

During this time, I was active with the local chapter of MENSA to help build my ego. I played bridge with Parents without Partners (PWP) group as well as some MENSA members. One of the PWP members reported me for not having any children because I did not date her. I decided to form my own Social Singles Bridge Group.

This MENSA chapter under the leadership of Jennifer Brown had some very creative and entrepreneurial members. It was too bad that I was not receptive to any of their new venture ideas. During 1974 signs of impotency showed up. I ignored them. I did not seek medical help.

The new bridge club drew members from various groups because we knew how to party, play bridge and maintain an approximately 50/50 split among men and women. We met at people's home and at the Unitarian Church. Members were generally professionals in the 45 to 50 age bracket. It was like a private club. Members were voted in for membership only after attending three functions. We had at least three marriages the first year among the members. The members were still married 10 years later. The male of one older couple, Frank Schneider, did die after five years of marriage. One of the first members was Suzanne Barley who also got me involved as a volunteer in taking phone calls from distress people. Suzanne also introduced me to a maverick and a most giving Episcopal minister.

I understand the club is still going strong without me but the membership is skewed heavily toward female members. Some of original members died, moved as I did or quit when the club went very serious with their bridge- playing.

I was not successful in finding a suitable mate from the club because I was still depressed from my divorce experience. On several occasions I was second choice so I helped out during the marriage transition period. In one case, I spent all night with the father and new wife when his son got drunk and killed a person in a car accident. The son was depressed because he thought his father married much too soon after the death of his mother who was extremely loved by the church and the community. The boy served six months and then graduated with honors from Carnegie Mellon University.

I met Laura Diskin at the Unitarian Church. She was among the very best school teachers in the Pittsburgh area. Laura worked as a teacher with a brilliant principal, Dr. Lewis Venson, in an experimental Beltzhoover ghetto school on the south side of Pittsburgh. She was instrumental in bringing top speakers from all over the world. The results were outstanding. This shows me that good teachers and administrators make a difference with students. Her enthusiasm for Galapagos resulted in Laura taking twelve trips to this enchanted place. She retired to painting when Dr. Venson was promoted to supervising six such schools with less success. He retired in Florida.

Laura was a bridge player. I suggested she join MENSA. She did and joined the upper 1% group, Intertel. She was president of that group for many years. We continued to be friends. She was in love with a nuclear engineer who was a bridge club member. Therefore, she introduced me to her friend Connie Long, a social worker, at a Parent without Partners function. I still hold dearly the two large water colors she painted to match my furniture when I left Pittsburgh.

The previous two winters in Chicago had very little snow so I did not do any skiing. The next winter in Pennsylvania was also light on the snow. However, it started to snow when Connie and I were at a late New Years Eve cocktail party. We decided to go skiing so we went to pick up our skies. We got to Seven Springs at sunrise and after a few practice runs on the small slope we proceeded to the big one.

 Seven Springs used artificial snow which turned to ice. The high wind blew away the new white power on the top 25% of the mountain. Connie said that she wasn't going down that sheet of ice but would take the long route to the base of the mountain. I told her I would meet her down there. I did not make it because I had to be carried downhill on one of the ski patrol's toboggans to their infirmary. Once I hit the powder, I fell and my rusty binders did not release. I got a beautiful spiral break on my tibia and fibula.

The bones were immediately set at the local hospital with a hip cast and the hospital's therapist forced me to walk with that hip cast the very next day. That was very, very painful. The therapists must have had ear plugs as I kept telling them that they were sadistic. However, I never had arthritic problems as a result of this accident and the bone alignment was almost perfect.

On the fourth day, I was picked up at my home to play bridge (alcohol was always available at our bridge functions) even though I was doped up with pain killers. Don't remember how I did at bridge.

I met Connie's parents several times and to her surprise, they liked me. She blamed the first marriage on her parents- she was forced to marry a man from Oil City even though she did not love him. Her father was the corporate attorney for the oil company.

Connie did not want her parent's approval because she was rebelling so she just canceled our wedding plans even though we had purchased wedding bands together. She never married again, raised and educated two daughters, Linda and Suzanne.

The oldest daughter, Linda was in a wheelchair from birth with an artificial kidney and other disabilities. Linda graduated from a top law school, practiced for awhile but found out that she did not like it. She then got a degree in Public Affairs at Brandeis and has been working on a PhD dissertation for years. She is married and has a baby boy.

The second daughter, Suzanne Long, moved to California after graduating from Cornell and is working for a publishing company. She has two children and is newly divorced. She is also writing a novel about two sisters and is actively trying to get it published.

I also met Ann Dunlap at the Bridge Group. She was a chemist at Westinghouse's Research Center and taught Chemistry Lab at Duquesne University in Pittsburgh. She was divorced with two boys to bring up. Her father was a successful stockbroker.

When she was laid off at Westinghouse, she decided to work for her PhD at Duquesne University and taught one or two additional Chemistry courses for income. To the best of my knowledge, she never finished her dissertation. Ours was a funny relationship – we like each other but both were afraid to get close for fear of being rejected.

I met Janet Simberg at one of the social functions in Pittsburgh. She seemed quite depressed because she had to go to a divorce hearing alone with no family support. I told her that I also had to experience that alone back in the 70's but offered to be her support. She accepted and I was there. I don't know how her husband got away with not being present because he was the one seeking the divorce. His attorney represented him.

After the proceeding, I took her to a restaurant on Top of Mt Washington for lunch, talk and a few drinks. Her husband was a well known attorney in Pittsburgh. He and his family were embarrassed with Janet because she could have an epileptic seizure. Earlier he dumped her in a Montreal Hospital (only hospital that performed this very delicate and complicated surgery) and left to file divorce proceedings. She was totally alone during and after the surgery but it was a total success. His family with the exception of her brother-in-law Edwin B (also an attorney) ignored her even after her surgery.

After the divorce, Janet was very successful writing children books. She was also affiliated with University of Pittsburgh. I kept in contact with her and her brother-in-law for a few years after I left Pittsburgh.

I had my eyes on Gerri Titchworth while in Pittsburgh but unfortunately she had her eyes on another bridge player. Neither of us married again

Linda (Lakshmi) Segall, a City Planner for the City of Pittsburgh, would lead a carload of people seeking spiritual guidance's to the Jain Meditation International Center on East 86th Street in New York.

Linda, her sister Susan and a Public Relation person, Leigh Chrystal-Feeney from North Hill of Pittsburgh eventually quit their job and moved to NYC to join the cult full time. Unfortunately Mr. Segall lost his only two children to this cult. The public relation person, Leigh Chrystal Feeney, left her affluent husband (US Steel Executive) for Gurudev Chitrabhanu. Being a writer, she wrote books on yoga (I still have a draft of her first book) and meditation. The irony was her blind double standard; she didn't mind when Gurudev cheated on his long-time student and wife, Pramoda but immediately left for South America when she caught him sleeping with one of the other cult students. She thought that she had him exclusively.

Gurudev Chitrabhanu was able to attract many unemployed executives in the Metropolitan New York area. He claimed to be the first Jain monk to come to the West and accepted an invitation to the Third Spiritual Summit Conference at Harvard Divinity School in 1971.His philosophy was world peace and nonviolence, emphasizing the need to appreciate the sanctity of all life and to build solidarity in the larger family of mankind. He was not only a Master, lecturer, but an enlightened spiritual teacher to the unemployed executives in search of the truth and self-realization.

At times we would have retreats in their follower's large homes in places like Huntington, N.Y. There he emphasized that the "principal essence of karma is awareness of the fruits of one thoughts, words and deeds. It is action-oriented and cannot be reduced to fatalism. Instead, it involves taking responsibility for one's actions. And taking responsibility means assuming control of one's life. It is such control that conquers inner weaknesses and brings equanimity and harmony"

Gurudev Chitrabhanu was born on 7/26/22 in a small town of Rajasthan, India. He left home at the age of 20 to become a Jain monk. He spent the first five years of his monastic life in silence and meditation. With this experience, he realized that the ultimate purpose of life is to expand one's awareness and to liberate the consciousness from attachment and aversion.

This enlightened spirit brought wisdom, and lucid language and eloquent speech. He witnessed the successful nonviolent struggle independence led by Mahatma Gandhi, He helped us address the challenges of our time by the power of nonviolence dating back from wounds left by Hiroshima, the Kennedy and Rev Martin King assassinations, subjugation of Vietnam, terrorization in Cuba, the Mid-East and Iran.

He addressed other leading institutions such as Princeton, Sarah Lawrence, Yale, Cornell and State University of New York. He now has 67 Jain Centers in North America and others in England, Africa, Japan, Singapore, Dubai and India.

BOISE CASCADE 1977 - 1979

It is an absurdity that he should rule others who
cannot command himself. Latin proverb

My stay at Boise Cascade as Market Development Manager began in 1977. The adjustment from the Plastic/Chemical industry to the Paper Industry was great. Politics was more important than results. I was lucky that the Beaver Falls operation was a hybrid – of chemicals and paper. I was also lucky that my boss, Bob McCabe was a good marketer and was dedicated to the firm. I was successful in developing new business with existing products and commercial development effort on several new products such as sandpaper backing. We also increased international sales substantially with the help of a consultant. This division was by far the most profitable operation for Boise Cascade.

I would have been demoted or fired by the corporate Personnel Director because there was an edict that no Harvard graduates were ever to be hired nor should anyone ever be holding a marketing title in the organization. Earlier Boise almost went into bankruptcy and blamed a group of Harvard Business School graduates for this catastrophe.

Before I left Boise Cascade I did an-in-depth Quantitative Territory Sales Analysis for our operation. This study caused a defensive uproar by some salesmen. One colonel reservist wanted to punch me in the nose at the sales meeting. "Who was I to evaluate him?"

I took him aside and discussed the many good things cited in the report that he was doing and there were only a few areas for needed improvement... He returned back to the meeting calm and collected.

The General Manager of our operation who didn't particularly like my boss, Bob McCabe, sent a copy of this analysis to John Wasserlein, Division GM in Brattleboro, VT who sent it to everyone in his division and to Terry Lock, Group Vice President of the Paper Group at Boise. John Wasserlein wrote "Whenever an in-depth analysis is done, we always find things that are somewhat embarrassing, but in my mind the openness to find such issues is the foundation of beginning to get them corrected."

During this time Bob asked me make a few calls on the Book Cover Publishing Industry with the salesmen. This was Bob's "baby". It was a very successful and profitable operation for our division. We had no competition. I learned very quickly that competition was just on the horizon with a superior and cheaper product. The salesmen already knew this and warned me to tone down the report as this is Bob's baby. "Don't tell him what he doesn't want to hear".

I had just come back with several broken ribs after I tripped and fell over my suitcase while running in Lake Placid's Holiday Inn parking lot on a very cold and icy day. I received a call from Bob McCabe He said that I was trying to usurp him and that the info in the reports can't be true, ("I'm Fired") I had to turn in my car immediately and get out of the company owned house in 45 days.

In a small mill town, Bob's name became mud. The town punished Bob for this action. When Bob left the firm for an advertising agency, Conklin Labs and Beebee, Inc., in Syracuse, NY, he couldn't sell his home in Beaver Falls, New York for several years.

During my stay in Beaver Falls, I met Neal Warren and his wife Shirley at the Unitarian Church in Watertown, N.Y. He was teaching math at a nearby high school.

Without his family and my next door neighbor, I would never have survived this wilderness. The year I was there was one of their worst winters on record – snow was as high as six feet high at times and ground snow cover from October till May.

I did not participate in the local sport activities of hunting and bar hopping. My activities with Neal included hiking, canoeing, bicycling, cross country skiing, snow shoeing and driving 60 miles each way to attend the Unitarian services each week. The minister never looked at his audience while giving his sermon. I see Neal and his wife Shirley to this day.

CONSULTANT 1979 - 1980

During this period, I did a total review of the specialty paperboard industry for a client in Springfield, MA and Casterland, New York. The treasurer of the company returned to Harvard Graduate School as a Professor of Finance. He also founded a successful money manager group which managed a portion of Harvard's endowment money. In June of 86, Dr. Brown indicated interest in joining our Group meeting to discuss the formation of a new financial group. Travel schedules prevented the meeting

FINANCIAL SERVICES INDUSTRY 1980

All things are obedient to money. English proverb

In 1980, I had just completed a survey on the Specialty Paper Board Business in West Springfield, Mass. I was burned out writing reports under time pressure so I asked myself what I could do that would utilize my multi-industry economic planning skills and ability to interact with management at high levels. Stockbroker came to mind almost immediately. I had a false impression that industry leaders associated frankness with wisdom. I was also a successful investor in the 60s and as I recalled, enjoyed the work of evaluating, charting and picking stocks.

My associate, Pierre Matthews wanted to learn about the market so I became his teacher and he learned from doing my charts. I probably would have been much happier as an analyst but Wall Street, at that time, required an MBA from an Ivy League school because most of the research was done for the Institutional Investors. How things change!

In the mid 60s there were very few economists or analysts on the Street and they wanted to buy the economic forecasts that we did at DeSoto. What I should have done was insist that I talk to the president of the various firms rather than the personnel director even though it could have hurt me like it did with the Montgomery Ward buyer a few years earlier.

SHEARSON LOEB RHODES 1980 - 1983

None can play the fool as well as the
wise man. French proverb

I stopped at the Loeb Rhodes office in Hartford CT because I had an account with them in the 60's. Talked to the local branch manager and he said he would hire me –but he does not know whether he will be with the firm next week because they just merged with Shearson. There were two offices in Harford and one will be closed.

Loeb Rhodes had a history of being associated with many of America's emerging industrial giants, providing financial backing for Westinghouse and Western Union, as well as innovative consumer giants like the Polaroid Corporation. The firm was a leading house for John D, Rockefeller and enjoyed respect as a trusted adviser overseas.

In the early years, intermarriage among the German-Jewish elite was common so partners were closely related by blood and marriage. Things changed after World War II from relationship banking to a more aggressive, transaction- oriented Wall Street with underwriters entering the trenches and selling securities directly to the public.

Kuhn Loeb stubbornly refused to enter this arena so in 1977 merged with Lehman Bros. The Kuhn name was still first in recognition because of their international reputation. There was much internal strife, and because in 1984 the firm sold itself to Shearson/American Express. Just prior to this, there was a merger between American Express and Sandy Weill's Shearson Loeb Rhodes. The combined firms then dropped the Kuhn, Loeb name and became known as Shearson Lehman/ American Express.

The Loeb branch manager, Warren Meridan, suggested I see Michael Winters at the Shearson office in New Haven. Michael extended an offer to me immediately. I decided to go to the Merrill Lynch office on the 14th floor. Had a good discussion with the manager, Mr. George Cook and took his test. He liked everything but wanted me to come back for another interview to test my seriousness. The only thing that resonated, after I refused his lukewarm offer, was my thinking "You can't be God, Mr. George Cook because I'm God." Two strong personalities may have been the best thing for both of us.

This manager was on a roll at Merrill Lynch. He was promoted to a large Boston office. In 1983, he was shot dead by a broker he had fired.

Two years later, I again had an opportunity to join Fran Adams at the same New Haven Merrill Lynch office, when I was leaving Smith Barney. I was successful and happy at Smith Barney because of the manager and because I did have an office so my one ear handicap was minimized.

Prior to Drexel going under, an ML executive was soliciting me for months to join the Merrill Lynch office in Stanford. I was at Drexel's Darien office.

I accepted a smaller satellite office where my medical handicap of having only one ear would not have been as pronounced. They may have given me a satellite office (usually a broker reward for those not interested in management) if I had accepted an offer immediately before losing many of my pension accounts.

I was quite sure that Drexel would survive, and I liked their equity and bond research department very much. At that time, I was not aware of the tension created by background noise and of being totally deaf when I was on the phone.

Back to 1980, I took the Shearson offer and moved to New Haven. I was supposed to study for the exam but had to do various manual office tasks because everybody had to do it when in training. It was a ritual.

This changed with the next trainee. The regional manager felt so honored to hire a Yale graduate that he told our branch manager that the Yale employee did not have to do any of the typical office chores, including getting the boss his coffee, making coffee for everyone, getting the mail, etc.

I met Betsey Hahn at the local Unitarian Church. We went to various cultural events in New Haven, and she noticed my head movements at concerts and at the theatre. She finally asked me if I was losing my hearing in one ear. I told her that I thought so but the medical profession thought otherwise – their past diagnosis was inner ear infection, asthma and allergies.

She persuaded to see one more expert. Betsey's deceased husband had been a noted mathematician at Yale so she offered to find a good specialist. The doctor, Dr. James M. Dolwaliby, and I hit it off because he was educated and thought like an engineer. He disliked engineering, went to medical school and became a very analytical doctor instead.

One hearing test told him that something was definitely wrong so he gave me a series of tests including the tilt test. (There was no MRI at that time.) I was then referred to Dr. Alvin Greenberg, neurologist who evaluated all the test results.

I had a CAT scan done just before I left for a one week prep course for the Series Seven Broker's exam in NYC. In class I got an urgent call to call Dr Greenberg immediately. He wanted me in the hospital the very next day but I convinced him to delay the operation for a week so I could take the SEC exam.

Took the exam on Saturday, passed, and I called my multi-faith friends and relatives to say a prayer. I didn't know which religions were in favor with God at that time so I tried to get covered by them all: Christians (Protestant, Evangelist, and Catholic) Jews, Moslem, Hindu, Buddhist, Unitarian and Agonist.

The tumor was as big as a golf ball. I checked in the hospital Sunday afternoon.

On Monday June 30, 1980, I had a 12 hour left suboccipital caraniectomy with total excision of left acoustic neuroma – approximately 4 cm. Apparently I had a rendezvous with death during the operation and again while I was in intensive care. I am sure the prayers, meditations and positive feelings of my friends contributed greatly to my miraculous recovery.

It is like I returned to tell of the road, of the spiritual feeling, of fellowship and love extended to me by the two office secretaries, my boss and associates as well as my brothers and sisters-in-laws, also helped in the speedy recovery. The only permanent damage was total deafness in my left ear and a 5% loss of facial muscle control. (I will have to take a brain scan test once a year for the rest of my life.)

I spent two weeks post- surgery with my brother Bernard and my sister-in-law Judy at their home in Waterford CT. I began walking a little at a time so I decided to try moving back my to my New Haven apartment. I didn't want to overstay my welcome with Bernie. I was tough-minded, a survivor without then necessity of complaints.

 Neighbors and church friends helped with shopping as I was not allowed to lift anything for several months. When a church friend, Betty Bockleman helped me buy a TV at Caldor's, we elected to bring this 75 pound item home ourselves to save the delivery charge. It was foolish.

Every day I would walk a little more than the previous day. The goal was to reach the top of Sleeping Giant hill, slightly over a mile of winding roads to the apex. I made it to the top about 15 days later. (My ecstasy was like having good sex.). I again exhibited my Pittsburgh tough-mindedness and values.

 I lost my hearing because those hearing nerves were encapsulated in the tumor. It took over 15 years to adjust to this physical and psychological loss.

  Ten years later, I finally went to Gaylord Rehabilitation Center about getting some kind of hearing aid. They did have a unit that would pick up the sound on my left ear and transmit the sound to the right ear.

The one disadvantage of this unit was that in a noisy place, the sound would be amplified. I was afraid of losing my right ear hearing by putting the left ear micro into my good ear.

I was supposed to stay at home for six months but after two months I started to come to the Shearson office for an hour or so. The stock market was basically dead at that time. There was no activity whatsoever. We would take turn reading stories on the old telex machine. If and when there was anything newsworthy, the person on duty would read it ```aloud so everyone could hear it.

Since I hated cold calling and had little respect for any salesman, I decided to find a business niche. I decided on small business pension plans where I would be a match maker. There were several consulting firms evaluating money managers for the very large plans but none for the small to medium size plans. Therefore, I analyzed the performance of some 50 money managers specializing in fixed income and equities. I was a good technician but quite naïve. I never thought that politics would influence employee pension monies. I used bright young Yale students to help me with the part-time clerical work. I paid their salaries.

Working for Shearson, one of my first contacts was a paper company in NJ that had a $100,000 pension plan. I worked with the treasurer and we found a mutually compatible manager.

It was a big mistake going to an in-house manager.

He went to the president for approval and was told to give the business to a Shearson broker who also was a Shearson manager in Paramus, NJ. Since we were in a recession atmosphere, he did not question this decision.

I complained to my manager, Michael Winter, who did nothing. I requested permission to see Sandy Weil, the President of

Shearson. We had a nice chat but he then asked for written proof that I indeed worked with the paper company. I did everything verbally, not in writing.

He should have been proud of this procedure – promise the world but not in writing. I'm sure he was aware that our office had only one receptionist and office manager who also acted as a secretary to the branch manager and twelve brokers.

Phone records could prove that I was in contact with the firm and the money manager. This manager's fee was a commission (8%) and there could be about 30% portfolio turnover. A windfall for me, the manager and the office as the commissions were not discounted at that time.

Never did Sandy Weill suggest any compromises like splitting the commission with his producing manager in Paramus N.J. who obviously had some pull. The only good that came out of this was that I was to have my own secretary. I was very fortunate to find Pat Darly who had the fortitude to divorce a Norman husband. She had custody of her child.

She was a very bright and career oriented person who had worked in a doctor's office in New Haven. I remember that if a client was upset with me for some reason or another, she would calm the person before I picked up the phone.

The private secretary did not last long because I had to share with the high producing broker who was the previous branch manager. One secretary was shared by three brokers when the other brokers complained. Hiring assistants was a God-send for the office. There was a synergistic effect on production because the broker spent more time producing commission dollars instead of paper work.

Pat was on a roll. After leaving Shearson, she obtained a managerial position at Yale. Then to Atlanta Georgia.

I was told by the Boise President that they were looking for a $500,000 fixed income portfolio manager. I suggested a Shearson's In House Money Manager –Shearson Loeb Rhodes Asset Manager. I was told that they would use Russell Consulting Services but they would have to personally send the president a report on why we were not picked if that would occur. I suggested that I join the Shearson Money Manager in the presentation. I was thanked for the excellent lead but they would now take over. They blew it. It could have been a golden opportunity for me, the firm and the Money Manager. We certainly had to work hard to lose the business because Boise was trying to repay an IOU. They blew it. They may have overdone their Harvard credentials.

This could have been why Merrill Lynch was always after me because any large pension plan activities are well known on Wall Street.

Right before I left Shearson for Smith Barney I hired Shearson's third in-house Money Manager, Shearson Asset Manager for the Jewish Home Pension Plan in New Haven. Naively, I told the money manager, Lester P that I was leaving Shearson for Smith Barney and asked if I would be able to transfer the portfolio to Smith Barney. Lester reassured me but before I hung up, he was already dialing the client and selling him on the idea to stay with him at Shearson. I know this because the secretary at the pension plan told me that her boss was now talking with Shearson's money manager when I called. (Will I ever learn?)

It was too early for Shearson to give me permission to do discretionary accounts for professionals and executives. I was contemplating writing a financial newsletter.

Michael Winters joined Bear Stearns in Boston shortly after I left, broke up with the divisional VP's secretary and married the sole heir to Stop & Shop before they were sold to a European firm. He briefly set up his own brokerage firm clearing through Bear Stearns but returned as a high producing broker at Bear Stearns in Boston.

Since Sandy Weill became the big deal maker on Wall Street, his history might be appropriate.

SANFORD (SANDY) I. WEILL

Anyone could hold the helm when the
sea is calm. Publilius Syrus

How I wish that I knew more about Mr. Weill before my meeting with him back in 1980. He could have been an excellent mentor. The moral of the story: know your boss's background before you meet him.

Weill's was born in Depression-era Brooklyn N.Y. to two Jewish immigrants. His initial goal was to be a pilot after graduating from Cornell.

His first Wall Street job was as a runner for Bear Stearns in 1953. There he became friends with Arthur C who was working with Lehman Bros. He became a licensed broker in 1956. He also disliked making calls or personal visits to solicit clients. He loved poring over companies' financial statements and disclosures made to US Securities and Exchange Commission.

Sandy formed his first partnership in 1960 with his neighbor Arthur C and two other friends. From 1965 to 1984, he completed over 15 acquisitions, one merger at a time, to become the second largest brokerage firm. Included in those mergers were Hayden Stone, Loeb Rhodes and Hornblower.

Sandy's first setback was selling to American Express where his ideas conflicted sharply with then Chairman James R. Mr. Weill quickly realized he would never be named CEO.

He also failed to become CEO of Bank of America and take over Merrill Lynch. He quickly persuaded Control Data Corp to spin off their troubled subsidiary Commercial Credit. He invested $7 million of his own money into the company, cut costs, and reorganized, resulting in a successful IPO.

In 1993, Sandy reacquired Shearson from American Express and completely took over Travelers Corp. This was followed by complete takeover of Citicorp on October 4, 1998.

Sandy was replaced as CEO on October 1, 2003, after the company was hit by a series of scandals that followed the market downturn of 2002.

Quite a list of accomplishments for a son of two Jewish immigrants who wanted to be a pilot after graduating from college.

SMITH BARNEY 1983 - 1986

No fat charioteer; no lazy person as manager. Latin proverb

After many years of frustration trying to change peoples' attitudes and philosophies, it finally registered that it is wasted energy. Accept the rules and structure that exist as one is just a pea in a huge pod. If one can't digest a person or department, avoid them. This was the attitude I was going to start with at Smith Barney. Indeed. I was most successful there financially, and gathered interesting clients who would be friends most of my life.

I joined Richard Pignone, Resident Manager for Smith Barney in New Haven that later merged with Shearson, then American Express and finally Citicorp.

Fran Adams at Merrill Lynch's New Haven office also extended an offer to me at that time.

I was an active member of the CT Venture Capital Group; Sigma Xi- the Scientific Fraternity, New Haven; Stockbrokers Association; American Chemical Society; Engineering Society of Western Pennsylvania; Commercial Development Association and MENSA.

I was noted for consistency in production at this office. I had an office so I was not as distracted or stressed out with noise.

I personally hired several Yale students part time to do cold calling and send personalized financial information to my prospective clients. Sarah Slover, compared to her peers, had tremendous originality. She quickly grasped new assignments with minimum direction. She had the ability to get the most out of what she had to work with; doing a job as economically as was consistent with the objective I set for her. She was forceful and effective with her Yale peers. She applied and received a scholarship at Georgetown University's Foreign Service School. I was pleased when she asked me to write a recommendation for her. She also asked me to give her a recommendation for admittance to Columbia Law School in 1989. I kept in contact with her while in school.

I'm not sure how well my personality went over with some of the brokers in the office but Dick was very happy with my ability to close a sale and my consistent production. I used to kid him that he was a socialist because when he gave a raise to office staff, he gave it equally no matter who worked harder or was more efficient. It took years for me to recognize that for the financial service industry, he may have been right. He was very secure in himself.

I used to ridicule him somewhat because papers were always about ten inches high on his desk but he knew exactly where every paper was located. He was a Central Intelligence Officer in Viet Nam so he was exercising his brain memory cells every day and too involved to file things away immediately.

One of the investment blunders I made was selling Damson Oil Limited Partnership to some clients. I sold some after my manager, Dick Pignone, asked me to take another look as he purchased a large amount for his child's college fund. This probably became one of the most corrupt partnerships but to the best of my knowledge they were never sued or punished. They used numerous financial gimmicks after the partnerships were formed. Damson's previous investment banker dropped them and they were searching for another "sucker." Smith Barney was hurting financially at that time because they suffered from bond inventory losses in a high inflation environment. The Saudi saved Smith Barney with a large infusion of cash. Normally, I don't think SB would have taken the Damson's Investment Banking account.

SB's brokers were the very last on Wall Street to know the perils of Damson Oil. Clients who purchased the partnership through other Wall Street firms were able to get out whole or close to it. The key producer at this office, Tom Fusco left for this very reason. So did I. He returned to Smith Barney a few years later.

Dick Pignone stayed at Smith Barney for eight more years but left for A.G. Edwards and Sons in Hamden CT when the new SB management installed much higher production quotas. He recently retired as branch manager but is still a producing broker.

Four brokers who were either with Shearson or Smith Barney and still employed there are:

1. Tony Passarello

2. Ernie Astrelli

3. Tom Brundage

4. Billy Fusco

My vacation during this stay at Smith Barney began December 24, 1983. I left for a ten day vacation to Phoenix, AZ for hiking, camping and sight seeing at the Grand Canyon.

At Smith Barney, I had interesting clients who became close friends: Joel & Dorothy Blum, Dorothy Bates, Albert Bates, Maude Bliss, Robert Breitbarth, Robert Ferris, Howard and Carla Runda, Howard Levin, Sam Levine, Harriet Sims and John Wilkes.

JOEL AND DOROTHY BLUM

A handful of life is better than a bushel of learning. Scottish proverb

During 1982, I was calling various business establishments in Fairfield County. Among those targeted was the Four Star Family Diner in Norwalk, Connecticut. I presented a corporate bond paying 17%. Dorothy listened to my story and said she would talk to her husband. They purchased the bond. Their next investment was 50 shares of GE which turned out to be worth $250,000 on 1/31/07 or a gain of 1,011% plus 3+% dividends during this time. Five hundred shares of AT&T were purchased on 12/15/1984 for a total cost of $59,313. Today, 11/06/07 those shares were worth $181,837 plus 54 shares in Avaya, 239 shares of Comcast Cl A, 35 Idearc, 31 NCR, 355 Quest Communication, 707 Verizon Communication, 438 Vodafone Group PLC and $34 cash out for partial shares. Many of these stocks were paying in excess of 3% in dividends during this time. The other blue chip, high yielding stock that was purchased was Exxon on 11/17/1987.

The adjusted purchase price was $3.48 giving a 2,560% gain plus a good dividend.

These investments resulted in a deep friendship and very successful client relationship. They left only for a year or so when they went to Smith Barney with his brother-in-law's broker. Dorothy was interior decorator for my New Canaan apartment and she made me a life member of Hadassah. When I retired in 2006, I continued to be their financial consultant. I believe I am closer to Dorothy and Joel than I am to any of my relatives including my brothers!

Joel was a survivor of four years in a German labor camp in Russia. His brother Wilhelm was a deported to a labor camp in Czechoslovakia. Both parents and his younger brother died on arrival in Auschwitz. His older brother died in a labor camp and his youngest sister died soon after liberation.

In Russia, Joel dug up live mines and buried dead German soldiers. Thanks to a German officer, he was a survivor of back and front shrapnel wounds he suffered when digging up the mines. He and several others also tried to escape in Poland. The only reprimand was that they shouldn't try it again "because you could be liberated."

During the winter of 1944-45, as the Russians advanced in Germany, he and 10,000 others were marched to Gunskirchen Lager, a German concentration camp near Lambach, Austria. 8,000 survived the walk. Joel was liberated by the71st U.S. Infantry in Austria on May 4, 1945.

Wilhelm was sent to concentration camp Theresienstadt (Terezin) late in the war because of a head injury. This camp was operated by the Gestapo as a front, a model Jewish settlement but in reality a concentration camp and a transit camp for European Jews reroute to Auschwitz and other extermination camps. The Red Cross took control of the camp on May 1, 1945 and it was liberated by Soviet troops on May 8, 1945.

Dorothy and her three sisters Rose, Helene and Susan were survivors from Auschwitz II, Czechoslovakia. The family was lucky in that they did better than most of the Jews that came from their birthplace, Negrovo, a remote part of Czechoslovakia which was taken over by the Hungarians early in the war. Dorothy lost both sets of parents and two siblings. Their families weren't deported until Passover of 1944. Dorothy's oldest brother died of illness in a camp.

Her mother and nine-year- old brother were gassed on arrival at Auschwitz. Dorothy's father died in Auschwitz just before the war ended.

At Auschwitz, Dorothy and her three sisters Rochel, Chaya and Sarah sorted clothes sent to the German people at home. The Germans asked everyone to undress before they sent them to be gassed. They told them that they were going to take a shower but the shower was poison gas. There was no way to escape or hide. The Germans had dogs and guns. Anyone who stepped out of line was torn up by a dog. The prisoners who worked in the crematoriums were killed by the Germans after three months because they did not want to take a chance that one of them might escape and talk about what was going on at Auschwitz.

As the Russians were advancing, Dorothy and her sisters were forced to march from camp to camp closer to Germany. Rochel was able to smuggle potato peels out of a kitchen. She was caught once and punished severely.

Rochel got typhus from lice. The three sisters dragged Rochel along. Each made sure the other would go forward even when they wanted to give up. Fortunately this turned out to be the last leg of their march. The inmates received a daily ration of half a piece of hard bread which was further reduced when the few remaining Auschwitz prisoners were marched about 30 miles daily from camp to camp ahead of the advancing Russian army.

After liberation, Dorothy and her three sisters made their way home to find her parents' house in Negrovo. Dorothy and her sisters dig up the prayer book that their mother had buried in the back yard. They tried to recover some of the items left in their hope chest. The Russians took things that were of value. They stayed in the area for about two weeks and then left for Budapest and stayed at a dorm. Two sisters wanted to go to Prague. So they all left for Usty Laben where the survivors received apartments. The oldest sister became a cook and the two middle sisters, seamstresses. The youngest one went to school.

Joel went home to Batyu to find his brother Willy already there, trying to repair things. Joel convinced Willy that there was nothing left for them. Joel and Willy left without talking to anyone, and headed for Prague.

In Prague, Joel met and befriended Dorothy's ex-boyfriend. Before the war, the ex-boyfriend asked for Dorothy's hand by asking her father who replied that he should ask her but he didn't. He asked for her hand again but was refused again so he introduced his friend Joel to Dorothy at the Prague YMCA. Joel purchased a second hand black suit and got married in February 1947.

Annette was born in December. They moved west and were granted visas to enter the US. They traveled to Gothenberg, Sweden with Joel's sister Dina. The day the boat left for the US, a full page photo of Annette being held by Joel was printed in the local newspaper. The picture was captioned "Refugees Leaving for America." Their ship arrived in New York in January 1949.

In New York, Joel got a job in a lumberyard. A relative in Connecticut lend them money to start a business in 1950. They purchased a small decrepit trailer diner in Norwalk CT. Joel became "Joe". According to Joel, a customer had to show him what a hamburger was and how to make his first one.

In 1956, they tore down the old diner and built a new one. (Nobody wanted to buy the business.) The new unit was pre-fabricated aluminum and fiberglass. This became the Four Star Family Diner on Main Street. The menu was American, Hungarian, Irish and Jewish (Especially Jewish). They were one of the very few diners in the US that served gefilte fish, cold borscht with a hot boiled potato, home made potato pancakes and cheese or blueberry blintzes.

Annette and Joni did their homework in a booth while Dorothy helped out during dinner hour. While growing up, both girls felt peer pressure around Memorial Day. Their friend's fathers were Jewish veterans of World War II and their children got to ride on the float in the parade.

By the 70s it was in vogue to be the child of Holocaust survivors.

Dorothy refused to remove the number on her forearm that was tattooed when she entered Auschwitz.

Working 150 hours a week between them, they were able to send both daughters, Annette and Joni to law school. Annette started law school at Columbia. Her undergraduate work was done at Bryn Mawr College. Joni also started her law degree at Columbia but finished up at Harvard when she got married to Daniel Hassenfield.

Annette became chief counsel to the U.S .Dept of Health and Human Services in New York. Retired, she is helping her Russian husband Sam Landa in his dental practice in New Haven, CT. Joni teaches Legal Reasoning, Research & Writing at Boston College Law School.

Joel and Dorothy always supported Jewish organizations including UJAZ Federation, the Jewish Center and Congregation Zerah Kodesh, Temple Beth El and Beth Israel Synagogue.

Dorothy was very active in Hadassah. She was honored as Hadassah's Woman of the Year and chosen as honoree for the Hand of Healing in 1981.

Joel is a Hadassah Associate, and a member of the National Holocaust Commission. Both Annette and Joni are Life members of Hadassah.

Recently Joel's grandson, Elie Hassenfeld, a hedge fund analyst and his partner Holden Karnofsky gave up their six figure incomes to form Give-Well. They study charities in given fields and rank them on their effectiveness. Give-well is supported by a charity they created, the Clear fund which makes grants to charities they recommend in their research.

DOROTHY BATES

A single day among the learned last longer than
the longest life of the ignorant. (Seneca)

I met Dorothy Bates just before she sold her real estate practice in Wilton CT. I happened to call at the right time, and we hit it off almost immediately. She was a prominent real estate professional with her own agency teaching real estate ethics and establishing local and state Boards of Realtors, serving on the National Board -- and writing college textbook (*How to Run a Real Estate Office*).

Dorothy grew up in Sioux City, Iowa, daughter of the late Dr. Frederick Roost, a physician and the late Helen Roost, once a soprano with the NY Metropolitan Opera. Her first book, *Adventures of Andrea* was penned and illustrated by her at the age of 9. She was assistant City Librarian in Sioux City at 14.

She enrolled at Iowa State University at 15 majoring in home economics and minored in journalism.

She was one of my clients who didn't complain about commissions. She continued to be my client when she moved to Summertown where son Albert was starting his own family on "The Farm"(10), a large spiritual community from the sixties counterculture movement.

 In 1979, Dorothy began building a cutting-edge solar house near the commune on 40 acres. It was completed in 1981. She wanted to sell me a small plot near hers in the early 90s when I visited but I was not ready for communal living.

 In this rural community, she went on to several new careers: tax preparer, investment strategist, financial advisor, editor and publisher of sixteen vegetarian cook books, and high school literature teacher. She revitalized The Farm's small publishing house, The Book Publishing Company (BPC), when it was facing extinction toward the end of the Eighties. BPC had a niche in publishing Native American lore, eclectic spiritual topics, midwifery and a few cook books. To revitalize the company, she created new titles, updating popular old titles, writing her own titles, and bought rights to *The Bernard Shaw Vegetarian Cookbook*. She also hosted visits from new vegetarian authors, inviting them to complete their work in her home. She coordinated food photography sessions, promotional tours, interviews and television appearances.

Currently they have some 300 books in print with distribution throughout the US, Canada and parts of Europe. Initially she financed the cost out of her own pocket but later she instituted a two- year borrowing program at current bank rates.

During November of 1999 Phyllis and I joined her, her friend Kippy Nigh and husband Ron, an archeologist, on tour of three different geographical sections of Mexico. My friend Phyllis was reluctant to go because Dorothy was scheduled for heart surgery at Vanderbilt University Hospital upon return. She held her own even when visiting the archaeological sites in Oaxaca. Her surgery was postponed until she got rid of her cough. Apparently for decades, Dorothy endured severe health problems but remained cheerful and indomitable in the face of every setback

Dorothy passed away on Friday, May 9, 2003. She refused using life support. She was a very tough woman. She wanted to look over her accomplished family from above.

Most people associated with the farm attended Dorothy's memorial service. -People came from as far as California and Alaska. The accolades were mind boggling. People around her appreciated her life of love, sharing good food and wisdom, good cheer and courage. To this day, people at the Farm still talk about her accomplishments.

Even though I was Dorothy's main broker, she did spread her investments around to other brokers and advisors which we consolidated to Raymond James on her death. When my nephew Brian had a new account quota to meet at Merrill Lynch, I referred several of my accounts to him: my regular and IRA account; my sister, Catherine Gorscak; a widow of an associate from Lucidol, Jenny Wylegalia; my nephew, Richard Gorscak. My sister's account was transferred to one of Brian's associates because it was small and inactive.

I was not pleased with Merrill Lynch's Buy /Sell recommendations at that time. This was the peak time in which there was a conflict of interest between the analyst's recommendation and investment banking.

ALBERT BATES

*Learning is a treasure which follows a owner
everywhere.* Chinese proverb

Albert became custodian for all Bates accounts. He is as interesting as his mother Dorothy. Albert earned his B.A. at Syracuse University in 1969 and his LL.B (Bachelors in Law) and J.D.(Juris Doctor) at New York University.

Other educational accomplishments include: E.M.T.(EMERGENCY MEDICAL TECHNICAN) State of Tennessee, 1974 and Perm culture Certificate 1996.He made Who's Who listings including: World, American Law, Emerging Leaders, Science & Engineering, South & Southwest, Executives and Professionals, Men of Achievement, and International Biographical Dictionary.

Albert joined the 680 acre Farm located in Summertown, TN in 1972. He took a 1,000 mile trek on the Appalachian Trail, New York to Tennessee.

The Farm is one of the largest and durable communities formed during the so-called "hippie" movement of the late 1960s and early '70s. Albert and his mother helped this spiritual community transform itself into a cooperative with a hybrid economy.

Albert has written several books, the most recent being *Post Petroleum Survival Guide and Cookbook* (New Society Publishers). He also has his own blog that can on the Great Change website. A profile by Jim Windolf appeared in the April. 2007 issue of *Vanity Fair.* Much of his writings on Ecovillage and Sustainable Community; Politics and Power and Human Rights and Dignity are available on line. He was also a contributor to Al Gore's book and film on global warning.

KATHRYN HILL.

Learning is better than house or land. Irish proverb

Kathryn Hill, Albert's sister, was my client until a Raymond James broker in its Cranston. RI branch was accused of bilking investors out of $16.5 million. Kathryn indicated that she would stay with me if I left Raymond James. Later she now claimed I did not respond to her needs for more income. She went to United Bank Shares (UBS) and is quite happy. She converted a 58-foot trawler to a live aboard home in Virginia. Recently put a sailing rig on her trawler and moved to southern, California where she volunteers full- time for the Avatar Meher Baba Center.

MAUDE BLISS

*A nod of the head is enough for an
intelligent man.* Chinese proverb

Maude Bliss was another client. Her deceased husband was a chemist who owned and operated a small paper company that manufactured the paper for the US Treasury's currency. She was a very proper, lonely and bright woman who indulged heavily in alcohol and cigarettes. From the pictures around her house, she was a very beautiful society gal in her time.

She was the only client who consistently gave me high quality Christmas gifts. I still have one of her costly neckties and a bottle of Taylor (10 years in the Wood) Port that she gave me. The client-customer relationship was usually excellent. At times I would receive her late- night, "I love you" calls. She was, of course, inebriated, so I asked her to change brokers. But she came back. I kept in touch with her son in Massachusetts a few years after her death.

ROBERT BREITBARTH

*Unless the water is deep (i.e. unless the leader is great,)
the fish will not gather in a school.* Korean proverb

I met Bob by cold calling when I was with Smith Barney. He was president of General Cable Corp in Greenwich CT. H e became a good client and friend. He liked Merrill Lynch's full service investment money account and did not want to go through the same the process with Smith Barney.

He referred me to several of his executive friends who became clients. After retiring from General Cable, Bob became active with the United Nations. He was also active for a year with the Metals Partnership that we had formed. Bob's wife, Laurel was active in The Westport Theatre Group. She died around 2005.

HOWARD AND CARLA RUNDA

We live and learn; we learn and live. American proverb

I met Howard through a cold call when he lived in Stamford CT. He was with Booz, Allen & Hamilton, Inc and kept active by consulting with various small firms in and Ohio where he retired. Since he had several sons quite successful in technology he tended to skew his investment interests into that area. .He invested in the Metals partnership with Bob Breitbarth and me.

I did not realize till later that Carla Runda, his wife, was a market researcher – in fact she was Manager of Market Research/ Information at Booz, Allen & Hamilton in Europe. She tried being an independent consultant prior to going to a division of Johnson and Johnson in Germany. Currently she teaches German and French and does business interpretation and translations for a number of firms in the Cincinnati, Ohio, area.

SAM LEVINE

A nod of the head is enough for an intelligent man. Chinese proverb

Sam was special consultant to John Wasserlein, Divisional Manager at Boise Cascade, Brattleboro VT. All three of us got to know each other quite well on a flight from Beaver Falls, NY to Boise, ID in John Wasserlein leased small plane. I worked with Sam to build up Specialty Division's international sales. Boise Cascade got out of the paper manufacturing and into office products.

As a client, Sam was tough but fair. A perfectionist, he would calculate interest on his money market to the third decimal point. If his calculation did not coincide with the firm's, he would request a credit. Sam was one of the first clients to leave me because he was afraid that Drexel, my employer, might go bankrupt. The fact that his account was insured for $50 million did not comfort him much.

ROBERT FERRIS

Honor follows the unwilling. Latin proverb

I met Bob Ferris when he was Research Director for Sealed Air. He retired shortly thereafter and moved to southern California where he played golf daily with his wife. They took time off from golf when I visited them in 1989. Bob died in 1994

HOWARD LEVIN

Take honor from me and my life is done. Shakespeare

171

I met Howard and his wife Arlene when he was deputy program manager, Department 688, Electric Boat Division General Dynamics. He invested in high quality "good value" stocks.

Since he was concerned about commissions, I taught him how to trade options. Initially he would buy a high quality stock and then sell calls against them for added income. When I left Smith Barney, he stayed with the manager, Dick Pignone.

Today he only sells uncovered puts on stocks like General Electric, Pfizer, Home Depot, Lowe's and CVS Drugs and buys them back with a 2 or 3 point profit if they drop in price. He keeps sufficient cash in the account to cover if the securities are put to him. He does about 700 trades a year.

Since 1973, his wife Arlene owned and operated eight stores in Mystic Village Mall. She recently sold her last store, The Country Store.

Howard is still a gun collector and a daily poker player at the casino. He likes poker because one does not have to play against the house but only against the other players.

HARRIET SIMS

Learn young, learn fair; learn auld (old),
learn mair (more). Scottish proverb

Harriet was an accountant by profession graduating from New London Business College in 1935. Harriet's initial job was with Dougherty Accounting Services. She then joined the Housing Authority of New London as Office Manager and Comptroller. Three years prior to her retirement, she became Director of this Housing Authority.

She was easy to work with because she was decisive and willing to learn. She was a value investor, one of the first to jump aboard our Super 18 and Super 25 Program.

When she died on 8/19/97, her estate was divided among two relatives – nephew David and first cousin Doris. Because David was a trader, the nephew stayed with Buell Securities when I left the firm. Her first cousin, Doris Sobiech, stayed with me but was reluctant to make portfolio changes. She feared making an investment mistake! Her accountant sold her on the safety of a deferred annuity. She was given false or misleading statements that some investments never lose money yet give excellent returns. I'm sure neither liquidity nor cash flow was thoroughly discussed with the client. It was fortunate for that accountant that her stock portfolio gave her sufficient cash flow to meet her immediate cash needs.

It is unfortunate that, for certain older clients, some annuities are a poor investment for them regardless of the after- death returns. Accountants and tax attorneys should refrain from selling investments. Better to give their clients objective checks and balances.

Raymond James had a few brokers who sold the higher commission policies with a total disregard for the client's immediate needs. I was, however, proud of RJ's courage with their recent annuity product sales program. They stood up to some of their esteemed colleagues by refusing to carry the high commission products in Raymond James' portfolio and forcing the insurance vendors to reduce their fees as well as simplifying the policies.

Earlier, Raymond James did not do due diligences on each of the companies they did business with. They left it up to the broker's branch manager to make sure the product was suitable for the client's goals and objective.

The flaw for the marginal manager is that he or she must make the production numbers. Otherwise they would not be with Raymond James "tomorrow".

For a short time after RJ was fined heavily for lack of supervision, their insurance department scrutinized every policy application.

My former branch manager was in this bind. He needed to make the higher production quotas recently put to him by the high regulatory fine against RJ because of one bad broker in Rhode Island. In his mind, he justified every policy he wrote because it guaranteed the client safety of principal but neglected to tell them that they had to die to exercise that benefit. (Or wait 5 or 7 years to receive the total return cash flow without diluting principal.

Under the earlier policy, the Home Office disapproved some annuity applications because of the client's age, goals and objectives. Revenue and broker pressure did not convert the entire department's ethical intention into ethical action regarding suitability. The new strategy will lower policy fees, create consistent commissions and reduced opportunities for confusion by simplifying the offerings.

I believe that this is an excellent start and just may save the insurance companies from themselves. If the bad and good policies are paying the same commission, the broker will naturally do what is best for the client. Simplifying the policies should be a godsend for the client because he would not have to give it to an accountant or tax attorney for interpretation.

JOHN WILKES

Men of learning are plain men. American proverb

Dr. John Wilkes was research director for Duracell Battery prior to it going public. John was able to have Merrill Lynch send some shares to me so a few clients were also able to participate. The firm was then purchased by Gillette and then Proctor and Gamble.

After the public offering, John retired and moved to Austin, Texas where he invested in real estate. He had a son and grandchildren in Austin. I added them to my west coast trip in 1990. They gave me a grand tour of Austin and wanted me to move there. They found their neighbors chilly. Eventually they moved back to Connecticut.

DREXEL BURNHAM & LAMBERT 1986 - 1989

He is not a merchant who always gains. Dutch proverb

The switch to Drexel took me to a more dynamic firm which would permit me to try to do venture capital, private placement and other investment banking business. They gave me good backing evaluating various money managers throughout the country for high- net worth individuals and small- to- medium size retirement plans. Their quantitative stock and bond research and their asset manager's evaluations were superb.

The atmosphere in their NY headquarters was very broker friendly and they had excellent operational support. They also had a generous payout. I was told that brokers had the ability to get stock ownership in a firm when it was quite profitable.

My branch manager was Arthur Katz, Shearson's branch manager at Paramus, New Jersey. It was because of him, that I had the opportunity to meet Sandy Weils.

I was surprised to be approached by a headhunter only seven months on the job. Little did I know that in short order the firm would be receiving a stream of unwanted publicity. I didn't think it would hurt me much with individual clients. But it would hurt the firm, no matter whether Mike Milken or any of his staff is guilty or not. I was wrong.

Mike Milken took the hit for the junk bond fiasco. The president, Mr. Joseph, didn't fire him before the publicity- hungry Rudy Giuliani forced the firm into bankruptcy.

Drexel never would have survived as a firm without Mike Milken. They were an innocuous second- tier firm until Milken, a Wharton School of Finance student, and his professor, came up with the junk bond idea. Milken's junk bond idea brought huge revenues and profits to the firm.

A short history of Drexel, according to my friend, Harry Block: Around 1978, Burnham and Company bought Drexel Firestone. Drexel had been an old white shoe firm. At one time, it had been Drexel Morgan.

When Glass Steagall was enacted, J P Morgan said that Drexel could keep the brokerage firm and he would take the bank. Drexel needed money and the Firestone Tire Company put money. It and it was renamed. When Burnham took over, Drexel was a bit controversial since Burnham was, middle -of –the- road firm, and considered a Jewish firm.

Other major- bracket underwriters were not happy but had to go around. The brackets were done alphabetically. They did not want it to be Burnham Drexel which is why it became Drexel Burnham.

Mike Milken was working with Drexel while going to University of Pennsylvania. He was very sought after even then. He was about to go to Goldman Sachs but there was a hang up because his wife was pregnant and Goldman Sacks could or would not cover maternity costs. Since Burnham was acquiring the firm, they "bridged" the coverage so Mike Milken came over.

In the beginning he used to commute to NYC from Cherry Hill, NJ. When one of his children developed asthma, he decided to go to warm weather. That is why he moved to California.

Baron Leon Lambert was the majority owner of Banque Bruxelles Lambert was a shareholder in W E Hutton which Burnham bought. He then made an investment in Burnham. At one point he tried to make a run at taking over the firm but they fought him and won.

One middle management person from Merrill Lynch continuously knew weeks in advance what was going to happen at Drexel. Investment bankers badly wanted to get into the junk bond business. Rudy Giuliani never brought the insider trading charges against Drexel that he so publicized in the press.

During this turmoil, I lost several pension fund clients and personal clients. I stayed with the firm to the end. (I'm usually the first one to leave at any sign of trouble.) I also had Merrill Lynch courting me before things really got ugly at Drexel.

One pension plan loss was a relative. One June 1, 1987 he opened an account for slightly more than $100,000. Being a relative, conservative and with little financial experience, I chose a money manager, Centurion Capital Management for a 1% per annum fee paid quarterly. The manager's specialty was telecom stocks. He had worked for AT&T before they broke up into seven regional Bells in 1984.

There was consistency of real returns on these foggy equities when measured over a period of twenty years. They produced good dividends, many splits, spin-offs and cash distribution giving a total return in excess of 10% per annum. (Please refer to appendix for details for AT&T's Stock History since 1984.) The Bell's almost made a full cycle – breaking up of AT&T into seven companies on 12/31/83, with a few exceptions, reunited in 2007.

Some investors also fall into the trap of over confidence in their own abilities by success in their own field. There was a grand bull market that started in August 1982 through March 2000. The temptation of high flyers and fads can indeed overwhelm the need to be a long-term investor even among the most conservative. The client lost over 1,000% on his initial investment which also produced good income along the way. This effectively demonstrates Jeremy Siegel's argument of the consistency of real returns of equities. On or about this time, the Super 18 Stock Picking Program was conceptualized.

The only significant long-term account that I obtained while at Drexel was Arthur Klaben, He thought he was big- times, always wanted more discounts. He requested operational changes in his accounts. He suggested that I open a conservative account for his wife.

When I left the Darien, Connecticut branch which was purchased by Paine Weber, Arthur came to the office with his wife requesting special discounts. He was surprised when the manager walked away.

Part of his accounts transferred with me to Smith Barney/American Express. He died of a massive heart attack in January of 1994. His death triggered an IRS audit. His wife Phyllis and I are still very good friends.

Drexel sold its retail business piecemeal well before the bankruptcy. Smith Barney and Paine Weber made a bid for our Darien office. Lance Bailey, a previous Paine Weber (PW) broker, promoted his ex-firm. I promoted my ex-firm, Smith Barney. The office voted to become affiliated with PW. I left for Smith Barney, New London.

Arthur Katz had several subsequent jobs, mostly at Smith Barney. Lance Bailey became assistant Branch Manager to Chet Safian at the new Paine Weber office.

I'm still friends with Harry Block who became the operations manager in Darien just before I left. He was, in my opinion, most competent, a very strict but fair Compliance Officer. My transition from Pain Weber to Shearson was smooth, thanks mainly to Harry Block and my secretaries Mary D and Patty R.

During 1986, I visited my brother in Arizona, my Boise Cascade friends and neighbors in New York and friends in Montreal Canada. I also visited my client Mac Cleary in Fort Lauderdale. A retired GE executive, Mac was the person who initiated the Super 18 concept.

I came very close to purchasing a house in North Norwalk – the loan was approved but I requested a $4,000 allowance for some improvements based on the house inspection. The owner refused but sold the house for $15,000 more than I offered.

SMITH BARNEY/AMX 1989 - 1990

In business, one must be perfectly affable. Chinese proverb

Except for one client, Peter Perry, nothing memorable happened here. For me, the working conditions were not good. My office was totally in an open area. A complete change in management style was really bad news.   Earlier they might have done little for you but at least they listened but now numbers were the only thing that mattered. Produce, they may listen and you may get what you needed. Don't produce and you are out.

I was glad that the Darien office went with Paine Weber as they seemed to be more broker- friendly. I don't think many of the brokers there would have survived the new Smith Barney management style.

I got Peter Perry as a client by accident.. Peter's secretary thought I was his son when I first called Peter so she told him I was on the other line.

Peter was tired of the BS the stockbrokers were giving him when they called.   He quit taking their calls even though he needed their help with his ESOP. He asked me a specific ESOP question and I told him that I did not know but I would find out and call him back. He was impressed, so he became a client.

To this day, we are friends even though he moved his account with my nephew. Peter needed stability, and my nephew needed assets on his book- a good marriage!

We jointly worked on finding stocks for his ESOP Value portfolio that met the following criteria: High quality and expected to continue earning and dividends predictability. Because this was an ESOP with tax consequences, he did not want to replace an issue with much higher appreciation potential and/or diversification into a growth industry not represented in the portfolio.

He also did not want to take profits and/or go into a higher cash position regardless of the economic conditions. Even if a stock became a Fallen Angel he did not want to sell because of capital gain consequences.

Ten years later, the securities in his portfolio mostly met the criteria's we set forth.   Two exceptions were Time Warner and Boise Cascade. The latter finally broke even.

This modified Graham & Dodd's strategy was good for the client but not necessarily good for the broker or the investment banking firm. The initial transaction was great but the only commissions generated thereafter were from the dividends that were invested.

I believe this strategy and stock picking process was the embryo for the Super 18 and 25 programs that we developed a few years later.

During this time, I met and dated Beb Kennedy at the Unitarian Church in Westport CT where we both were active members. She had two adult daughters and an adult son.

Beb had some very interesting friends. In 1999 we attended a large Chinese wedding in NYC where the bride changed into beautiful new wedding attire after each meal course. My second wedding in Long Island was a very meticulously planned ceremony at the Coast Guard Academy. Both the bride and groom excelled as strategists.

My nephew Brian rented a room at her home when I moved from New Canaan to Old Mystic. Brian had shared my apartment in New Canaan.

PHYLLIS KLABEN

It is the things in common that make relationship enjoyable, but it is the little difference that makes them interesting. Todd Ruthman

I started dating Phyllis Klaben during the spring of 1995 – approximately a year after her husband's untimely death. We shared interest in bridge, finance, medical market research, foreign movies, theatre, and travel and to a lesser degree hiking, opera and bicycling.

Initially I traveled with Phyllis to her various Medical Research conventions and meetings in Chicago and New York. We also participated in several family member weddings and bar mitzvah or bat mitzvah in Ohio and New York. In February 1999, we went to the Money Show in Orlando and visited some of my Florida clients. We also attended the Jazz Festival in Montreal and visited one of Phyllis's top medical research writers while there.

In November of that year, we joined Dorothy Bates and Kippy Nigh (who lived in Mexico for thirty years) on an eight day Mexican tour to Oaxaca, the Mexican seashore and Mexico City. My favorite memory of this trip is the people: the organizers, their children. The Mexican people: from the archeologist, weaver, woodcarver, cab driver, waiters, massages', boat captain

Other things that were memorable include the archaeological sites, National Museum of Anthropology and Day of the Dead celebration.

In 2002 we took a wonderful Elder Hostel tour of the Getty Museum in Los Angles followed by an opera tour in Sarasota, Florida, February of 2003.

During the winter of 2005, I spent several weeks with Phyllis looking at property and helped her in the price negotiation of her current home in Florida. Two weeks later, she could have sold the home for a $50,000 profit. That was an excellent synergistic team effort.

During the winter of 2006, I explored the possibility of moving and working in Vero Beach. Neither worked out so I returned to Connecticut and retired.

During the fall of 2007 Phyllis stayed in CT and worked out the details to move her older sister Shirley into the Assisted Living Section of Seabury Retirement Community in Bloomfield, Connecticut. She also stayed in CT, even though she hates cold weather, to receive breast cancer treatment. Phyllis, John Rim and I plan to spend two exciting weeks in Croatia next May.

ANNA PISACICH

All happy families resemble one another; every
unhappy family is unhappy in its own way. Tolstoy

During the early 60s, Brother Ed brought Mom and Sister Anna to Phoenix. Anna adjusted to the new environment quickly. Mom could not adjust to someone else being in command. Anna was given reading and arithmetic lessons. She went to social dances with a neighbor.

We learned that she was not retarded but slow with an IQ of 70. She enjoyed visiting the Grand Canyon with Ed and Eva. Mom felt her command over Anna was being threatened so she returned to West Mifflin with Anna.

After mom's death on October 7 1978, Ed and Eva brought Anna back to visit Disney Land (Anaheim), Las Vegas and Tucson. She lived in the family house (West Mifflin) for awhile but then moved to an apartment near Sister Kate.

During the fall of 1990, I spent a week in Pittsburgh to study the situation because Sister Anna tried to take her life when she learned that we were breaking up her apartment for a group home at the suggestion of Mon-Yough Mental Health Clinic. Being a people person, it appeared that she did adjust quickly to her new environment. My sister Kate suspected that Anna and many of the other residents became addicted to drugs. That was a way of keeping them docile.

In 1993 brother Ed brought Anna to the Mayo Clinic (Scottsdale AZ) for a thorough physical as he was concerned about many medications that she was taking, a flat look to her face, and episodes of tongue thrusting and twisting.

The doctors at the Mon-Yough Mental Clinic were sent this Mayo Clinic report on November 16, 1983 with test results, diagnosis and recommendations.

They acted on a few recommendations. When Katherine complained to Anna's psychiatrist, it was to no anvil. When Anna complained, they gave her more psychological drugs without questioning and investigating. Nobody checked the abnormal module on her right breast. Nobody checked probable candida vaginitis.

The Medicaid program in Pennsylvania spent dollars but the quality of care was mediocre. It was not much better when I moved her to a nursing home in CT near my home. Medicaid patients in a nursing home have no doctor's choice if seen in the nursing home. I finally insisted that she be able to go to a doctor's office that was accepting Medicaid patients. `They caught the cancer two weeks before she died on March 8, 1998 at the age of 68.

Her body was shipped to West Mifflin, PA to be buried in the family plot. It was surprising to see how many friends and acquaintances took time to offer their condolences. Her old neighbors and friends took care of and watched out for one another to the very end.

She was not brilliant but a people's person to the end. We had a Memorial Service at the Nursing Home a few months later with a guitarist, Carlton Kish, from Boston.

ADVEST 1990 - 1992

As the master is, so is the shop. Polish proverb

Earlier in my career, I was offered a position with the Boston office of Advest which I think would have been excellent for me despite higher living cost. The Middletown office would not have been a mistake if my joining the firm was a joint decision of the corporate office, regional manager and the branch manager. Perhaps then the branch manager would have been more communicative about their plans to move into new quarters with additional office space. My desk was in an awful area with no noise barriers and privacy. There was absolutely no concern for a person's handicap or potential. Also, all parties including me were guilty in not communicating well. I think I could have made a terrific difference at Advest.

When my nephew Brian had a new account quota to meet at ML, I referred several of my accounts or relatives to him: my regular and IRA account; my sister, Catherine Gorscak; a widow of an associate from Lucidol, Jenny Wylegalia; my nephew, Richard Gorscak. Brian and Dorothy Bates never hit it off so the account was eventually closed. My sister's account was transferred to one of Brian's associates because lack of activity and size. I was not pleased with ML's buy /Sell recommendations at that time. This probably was the peak time in which there was a conflict of interest between the analyst's recommendation and investment banking. My nephew Richard's account is still with him.

One noted new account was my high school classmate and neighbor, Ronald Kish and his wife Vi. Ron was a nuclear physicist who specialized in health safety at graduate school and a premed student in undergraduate school. His initial position was with the Bettis Atomic Energy Plant in West Mifflin that was managed by Admiral Rickover. Subsequently he held a series of consulting nuclear hygienist positions that were based in New York and Ohio. Ron was an accomplished violinist in high school. He also played the organ.

I kept in close contact with Ron and his family throughout the years. At the Bettis plant, he also worked with a classmate and neighbor since 3rd grade, Glen Lowery. We used to raise, breed, trade and sell various animals like pigeons, rabbits, mice, hawks, etc. The last time I saw Glen was at Ron's home in Mt Pleasant, PA after a heated debate concerning rifles. It was Ron and me against Glen. We may have won the debate but lost contact of a dear childhood friend.

Ron never became a large client because he wanted to spread his portfolio around to keep it a secret from everybody including the family and his financial advisors. This became a problem and a lot of work for me to reconstruct upon his death. Unfortunately the wife and family followed in his footsteps regarding finance.

Ron died January 3, 2003 in Ohio from a painful death of multiple my Loma. The irony is that the various federal government agencies put the burden on the widow to prove that he had excessive radiation exposure. Ron rarely discussed his work with Vi perhaps (my nephew is a senior engineer at Bettis- he also never discusses his work outside of the plant) he felt it was too technical for her, it was classified secret or top secret and/ or he was too much of a male chauvinist.

The company, Advest, originated in 1898 when two young engineers that had knowledge of the new technology, electricity, established an investment banking firm called Perry, Coffin and Burr to help electric utilities with financing. A series of partnership followed: Newburger, Henderson & Loeb of Philadelphia (1899); Sartorius & Co of New York (1899); Richter & Co of Hartford (1905); Doolittle & Co of Buffalo (1917) and Vercoe & Co of Columbus (1922)..

In the wake of 1912 recession William H. Putnam, a Richter & Co partner, gained control of the company changing the name to Putnam & Co. The partnership enjoyed decades of prosperity as well as periods of depression and wars. In the 60s, and the 70s the firm began a merger campaign of its various partnerships and changing the name to the Advest Group in 1977.

The company went public in 1980 and extended its market reach in Maryland, Washington, D.C., New York, Rhode Island, Virginia and Ohio. They also opened a saving and loan bank. The decline in the stock market in 1987, a deep recession in real estate and severe trouble with lending institutions caused the stock to drop to $1.75 from IPO price of $10.75 in 1980. The company recorded a net loss of $9 million in 1990 and the losses continued for an additional three years. Allen Weintraub, CEO turned the company around to positive earnings by mid 1990s and the trend continued. He retired as CEO on April 1, 1999.Grant Kurt took that position in 1999 followed by Dan Mullane.

All three CEO's were presidents and active with Connecticut Rivers Council.

On September 14th, 2005, Merrill Lynch announced that they were purchasing the Advest Group, Inc a subsidiary of AXA Financial for $400 million. Just think, if I stayed at Advest, I finally would have been part of the mighty Merrill Lynch. Dan Mullane left the firm shortly after the merger.

COBURN & MERDITH 1992 - 1994

Through obedience learn to command. Greek proverb

This equity firm was founded in 1934 under the name of Coburn and Libby. Tom Meredith became a partner about twenty years ago. The firm clears through Pershing Trading Company. The company moved to 150 Trumbull Street and then to 225 Asylum Street during the past ten years. I recently asked one of the firm's old timers what their niche or greatest asset might be? His reply was "they are a typical brokerage firm with their greatest asset being the broker". The two young Coburn's also appear to have developed the firm into a professional financial service firm with an excellent platform. They appeared not only talked the talk but walked the walk. I hoped I contributed some to this transformation. The firm did have a high percentage of bright brokers and staff that performed relatively well in trying times.

There was little interest in my Super 25 stock selection program at that time. They were purchasing Dorsey Wright Technical Analysis service and were quite happy with its performance.. They also used Pershing's equity research and Value Line research. I also used Value Line's data base for my Super 25 program. They were also trying to build up their own syndicate department. It was fortunate that none of my clients participated in their first two public offerings. Today they appear to have extensive research access and product mix availability equal to and/or exceeds just about any wire house.

My getting Graham Walker as a client probably forced the firm to specialize in the many facets of restricted securities. An irony in that I was able to close the deal in getting Graham Walker, CEO of Dexter Corporation as a client while Barry Coburn was working on him for several years with little success. Working with restricted securities is a strong niche for the company as it requires a good attorney or an equivalent to complete all the paperwork accurately and in a timely manner. The old Smith Barney and Drexel were masters in providing that service to their clients.

BUELL SECURITIES 1994 - 2000

*Who knows not to obey knows not to
command.* French proverb

Buell Securities was registered with the SEC on 11/17/1977. It was mainly an equity firm with a good track record in picking stocks. The firm had an added advantage for me of being very close to my home. When I joined the firm, Christopher D. Berris was the president and major owner. Chris and his minor partners James Cullen, William Cusack and Gerald Uricchio told me that they were receptive to my doing my own research on the Super 25 Investment Program as long as it did not cost them or the firm any money.

Our previous three years of research and test marketing told me that selling the research to the larger institutions was not appropriate because most of them wanted their own proprietary computer program. It was further determined that the acceptable portfolio size for 1995 should be $100,000 with five portfolios. I was planning to spend less time on administrative things and more on analysis and improving my lifestyle and health. During this period of time I worked quite diligently with Peter Perry and a local Public Relation person that was also located in our building for promotional material. I obtained compliance advice and suggestions from my compliance friend from Drexel.

During the fall of 1994, I visited my long time friends John and Joella Rimberg in North Carolina. I visited the Science & Math High School for gifted children, Duke University at Durham, University of NC at Chapel Hill, attended several classes of John's at Pembroke University, saw real democracy at work in the election process of a Tribal Chief for the Lumbee Indians; walked the cleanest beach I have ever been exposed to; and saw among other things the Borough's Welcome Research Building at Triangle

Research Center. This was one of my best sightseeing vacations as were the discussions on education, science, sociology and politics with John, Joella, and their friends and staff members.

As the market began to improve in 1995, the firm expected me to increase my production. The challenge of higher production, Super 25 Program, Health and Social Life exceeded a 24 hour day. I already dropped Bridge because I just could not afford the time to upgrade myself to the level of my bridge friends who play daily and took frequent lessons.

RISK: THE SNOWBALL IN HELL

LIFE-THREATING MEDICAL PROBLEMS

He who has not health has nothing. English proverb

This was a period of marginal health for me as well – In June of 1994, I went to the Mayo Clinic, Phoenix, Arizona for a complete medical check-up. I needed consultation for my imbalance and eye blurriness as well as headaches and memory deficits. Fortunately I only had a mild cover over portion of the retina in the right eye and my intellectual function was not typical for dementia or memory deficit. Simple eye drops for dry eyes, a series of balance exercises and reduction of drug intake were quite useful recommendations. During the rest of the time while at the clinic, I spent touring the South West of the country and visiting with my brother and his wife Eva.

In 1997, Dr. Robert Duckrow, UCON Medical Center suggested that I have a brain lesion removed (Excision of right frontal cortical oligodendroglioma). I became sold on the idea when he suggested that it also might resolve my impotency problem. We tried the psychiatrist a few times and was not successful. The operation was done at Yale New Haven Hospital by Dr. Spencer on 9/2/1997. Again, the post hospital stay was at New Haven Medical Center and ten days of loving care was given to me by my sister-in-law Judy at Brother Bernard's home. I recovered rather quickly and returned to work in about seven weeks. There was no post rehabilitation prescribed for this traumatic brain surgery .I never had a seizure again. Too bad this was not possible back in the 50's. However one of my friends from Pittsburgh had her's done in Montreal in the early 70's and became a noted publisher.

Again in 1999, I had a two-vessel coronary artery bypass at the suggestion of Dr Michael Blum of Yale. Dr. S. Jack Landau of New Haven was my earlier cardiologist. In 1985 I underwent a cardiac catherization by Rene Langou at the suggestion of Dr. Landau. It was determined that I had coronary disease with two lesions in the left anterior descending. One was 30% obstructed and the other not clearly defined so I was treated medically. It is just possible that subsequent and perhaps the current complaints were gastroesophagel reflux rather that heart related disease.

The two-vessel coronary bypass was done by Dr. Sabert Harsham at Yale Hospital on 4/27/1999 based on the results of a prior catherization. The post five day hospital stay was again at New Haven Medical Hotel. I again stayed for two weeks at my brother's Bernard home in Waterford, CT under the care of my sister-in-law, Judy Pisacich.

The recovery period may have been shorter than three months because of the superb rehab program at St. Francis Hospital in Hartford and walking my black cocker spaniel dog Quake at least twice a day. The end result of this most painful and longest recovery period operation was low blood pressure.

NUTMEG SECURITIES 2000 - 2003

Who knows not to obey knows not to command. French proverb

Nutmeg was founded in 1986 and is located in Westport, CT. Nutmeg has clearing relationship with Pershing LLC, A Bank of New York Company. They an equity firm but expanded to a few other financial services during my stay with the firm. The operations director Ed Vioni (formerly an attorney and with Merrill Lynch experience) left shortly after I joined the firm. His goal and business model was to expand the retail business from the current 40% of revenue by expanding the product platform and improving the quality of the business.

The firm was hit with a succession of business changes in a very short period of time: The compliance person was a broker with her own book. The firm lost its direct access computer developer. His replacement had to learn this new system in short order. The industry was being bombarded with many new compliance regulations due to the many ethical scandals frightening even the most experienced compliance officers.

I had trouble connecting into Nutmeg's direct access system at my home because I had to segregate business and non business emails. I also needed a new computer so I could update my operating system so that it would be compatible with the firm's system. Better communications may have expedited the change. Nutmeg wanted to leave the Retail business because of the high regulatory costs.

I was not permitted to promote my Super 25 Program to new or existing clients. Therefore, I offered my Nutmeg clients and prospects not only research from Pershing, but second opinions from their choice of: Standard & Poor's, Merrill Lynch, Zacks,

Worden and ABN Ambro, Inc. This research was paid for by me. No additional cost to Nutmeg.

If they chose Zacks, they were to select one or two continuously weekly item updates: Focus List, Timely Buys, and Stock Pick of the Month, Number #1 Ranked Stock, Value Portfolio, All-Star Analyst Portfolio, Brokerage Analysts Top Pick and Brokerage Firm "Buy List".

The clients would also receive Taxable and Non-Taxable Fixed Income IPO's and Secondary Offerings from Pershing and Equity Linked CD's with 100% participation in the positive performance of the blue chip stock at maturity from LaSalle Bank.

This package of services, in my opinion, could not have been equaled by multimillion accounts with firms such Morgan Stanley, Pain Weber or Merrill Lynch. If my test market worked, the program would have been passed on to the other brokers that were willing to participate.

Most of Nutmeg's previous growth had come from small cap block trading. Their experience and relationship within the small cap institutional community enabled them to cross a large number of smaller illiquid stocks with little or no market impact.

Approximately 60% of Nutmeg's revenue was Institutional and 40% Retail. It was Ed Vioni's goal when I joined the company to increase the retail revenue but upon his leaving the ratio remain stagnant, at best.

The institutional orders use special software for money managers and plan sponsors trades. These are agency only, conflict free execution and settlement services. Using this tool for large Nutmeg's retail clients probably would have given them a distinct advantage in gains and more profits to the firm.

 They had a women president when I was with the firm and they heavily promoted the fact that "Nutmeg is recognized by many states, municipalities and corporate pension plans as a minority owned and operated business (Women Business Enterprise).

They are certified as such by the Women's Business Enterprise National Council (WBENC) and the State of Illinois Central Management Service (CMS)". I thought that this was an excellent marketing tool to be addressed to the growing number of women clients that are interested in finance.

RAYMOND JAMES FINANCIAL SERVICES 2003 - 2006

A good leader makes good follower. Latin proverb

Command shows the man. Greek proverb

The firm is a full-fledged securities firm with respected research department, investment banking unit and asset management offering, offering proprietary mutual funds and alternative investments programs. Research emphasis was generally small and midcap securities but they also had Goldman Sack's research (mainly large cap) when I first joined the firm. They now use UBS for their large cap research.

 When I joined the company, their Syndicate Department's distribution policy was probably one of the fairest on the street for the clients and brokers. This however changed as the firm got larger. They also recently announced an unprecedented move to require the restructuring of variable annuities. They will require all their approved annuity providers to offer an alternative pricing structure that reduces costs without impacting standard or optional benefits. This should lower policy fees, create consistent commissions and reduce opportunities for confusion by simplifying offerings. At times, execution of trades seems to be a problem.

The Cranston, Rhode Island alleged fraud tarnished the firm's excellent reputation. It caused the loss of one large account – Kathy Hill and some of her other family members. . She claimed that she would stay with me if I went to any other firm even though I was not completely meeting her total income needs. Initially Raymond James may have been a bit slow in informing the brokers on that story but made up for it later.

Raymond James incorporated in 1962 in St. Petersburg Florida with revenues of less than $100,000 for the first fiscal year. They started humbly selling mutual funds. Membership on the Philadelphia-Baltimore-Washington Stock Exchange allowed them to fill orders for stocks and bonds. They gained membership on the NYSE in 1973.

Tom James joined his father after his 1966 graduation from Harvard. He immediately became CEO and recruited other Harvard's MBA's including Frances "Bo" Godbold who became president in 1987.

The firm was hit hard in the 1973-74 recession and stock market crash created havoc for small stocks and, consequently, RJF. Thus the firm's emphasis changed from sales to administration and finance. They became an expert in alternative investments – especially in the energy sector. In 1979 the firm was cited for its leadership in areas of financial planning services to small investors. (I wished I knew about Raymond James in 1980.) They opened a Paris office in 1987 and Geneva, Switzerland in 1988.

During the late 90s and early 2000, there was a merger epidemic. Thirty broker dealers had dropped off the radar since 1997, the majority due to consolidation. RJ and its chief competitor AG Edwards & Sons warded off suitors.

When the bear market hit again a new wave of consolidation occurred; this time by brokerages hurt by declining commissions and investment banking fees Lack of capital, increased competition, and need for larger distribution systems made larger look better to some independents but not to RJF and its chief competitor AG Edwards. They stuck with their traditional retail brokerage business despite the capital market downturn and subsequent drop in consumer business. Legg Mason, on the other hand, recreated itself as an asset management firm. Wachovia Bank recently announced their acquisition of AG Edwards.

Hindsight, one apparent weakness exhibited by RJF may be the lack of training and screening of branch managers in ethics and supervisory responsibilities rather than just production. Branch managers should also be protected from themselves and not be permitted to supervise their own sales activities. Just maybe the concept at the various wire houses that the branch manager has all the responsibility but no authority is correct. At these firms, the regional managers are not producing and do visit the branch offices regularly for marketing, compliance and administrative advise. They should review each manager's portfolio of accounts for business quality, ethics, and potential as well as commission dollars. Perhaps larger offices and no or low producing managers could help resolve the situation. This would, of course, change the model away from the independent contractors whose time may have faded away because of the high regulatory costs. Looking hindsight, fines paid to the NASD and related government agencies for lack of oversight and supervision during the past several years may have paid for some of its implementation.

A few months after I closed my home operations in Cromwell, CT for the Vero Beach, Florida office, my branch manager left the firm. I also wonder if Chet Helck was a bit too quick in forcing out his co called independent contractors that were producing less than $150,000 a year to offset those nasty regulatory fines that developed under his watch. Just maybe he and his divisional managers could have developed a better plan. Good evaluation forms could be a start.

No question that Tom James was and still is the driving force of the company. Middle management, in my opinion, is not their strongest suit. They should visit the branches least several times a year and consult the broker eyeball to eyeball rather than just sitting behind a desk and communicating via email or phone. The firm does seem to have strong technicians that could, in time, become very good managers. Technicians should make better managers than good sales personnel because they are giving up less. A few bad independent contractors could forestall my prediction that the firm will be bought out within the next eighteen months. I understand they weeded out many of them along with some good ones.

My most memorable client while at Raymond James was Dr. Myron Fields. I met Dr Fields through his daughter Teresa and her husband Mark, an associate professor in geology at Yale University.

DR. MYRON & ANNA FIELDS

A learned man has always riches in himself. Latin proverb

The wealth of the mind is the only true wealth. Greek proverb

Dr Fields was born and raised in Brooklyn New York prior to World War Two. He grew up on the streets of New York, living in the tenements of the ghetto.

He went to Temple University on a baseball scholarship, but completed his undergraduate education at New York University. Because of economic reasons, he went to Italy to study Medicine, which was probably the most significant life changing experience of his life. Medical school in a foreign language, which he was completely ignorant of, was a work of love and determination. The Italian experience of their culture, their value system, their friendships, their history, and their food was a life changing experience. He met Anna there, and in spite of personal family objections, married her and has shared his life with her for over 47 years.

He returned to New York to do his internship, and surgical residency during which time he had three children. He got drafted into the military during the Viet Nam War, where he was a Flight Surgeon serving the soldiers in that conflict. Subsequently he moved to Rock Island Illinois where they presently live.

His three children are on their individual journeys; Teresa is a Lawyer in New Haven Ct, David a Professor of Marine Biology in Maine, and Jacqueline a Physician in Colorado.

Myron retired recently, spending his time with music, biking, boating and gardening, while spending the winters in Colorado Skiing, snowshoeing and ski skating. His motto of life is, "each day is a gift, which is meant to enjoy to the utmost, sharing with those who love us, and who need our love."

RETIREMENT

I officially retired as a stockbroker on April 1, 2006 but I shared managing the portfolios of a few of my larger accounts and close friends with the Vero Beach manager, Rose Spytek.

MORE RISK

He that wants health wants everything. French proverb

During the later part of 2006 and 2007, I was admitted several times to The Hartford Hospital for chest pains. I was released with no heart problems. However the second time this happened; I insisted that they try to identify the possible cause. They did extensive tests relating to the heart including possible stroke but nothing relating to possible gastric problems. An upper and lower colonoscopy indicated no health problems.

Something, however, started to go wrong with the body on April 28th, 2007: Bleeding, loss of consciousness for 24 hours, fatigue and low blood pressure. Internal bleeding ceased but standing blood pressure was still low.

After three hospital stays, multiple Endoscopy and colonoscopies I decided to return to the Mayo Clinic , Scottsdale, Arizona for comprehensive evaluation of the following complaints: gastrointestinal, cardiovascular, ophthalmologic and immune system I decided to go after our family reunion in Logan, Utah on July 18th and hosted by brother Ed and his wife Eva. I left Connecticut a few days earlier to pick up my sister Kate. She could not travel alone.

 Maybe the disease is old age and it can be more to be feared than death. However before I admit to that, I accepted the Spanish proverb that "the beginning of health is to know the disease." I did get answers at the Mayo and implemented some of them at Yale or UCON Medical Group..

The sequence of events for the above medical episode follows:

4/28/07 Normal BP sitting.   88/56 standing. Bad vision problems.

4/29/07 Low BP sitting and not recording standing. Black diarrhea. Fainted while urinating.

4/30/07 BP sitting: 86/47/71 Standing 58/38/50 Very dizzy, vomiting blood.

5/1/07 Continued low BP, hiccupping, slept or unconscious for 24 hours.

5/2/07 Large pool of black blood along side of bed. I drove myself to the emergency room at Middlesex Hospital thinking that I ate tainted fish on Sunday. They assured me that it was not food poisoning.

The hospital recommended I drop the use of baby aspirin and replace it with Plavix. My cardiologist rejected that idea but started it when several neuroophthalmologist told me I had a stroke and I replaced aspirins with Plavix.

My regular GI doctor readmitted me in his hospital, Hartford Hospital and repeated an Endoscopy followed by a colonoscopy. No definitive answer so they had me monitored by a visiting nurse for several weeks.

BP continued to be low, dizzy, weight fluctuated daily or hourly within a 5 pound range. At the suggestion of Dr Tendler, I increased the dosage of Florneaf to 0.1mg daily. The iron capsule was also reduced to 65mg.

The physicians at the Mayo clinic doubled the dosage of Protonix daily (30 minutes before breakfast and 30 minutes before dinner). They suggested ways to stop heartburns before they got started by avoiding juices such as: orange, grapefruit, cranberry and tomato and liquor, wine, coffee and tea. The foods to avoid were: mashed potatoes, French fries, raw onions, potato salads, macaroni and cheese, spaghetti with marinara sauce, sour cream, milk shakes, ice cream, regular cottage cheese, and ground beef, marbled sirloin, nugget-style chicken, Buffalo wings chicken. The fats, oils and sweets to avoid were: chocolate, corn chips, regular potato chips, high-fat butter cookies, brownies, doughnut, creamy salad dressing and oil & cheese salad dressing. Avoiding just a few of the above seemed to help immensely.

It should be noted that my Medicare drug provider, Humana, would not give me a script for Protonix unless we try other drugs in the formulary first. I had a similar problem with them using the drug Nexium. The less expensive drugs may have worked in combination with the food items to avoid listed above. It's communications again.

Avoiding some of the items listed above and Protonix resolved my stomach problems. The orthostatic hypotension solution was to constantly take 0.05 mg of Florneaf daily and constantly wear the 40-50 compression elastic stockings during the day. This was Dr. Tender's (UCon's Medical Center) initial recommendations. I put my bed on a 12 degree incline and they gave me a series of exercises to successfully help manage orthostatic hypotension.

The Mayo clinic suggested I have my cataracts removed and an astigmatism implant but the Eye Clinic at Yale said no. The Yale Eye Clinic said, based on my poor peripheral vision, I had a small stroke but my yearly MRI at Yale said no. (Talk to two different physicians and you might get two different test interruptions) The Mayo suggested that I commence using Viteyes Areds Advanced to preserve macular health and two different eye drops for dry eyes – Bausch & Lomb Muro 128 at night and regular eye drops in the morning. The eyes should also be washed with a warm wash cloth every morning. The macular degeneration can also be slowed by drinking red wine but this a no no for my gastric problems. Fish, flax seeds and pomegranate juice also improve the macular health.

The trans-hearing aid that Yale's Audiologist suggested was ineffective for me. I will look into a Baha hearing system that the

Mayo Clinic suggested for my Single Sided Deafness (SSD) when I visited them earlier. The system combines a sound processor (worn externally) with a small titanium fixture implanted behind the ear and works through bone conduction of sound to the inner ear. This treatment began in Europe in 1977 and was cleared by the FDA for use in the United States in 1996. There are over 35,000 successful recipients for this system. Maybe after 27 years of hearing hardship, I will be able to hear normally for the next twenty years. I still will trust my eyes more than my ears because what I hear strikes the mind less than what I see.

My heart was in excellent condition. The sleep study at UCONN confirms that I should continue using the Bipap's airway management system unit but with a humidifier.

I accomplished a great deal by solving many of my concerns at the Mayo Clinic even though it was in the heat of summer when there was a great deal of vacations and medical conferences. They excel in verbal and written communications.

PISACICH FAMILY REUNION IN THE USA

> *Govern a family as you would a small fish-*
> *very gently.* Chinese proverb

Brother Ed initially planned to have this reunion in Croatia but Katherine's complicated surgery intervened. Ed rescheduled it to Logan where he normally goes every summer to beat the heat and to participate in Logan's opera and film festivals.

I went to Pittsburgh first so I could travel with Kate. We were pleased she handled the trip well. She was in a wheel chair most of the time. Ed planned meticulously. Those attending this pow-wow were: Ed and Eva Pisacich, Bernard and Judy Pisacich,

Katherine Gorscak and me. We stayed in deluxe suites at Snow Hall Dormitory, Utah State University.

The schedule was full and varied. It was a combination of cultural activities, scenic tours, excellent meals, family discussions and a "pool" challenge from Bernie when there was free time. We also took walks when possible. We saw four performances at Cache Valley Opera Theater: Verdi's II Trovatore, Frank Loesser's The Most Happy Fella, Jerome Kern and Oscar Hammerstein's Show Boat, George Gershwin's Porgy and Bess. We also went to recitals in the Mormon Temple and Tabernacles in Salt Lake City and Logan.

The tours at Caribbean-blue water and sandy beaches at Bear Lake, the East and West Pioneer Trails, Utah State University and the affluent residences in Logan were of natural superiority.

Ed interviewed Kate about her life as a child in Croatia, her trip to the US, and early life in America. He also showed many family photographs.

The trip was a tremendous success because Ed and Eva did a terrific job. He was a good host. An ounce of blood is worth more than a pound of friendship.

RISK MANAGEMENT: A SUMMING UP

To sin we seem to rush, to virtue, we crawl. German proverb

Wall Street brokerage sins don't just occur in NYC or Chicago as told by a slew of recent books the latest being Cohan's *The Last Tycoons.* Sins occur on a local level with midsize and small firms from time to time. I will leave it to them and others to make war with these vices of ego, greed, lust, wrath and jealousy but I will try to make a few suggestions to help improve the situation even though the industry made considerable progress at the lower level recently-either voluntary or with a gun to the head.

However, very little was done at the higher level of Wall Street. Take Citigroup as an example, the damage that just a few leadership men without souls almost caused the demise of Citigroup by lax oversight and "high-octane trading". Some of the men involved include Sanford I. Weill who I idolized earlier in the book, Robert E. Rubin, Chairman of the Executive Committee and most recently Secretary of Treasury; Charles O. Prince III who was connected to 120 board members in 6 different organizations across 3 different industries; Randolph H. Baker, Managing Director, Fixed income with a annual compensation of $17,500,000; Thomas G. Maheras who was company president at the time of the sub prime mortgage crisis. Maheras' annual compensation was reported to be $30,000,000. Also included in those poor leaders was David C. Bushnell, Senior Risk Officer who was responsible for managing risk for Citigroup and all its member companies. Quoting Eric Dash and Julie Creswell of The New York Times "They make Warren Buffet look like an altar boy". Hopefully some of these leaders will be gone tomorrow.

The following low-level oversights are based on my 25 years of industry experience with small, midsize and large financial institutions as well 25 years plus of corporate experience.

The industry should spend more time and money on people and education or they too will be outsourced to India and China for reasons other than low cost labor. The people in these countries feel that anything in the world can be done with good instruction. They already did it in manufacturing and technology five time faster rates than the Japanese. America no longer has a monopoly on creativity and business sense. We too can blunder.

BRANCH MANAGER PROFILE CHANGE

The high cost of litigation and law suits will eliminate smaller offices and producing managers. They are becoming as obsolete as the horse and buggy. The managers will be more business than sales oriented. The regulators recently made it onerous on senior management to "overlook" major infractions .There are now specific rules that apply to producing managers that are comprehensive.

MIDLEVEL MANAGEMENT

Higher management will search for and train technicians rather than only successful sales personnel for any mid level management position. This may be a blessing in disguise for successful sales people who may dislike such a position because it limits their income, social status, freedom or entrepreneurship.

BETTER TRAINING/INSTRUCTION

Effective even though they may be more costly. Workshop type training rather than lectures by suppliers on topics such as ethics, motivation, communications, decision making and empathy are more effective. The industry should accept the fact that perhaps only 50% of the participants are likely to stay with the firm but the initial gains and the industry PR more than justifies the cost. Use GE as an example.

I remember the one decision- making seminar I attended at Stanford University. Jack Welsh, Commercial Development Manager for GE Plastics, was one of many attendees with whom I networked for many years.   Later, I tried to persuade him to purchase Smith Barney when they were in trouble but he wanted higher net worth clients and a more prestigious firm so he purchased Kidder Peabody. That was not one of his better decisions. Or was it?

WALK THE WALK ON ETHICS
WHEN MONEY SPEAKS, THE TRUTH
KEEPS SILENT. RUSSIAN PROVERB

Money talks in this as well as other industries so there was a tendency to close one's eyes to major infractions. They hit minor infractions hard to show that they are working diligently to preserve the industry's ethical standards. This could be the hardest problem to resolve. It is much easier to imply findings or claims verbally.   Putting it in writing could cause lawsuits but it is preferable to put it in writing so everybody understands the subject including the writer. That is what I recommend. I would also like to cite the unfailing boomerang quote by Earl Nightingale in Ethics-Financial Industry "Every time you do something less than honest, you're throwing the boomerang. How far it will travel no one knows. How great or small a circle it will traverse only time will tell. But it will eventually, it must finally, it will inevitably come around behind you and deliver a blow to you."

BUILT A PERSONAL CODE AND
WRITE IT DOWN ON PAPER

This signals a commitment. One is much more likely to stick to the code in every day scenarios of facing the stress of dollar signs and the need for short-term gains. There is a need for a fixed point of reference to tell you to stop. This is how Enron leaders got into trouble — moving from bad business practices to crime. No one stopped them along the way. This is also what probably happened with the recent mortgage crisis which almost destroyed the nation from within (without terrorists).

OTHER TRAINING FOR COMPLIANCE OFFICERS

I remember one compliance officer who was with Drexel Burnham Corporation. He was educated on compliance and compliance decision-making procedures with communication skills and empathy skills. His soft and fair words went far. A successful compliance officer should receive training in both these skills plus writing skills and compliance decision- making *procedures.*

When middle management gets into trouble with regulators and cannot fix the problem immediately, there is a tendency to criticize and blame somebody else. This is a costly and it does not work because procedures are well- documented so that specific individuals or positions have specific responsibilities .When things go wrong, it is apparent who is responsible. When a manager claims that one of the supervisees has done something wrong, it is still the manager's responsibility to detect and correct the problem. This would eliminate the next impulse which is raising the production quota of financial advisors- regardless of potential problems - to offset the fines.

When I was in the corporate world and something was wrong, management usually cut advertising and marketing research funds. In my market research seminars at the American Management Association, I stressed the importance of communications and writing skills whenever managers said that their recommendations were not accepted.

Today, with a current housing crisis, an analogy was sent to me by several of my friends who indicate that the stock market is a scam. I can understand their view- point. Two examples of corporate greed (where the public was duped by greed) are Enron and Drexel Burnham. Some of the mortgage tycoons forgot that big mouthfuls often cause choking or that he that grabs too much holds fast with little.

Matthew Perry

This is the analogy my friend sent me:

"Once upon a time, a man appeared in a village in the middle of the forest. Since there were many monkeys in the forest near the village, he announced to the villagers that he would buy monkeys for $10 each.

The villagers went to the forest and started catching monkeys. The man bought thousands at $10. Soon the supply started to diminish and the villagers stopped their efforts.

The man further announced that he would now buy at $20.

This renewed the efforts of the villagers and they started catching monkeys again.

Soon the supply diminished even further and the villagers went back to their farms.

The offer increased to $25 each. The supply of monkeys became so small that it was an effort to even see a monkey, let alone catch It.!

The man now announced that he would buy monkeys at $50!

However, since he had to go to the city on business, his assistant would now buy on his behalf. In the absence of the man, the assistant told the villagers:

"Look at all these monkeys in the big cage that the man has collected. I will sell them to you at $35, and when the man returns from the city, you can sell them to him for $50 each."

The villagers rounded up all their savings and bought all the monkeys. They never saw the man nor his assistant, only monkeys everywhere!"

Now you have a better understanding of how the stock market works.

In the financial service industry, I was most successful (as well as happy) while at Smith Barney from 1983 to 1986. Richard Pignone, my manager, was filled with charisma and integrity. He gave me latitude to do what needed to be done to meet his goals and mine. He was ethical with his employees and clients. He didn't just talk the talk but rather walked the walk. When he couldn't do that anymore at Smith Barney, he left for A.G. Edwards. His philosophy was to try to do the best ethically, and never stop trying. It is unfortunate, but people break laws under the influence of greed— or they do only what is best for themselves.

I am most grateful to him and Smith Barney for the, many new people on my client list at the firm. Some are friends and clients to this day. Good management paid off for me. I'm sure it could pay off for the industry.

I am most grateful to him and Smith Barney for the many new friends I acquired from my client list at the firm. Some are friends and clients to this day. Good management paid off for me. I'm sure it could pay off for the industry.

The need for an average broker in the financial industry is diminishing now that more and more investors are becoming resourceful. They are demanding value for the commission charged. This is because proliferation of business news over TV like CNBC News, and Bloomberg ;Financial magazines and newspapers as *Kiplinger Value Line* , *Business Week, Forbes,, Wall Street Journal, Investors Business Dailey* and *Financial Times* financial software programs by discount brokers, business networks, mutual fund services; financial clubs like *Zacks, American Association of Individual Investors*; How To Books and Magazines Articles; Financial programs of all types including helping you in determining the tax consequences of your decisions. A few years ago there was only professional publications such as *Wall Street*

Journal, Barons, Business Week, Fortune Magazine Financial Times, Value Line and Kiplinger. In 1970, Louis Rukeyser, a journalist, exposed millions of Americans on his weekly financial and economic news on public TV. His success caused a availability proliferation of all sorts of financial coverage for the public. I remember very well that in the early 60's. Wall Street wanted to purchase DeSoto's economic forecast and publish it as a multi-client study to help fill an information gap. Some long-term investors with portfolios in excess of $100,000 can even outperform standard American funds using discount brokers and save the fees for themselves. Bright brokers and financial advisors should also consider breaking free and utilize the many advanced services that are currently available.

The independent or small brokerage firm and even the larger firms will have to provide much more service than just titles. The large financial firms that collects, assembles and analyze data financial data supplied to them by individual corporations will continue to perform a meaningful function until the government decides to takes over that function. Interesting time. I'm glad I'm retired.

CROATIA; MY ROOTS

I tired to organize a family Croatian trip (excluding Katherine) but there appeared to be too many travel conflicts. I formed a new team with my friend, John Rim PhD from Estonia and my cousin by marriage, Donald Langenfeld from Pittsburgh. John also brought along his Estonian friend Nadezhda (Hope) Popova, MD and her son Sergi Popov. The purpose of the trip was to gather family information and photograph various sites she remembered as a child.

The trip started for me May 6th, 4:10 P.M on Czech Airlines from JFK International airport in NYC. This was my first international flight outside the continent. John Rim did much of the planning from Estonia.

He had done a lot of international travel from Estonia and New York.

My bridge friend and computer consultant, Don Vercheck, took me to the airport to save travel time and hassle. Unfortunately I left my medication in a cosmetic bag adjacent to the suitcase. Neither of us saw it there on the floor when I took the luggage to the car. The first in a series of travel snafus.

I noticed my medication missing when I landed in Prague early Wednesday morning for the continuation flight to Zagreb. I was unsuccessful in trying to send an email in the one café that was open at that time.

Hardly anything was open at that time in the morning and I could not find a policeman so I tried to call Don who was quite familiar with Europe because he worked in different countries with IBM before retirement. The cost of over- night shipping would have been in excess of $250 and no guarantee of delivery because of customs. He suggested buying medications locally.

I never dreamt that international calls would be so expensive. I also thought the calling card I purchased at Wal-Mart would work. It did not. You have to purchase them in the country where you are placing the call. Your cell phone must also be modified to work in Europe.

I took a cab to the Sheraton hotel where we had reservations. They told me I did not have a reservation but could accommodate me at a higher room rate. Further discussions indicated that there are two Sheratons. The other one just changed its name from Panorama to Sheraton. Hardly anybody, including the employees and cab drivers, were aware of this. I finally did get to the right hotel.

John and his friends arrived a day later than originally planned. I was very fortunate to meet Jean and Rudy Perpich by accident in the hotel lobby-- seasoned Croatian travelers from Clairton PA (Pittsburgh area). Rudy was the sports editor for the Croatian weekly newspaper *Zajdenicar* which means "the fraternalist."

They were also seeking instructions about medical drug prescriptions for Rudy so we decided to do it jointly. They both spoke fluent Croatian which came in handy as we had to go to a district hospital-- to various clinics-- for prescriptions. They would not honor my doctor's scripts from the US. I am indebted to Jean for traveling with me that night and the next day trying to get at least some of my medications. Jean and Rudy also helped me with my insurance contacts.

Part of the mission finally accomplished, Jean and I toured Zagreb together because Rudy was bedridden. Jean and I had a private tour of the gothic Cathedral of the Assumption of Our Lady, and the Mirogoj Cemetery because we were the only tourists in early May. The cathedral was being renovated but still very beautiful. The cemetery is considered to be one of the most beautiful cemetery parks in Europe and a noteworthy landmark. I jokingly commented to Jean and the tour director that I might some day be given a plot as a result of my book. The young tour director also taught American and British English to children of politicians, government servants and business people.

Dr. John Rim, Dr. Nadezhda (Hope) and her son Sergei Popov arrived from Estonia on Thursday evening and took a cab directly to the hotel. Hope took this trip even though she had a life-threatening cancer problem. Her doctors thought the trip would benefit her which it probably did as she eventually resumed her medical practice.

On Friday, May 9th John stopped briefly at the Croatian Ministry of Education to set up an appointment with Dr. Dragan Primorac to discuss secondary schools in Croatia. Hope accompanied him while Sergei scouted the area.

On Saturday, we all went to the airport to greet Don who was coming from Pittsburgh. He had been in Croatia once before, in 2000. Even though he expressed deep family love in joining us, he came reluctantly. He was financially strapped because of major home remodeling projects and his work load doubled because an associate was not replaced when he left. I probably should have contributed more toward his trip expenses.

We then went to Alamo National Car Rental to pick up the five-door, eight-passenger Mercedes van we had reserved. That was not available. We took a less roomy seven- seater (including two jump seats in the rear) Opel van with much, much less luggage area. This was a mistake as my new camera was broken, the very next day, taking luggage in and out.

Sergei was the designated driver. He knew how to drive a stick shift and had an international license. He got us to the Hotel La Gus in Varazdinberg (Turcin) where we invited Fabijan Pisacic and his wife Anica to join us for dinner. The food and service was excellent. Communication was much better than expected. Don translated quite well; Anica understood some English and there was much eye contact and body language. It was a very enjoyable event for all.

We learned that Dad and Matthew Luke Tuk were the only two to leave the Pisacic and Stulijan hills; Mom's family house (Stulijan) was torn down many years ago; Fabijan works in construction. His employer is Mr. Zdravko Cindori who is president of several companies relating to water purification (commercial, residential and municipal). He has a large pool in his yard (currently a rarity in the area) as a show-piece for the up-and- coming middle class moving in from Zagreb. Fabijan's wife Anica is a nurse at the local hospital.

Fabijan was active in politics from 1980 thru 1986. He immediately became president of the Village Council. He became fed up with politics–lost all enthusiasm for this subject. Anica is not active in politics but is quite opinionated in various facets of politics. The complaints are similar to those in the United States: Gasoline very expensive, traffic getting too congested, insufficient parking facilities, people are paid low salary but expected to work hard, too much tax money is being spent in Zagreb and Dalmatia rather than locally.

The next morning we met with Father Pavlek at Kraljice Svete Krunice (Queen Holy Rosemary Crown Church). Earlier he had been a chaplain, leaving the military service in 2003. He then became a parish priest and was assigned the religious leadership to the people of Remetinec. He also has the responsibility of maintaining the church property with the help of his housekeeper and volunteers. Most of the restoration from the 2004 earthquake has been completed.

The Father does not speak English. Don and Tomislava Koren were the translators. After exchanging pleasantries, the Father gave us a brief history of the church and his background. Also a tour of the church and some of the genealogical data I had requested through Fabijan. Before visiting the cemetery located in the back of the church, we all enjoyed the home- made wine and whiskey that was produced from the church's vineyard. I donated to the church reconstruction fund and the Father gave both Don and me an autographed book entitled *Remetinec I Ostrikce* which beautifully describes and illustrates church history (priests, nuns and members). The book also contains many color photographs of the community.

The Cindori family had at least four ordained as priest and one reached the monsignor level in the church hierarchy. Davor Stuljan was also ordained a priest in 1995.There were several nuns ordained from the Cindori and Topolko families. Early in my life, at about the age of twelve, I too wanted to enter a monastery, with a friend. He did enter the monastery but left after a few years.

The village of Remetinec officially entered written church history in 1467. A petition was sent to Pope Paul II asking a special blessing for the Holy Virgin Mary monastery. This Franciscan monastery belonged to the Hungarian Holy Redeemer Province.

It is believed that before the Franciscans came to Remetinec there already was a Templar monastery of the Maltese Order. The Counts of Celje played an important role in building a monastery – especially Ivanis Korvin and his wife Beatrice Frankopan.

The 16th century was turbulent for the monastery. In 1529 four Franciscan friars were martyred by the Turks. During the middle of the 16th century, Krsto Batthtany stole the treasury of seven Slawonian monasteries of the Holy Redeemer Province that was kept in Remetenic for fear of Turkish attack. Later in the 16th century, the church and monastery were turned into fortifications against the Turks. The shooting holes in the church and church walls remain.

In 1657 twenty friars moved in after a thorough renovation of both the church and monastery by Elizabeth Batthyany and count Juraj.

This was a pilgrim church drawing people by the miraculous picture of the Virgin Mary of Remetinec.

The Remetinec monastery was abolished in 1789 and the parish of Remetinec was founded. It was part of the old parish of Madarevo that was established in 1334. The new parish included neighboring villages of Kljuc, Ostrice, Preseeno, Orehovee and Strmec.

Andelko Koscak describes the church in his book *Remetinec i Ostrice* as follows: *The parish church is an imposing Gothic edifice. It consists of a star-vaulted chancel, highly pointed windows with traceries, pews, rosettes and a net-vaulted nave. The baroque chapel of Saint Anthony was built onto the south-western part of the nave, with valuable stucco work. The main altar, with a middle upper part (retabel) was carved in wood in 1470. It is one of a few in continental Croatia. The beautiful and magnificent pulpit was made in 1710.*

Three internationally famous Croatian painters of naïve art, Ivan Rabuzin, Franjo Klopotan and Stjepan Hajduk, were born in Remetinec.

Our group journeyed to the cemetery on top of the church hill overlooking Remetinec. The cemetery was nothing like I expected. It was a beautiful peaceful park, elegant with trees, flowers, walkways, statues and a variety of tombstones. The families really honor the memory, fame and deeds of family- forever. I was told by my sister that in her days as a child, the graves were only marked by wooden crosses and little mounds of earth. This is one of the most beautiful cemetery parks I have ever seen.

The only cemetery park that exceeds it was the one overlooking Zagreb, The Mirogoj Cemetery. There the famous families, poets, politicians, scientists, sport stars and wealthy Europeans are able to have their loved ones buried despite the high initial costs and maintenance fees. Mirogoj Cemetery is considered to be one of the most beautiful cemetery parks in Europe and a landmark in the city of Zagreb.

Tomislava Koren took some excellent photos of many of the Pisacic family plots and tombstones. I forgot to ask him to include the Stulijan and Cindori families. Fabijan also told Tomislava to give me all the photos of Mario's wedding. It will be interesting to find out if Tomislava is a descendent of the Count of Celje who started building the monastery prior to 1467.

Fabijan arranged for us to meet with the Cindori families at the place were Mom was born. That house was demolished and a new home was built adjacent to it. I had a nice chat with Dubravka Vrzel Cindori with Don as the translator. Her husband Zdravko Cindori was not at home.

John briefly met the Cindori's older son, Robert, who came home from his second-year electrical engineering classes at the college in Varazhdin. He told John that he learned conversational English watching movies and TV but learned translation and grammar in school. They talked about schools in Varazhdin County, including Varazhdin City, Novi Marof Township and Remetinec village. Robert offered to help us obtain his Family Tree data which will be published in my next book.

Robert's younger brother Mario (17 years old) was also not at home. They have no sisters.

We did not get to see the home that Mom had built with the money Dad sent to Europe while working in the USA. We were told that it was recently renovated by Fabijan's newly married son. We did look in vain for a house that was close to a railroad track and a church in Varazhdin City.

The day ended at Fabijan's home with some home-made wine and cordials. The Pisacic clan certainly made a successful transition from agriculture to suburban living.

Hope was holding up quite well as did I even though I did not have all my medications. Sergei also seemed to enjoy driving us "old" people around these scenic hills. Don was beginning to lose his voice. Lack of sleep did not help. John paced himself well and appeared to be in excellent shape and spirit. His was accustomed to long trips traveling back and forth between Estonia and NYC.

We returned to our Hotel LaGus for a group dinner.

The next morning Don and I tried to meet my cousin Krunoslav Pisacic at his watchmaker-goldsmith shop in Novi Marof. He is a professional and dedicated watchmaker. He apprenticed with his cousin who resided in Vinkovci, a town further east in Croatia. He is one of the few active clockmakers in the area. There are nine clock- makers in his family history of which four are still practicing this profession. Five years ago he thought of retiring but some older people in Novi Marof, who did not like the new digital technology, were concerned that they would not have a place to fix their old mechanical watches and clocks. He kept his shop – *urar* in Croatian - open for them.

In 1563 a king donated to family Pisacic an estate in Hizanovec that was part of Karlovac County. Petar Pisacic and his brothers Matija and Stjepan received a nobility emblem from King Ferdinand II in Vienna.

Correspondence indicates that Krunoslav Pisacic is deeply interested in genealogy – a rarity in our families. We met, exchanged pleasantry and he gave me a color copy of the Pisacic family Coat of Arms which I had framed in a shop across the street. He also gave me the name of the head librarian at the town library so I could obtain a copy of the text explaining the Coat of Arms. He also gave me a copy of a newspaper article about his watchmaking trade. We could not spend much time with him because he was quite busy with customers. He is one of the last time-piece makers in Croatia.

Don and I then walked to the public library to meet head librarian Mrs. Rain. We were able to obtain a copy of the Croatian text that was translated from an old German book about heraldry. Don later translated this into English for me. We then met our group for lunch at a local café. Somewhere that morning I lost my notebook with family and trip notes. I called around the following day–in vain.

I had promised my sister that I would visit and bring souvenirs of the Croatian National Shrine – THE MOTHER OF GOD OF BISTRICA where Mom and she pilgrimed. It is located on the north side of Zagreb Mountain, 30 km (19 miles) from Zagreb.

We got lost in those winding mountainous roads. At the next village we drove through, Sergei asked a priest for directions to the village of Bistrica. He told us to follow him and he went out of his way to deliver us to the national shrine.

Back in the year 1209 this land was in the feudal possession of Count Vartislav. The large manorial estate of Bistrica and its hamlets was divided in the 16th century into smaller possessions which were donated to deserving feudal lords by royal deeds of gift. When Ban Josip Jelacic abolished serfdom in 1848, Marija Bistrica became a district community, and judicial center. In the 20th century, Marija Bistrica was administratively connected with the Stubice region; it became a separate community when independent Croatia was established.

Since the end of the 15th century the people prayed, thanked and pleaded their request to this wooden black figure of the Mother of God who hold's God's Son and her own son in her hands – the God-Man, Jesus Christ.

The statue was first placed in the ancient shrine at Vinski Vrh in 1499, buried in Marija Bistrica in 1545 and rediscovered in 1588. It was forgotten again, walled in, and then refound for the second time in 1684. This sequence of events: the removal of the statue, its hiding, and two findings awoke a belief in its miraculous power. It was a consolatrix for Christians during Turkish danger, a helper in World War I and II as well as in the Homeland War.

The following are Dr. John Rim's first impressions of Varazhdin County, Varazhdin City, Novi Marof and the Village of Remetinec.

Varazhdin County is changing. This is nothing new. The area has been changing for thousands of years. People have lived in this county for about eight centuries or more.

Even the geographic features are changing. Slowly but surely.

While the river and hills remain pretty much the same over the centuries, the people \have been digging and digging again and again, resulting in tunnels in the hills, for buses, trucks and cars. For trains, too.

Also tunneling for water and sewer mains everywhere. For electric cable. For underground storage.

For foundations that support buildings and other new construction.

Digging for new underground electric pumps that push water around and also up the hillsides.

Digging for new roadbeds and railroad tracks.

Digging for archeological exploration and research.

Digging for secret underground military installations.

Along with all this digging, they are using explosives to blast rock and create rubble that is removed and used for many purposes. The historic landscape is being changed by the inhabitants.

As modernization continues apace in Varazhdin County, its leadership position in northern Croatia continues to change as well.

Once Varazhdin was the capital of Croatia. For 21 years, between 1755 and 1756. Before Zagreb became the modern capital.

Now **Varazhdin County** is becoming an industrial center in what used to be solely an agricultural area and transport hub. During this transition, Varazhdin had long been a place for handicraft and cottage industries and works of art and public education.

Nowadays there are colleges and universities in the area, affiliated with higher educational institutions in Zagreb. There is free secondary and primary education. High schools and elementary schools.

Education costs the taxpayer a lot of money and competes for funding with new highways and medical facilities and policing and even national defense.

The churches support religious education but their role in general education has diminished. They no longer provide instruction in mathematics, the sciences, the national languages and Latin as they once did.

To their credit, the churches were the first to educate the people, long before the government took over. The churches also provided some public administration and medical care and social services long ago, together with maintenance of graveyards and church buildings and other church properties. Including church lands.

VARAZHDIN CITY

Only recently, the city of Varazhdin was made a diocesan center for the region. In 1997, just a decade ago. There has long been a religious seminary in the city, together with monasteries and numerous local churches, such as the cathedral and a parish church called Saint Nicholas Church, and the Church of the Birth of Christ, and the Church of Saint Mary erected in the year 1729.

Much earlier, the city provided for its own defense from attacks by land armies originating in surrounding areas. Fortifications were built and continuously improved. Now it seems that these protective structures are no longer needed.

By the time of the *American Revolution,* General George Washington, and the Continental Army of the United States in 1775 and 1776, Varazhdin in Croatia had formed its own permanent City Guard.

This armed contingent, called the Purgars, continues even today as a ceremonial force with a public Changing of the Guard. Each Saturday, during the month of May and the summer months.

The city even chose to conduct its own foreign affairs and be a player in continental diplomacy and travel. By the year 1850, Varazhdin City was issuing **passports** to its citizens for journeys anywhere in Europe. Even today the city of Varazhdin will provide a complimentary souvenir passport to visitors!

Varazhdin has a tourist office although it hardly competes with the famous Dalmatian seaside resorts of Split and Dubrovnik. At this moment, the city has three hotels.

One hotel is in the city center. Another, LaGus where our group stayed and dined, is in the suburbs on a hillside south of the city. A third hotel was closed for a long time and has just been renovated.

Varazhdin City welcomes its citizens and any tourists each September, at the very end of the tourist season, with a variety of indoor and outdoor artistic, musical and cultural entertainments, called Varazhdin Baroque Evenings.

The theatre inspired construction of the Helmer Theater and the Croatian National Theater of Varazhdin City. At one time there were also lavish entertainments, social events and theatrical performances staged in the private homes of the local elite, including Count Adam Patacic and other noblemen of a bygone era who lived in buildings called palaces.

THE VILLAGE OF REMETINEC

The village is so close to Novi Marof Township that it may be swallowed someday to get better access to municipal services for Remetinec residents.

The annexation can also provide room for expansion when business-oriented Novi Marof needs more suburban space, especially for residential development – including second homes for the wealthier citizens of Zagreb.

This trend is already underway. People from the Zagreb elite are moving in for weekends and for the summer. Remetinec has attractive views on the hillsides and plenty of space for development.

The ancient tradition of hillside viticulture will be the first victim of gentrification and even urbanization in Remetinec. The land is too valuable now to be used for growing grapes to make wine for local consumption.

The inhabitants of Remetinec have many small plots devoted to viticulture but this number is sure to diminish as the rural culture continues to change. A single plot will prove to be sufficient for each household as land prices rise – and rise again.

Change is everywhere in the village of Remetinec. Water is now available on the hillsides. Communal sewage-removal, together with new gutters and curbing, has recently been installed in direct competition with septic tanks that depend on sunlight and always constitute a pollution threat to this pristine environment.

Installation of swimming pools is just starting but cars are everywhere, financed by leasing and secured loans from Austrian banks in Varazhdin City and even Novy Marof.

A new expressway now connects Zagreb with Novy Marof and Rementinec, greatly reducing travel time.

The main engine of change is television backed by massive advertising campaigns for consumer goods – cars, SUVs and trucks included.

Residents of Remetinec now have electronic wrist-watches, cell phones and other wireless phones that quicken the pace of interpersonal communication, with opinion leaders exerting their personal influence.

The large and active church in Remetinec is on the side of change. The aim of the village priest is to enlarge church revenue to fund continuous renovation and embellishment of the church building. Nowadays a golden altar in every church is not enough.

To achieve his ambitious financial goals, the priest needs more donations from the new people who live in Zagreb. He also looks to a higher standard of living resulting from the sale of viticulture plots for residential development.

The priest will continue to bless the first grapes and the first wine but on a smaller scale. Instead he will bless and perform weddings for more gentry-folk from Zagreb who buy land and build houses on the hillsides. These in-migrants substitute for the newborn locals whose numbers are declining as the birthrate continues to diminish.

The schools will be affected too. Small rural schools will be consolidated into new education networks as the number of children steadily declines – and declines. Offsetting this shortfall of babies is the growing number of elderly which means more support – including financial support – for the local church.

NOVI MAROF

Novi Marof differs from Varazhdin City not only in its size but also in its simplicity.

Whereas the city is complex and runs on double tracks, the town is a one-track kind of place.

Varazhdin City combines two styles, the Baroque and the Rococo.

Novi Marof has a single style. The contemporary style with an emphasis on function, not form. The focus is business. All business.

What used to be an old-fashioned store for clock-making and repair has become a store for rapid turnover of merchandise, meaning sales of the latest watches and modern accessories. The few grandfather clocks have become obsolete because most Novi Marof customers no longer buy nostalgia.

In Novi Marof, home cooking is out and restaurants are in. Even the town name, Novi Marof, suggests something new..

A single businessman in the town of Novi Marof owns and operates six coffee shops, one restaurant, one hotel, and one aqua park. The park has two swimming pools equipped with slides as well as three tennis courts. Most important is the parking lot for 200 vehicles!

You will not find a parking lot of this size in Varazhdin City. In the center of Varazhdin, called Old Town, the narrow streets do not accommodate even small cars.

Only ten miles separate Novi Marof from Varazhdin City but they are worlds apart in outlook. The national trend in Croatia seems to follow the lead of Novi Marof town rather than the city of Varazhdin.

BACK TO BEAUTIFUL AND INCREDIBLY COSMOPOLITAN ZAGREB AGAIN

We returned to the Sheraton because it was reasonable, we enjoyed their service, breakfast and computer facility. The young desk clerk ZZZZZZ spoke excellent English and was particularly helpful to me as a translator for local phone calls.

The first thing we did was return the rental car to Zagreb Airport. That took more time than normal and I swore to myself that was my last experience with them. I also spent a day or so trying to get my camera fixed, purchase disposable cameras as replacement and purchase the missing medications--with little success. I briefly toured the large open shops in central Zagreb with Don. He spent a lot of time shopping for family. He also planned to attend an opera that night. I told him I could not afford the time even though the cost was reasonable.

Another morning I decided to attend a Sunday Service at a church in the Jarun neighborhood, Saint Mothers of Freedom. It is a ten-year-old church seating over 750 people, mostly young. The music is moving and evangelical, similar to many churches in the USA. The church members also participate in the service rather than sitting back and observing.. That day was a very special service because the 3rd graders received their first communion – they were all in white. There was much picture taking.

I briefly met the priest, Father Stjepan Matijevic, after his celebration of this 12 o'clock mass. Since he only spoke Croatian, Italian and German (not American or British English) he immediately found a 4th year veterinary student, Davor, to translate for us. So very thoughtful.

The church has 25,000 members of which 18,000 are church-going. The church seats 350 but has standing room for 1,300, and accommodates 7,000 when they open the court- yard.

The church was built in memory of Croatian fighters lost during the Freedom War, 1991-1995. The church was blessed in the year 2000. The names of almost 16,000 fighters are listed on plaques around the church. A famous church designer, Nicolas Basic, was the architect.

The church is under the jurisdiction of the Salesian Order (new Italian order) which is known to work with youth. More and more youth are coming here to be with God. Less drinking of alcohol, less sex and more talking.

Croatia has been influenced by the Church since the 16th century when the Croatians defended the Christian World of Europe against Islam. This priest says Croatians are the strongest shield for Christianity in the world.

He felt that more and more youth are coming back to be with God. They need more than material things to be happy.

One of the best discussions ever with any priest. This includes the small mission church in which I taught Sunday school at Waynesburg Pa back in 1950. I believe he was a Franciscan priest. Very, very straight forward.

I also met an Englishman, Justin Barnes, at the church. He had worked with McKinsey as a consultant prior to relocating to Croatia. He has a Masters in Manufacturing Engineering and a BA in Mathematics. He is now in the property search business with his wife and would, of course would be glad to help me out if I was looking to invest in Croatian real estate projects.

Justin made contact with an English friend he knew who was living in Estonia. She had moved back to London but she in turn gave another contact. Because of time constraints, I was not able to meet her. Maybe next time if she is still there. The English certainly are excellent in following-up.

The next day, after I visited a police station to report loss of my driver's license and two credit cards, I was invited to an excellent cuisine lunch (near the Zagreb police station) by Marko Dragicevic, his girl friend Diana Konsuo(a school teacher) and Miro Glavurnic, a writer who translated six political books into Croatian. Diana laughingly told me that Marko was a Communist, certainly a dreamer. Marko appeared to be quite an intellectual. Among other things, he once was a TV producer. He studied Law but dropped out during his final year at law school.

He was vocal about the millions of dollars spent when USA President Bush visited Croatia. Secret service personnel were brought in prior to his arrival and over 5,000 military personnel were stationed throughout the country while George W. Bush was in Croatia, Marko said.

Marko plans to write a book about Dubrovnik – the most beautiful city in Europe according to him, and another book on what is wrong in Croatia today and what can be done to improve it.

Miro said very little – either a good listener or spoke little English or both.

I would not be surprised to learn that Marko will run for public office.

Marko and Diana both came from Dubrovnik. Marko's father has lineage and his mother was director of American Express operations in Yugoslavia.

I also met Veric Predrag, a free- lance photographer. He is a graduate of the University of Zagreb with a degree in geology. He claimed to know the Minister of Education, Dragan Primorac, quite well and was willing to talk to John about meeting with Primorac.

I missed John's meeting with Minister Primorac of the Ministry of Science, Education and Sports because I elected at the last minute to go to a police station on Strossmagerow trg 3 to report loss of my driver's license and two credit cards. I thought that would take a few minutes but it took many hours. It could have been longer but thanks to Mirjanna Kondor-Langer things were expedited; I got my police report and they contacted American Express.

The objective of John's meeting was: to speak about secondary education in Croatia; to provide a small number of students with the opportunity to further improve their command of the English language; to improve their knowledge and understanding of the West, including the USA with dormitory living for students over the age of 16 in such locations as Remetinec and Porec.

Since the Minister was not available, John met Anabela Sapina who is in the Department of Secondary Education. The meeting was successful, she said.

JOHN RIM'S COMMENTS ON ZAGREB

Zagreb is unique. There is no other city in Croatia that compares.

This is also true of such capital cities as London in England, Paris in France, and so on throughout Europe.

Unique just one of many adjectives that describe Zagreb.

Others include *prestigious, politically sensitive, notorious, documented, distinctive, famous, international, impromptu, biggest, high-profile, atmospheric.*

Prestigious Residents are proud to be living in Zagreb. Many have moved to Zagreb from other Croatian cities and towns for this reason.

Politically sensitive .Zagreb takes politics seriously. To the residents, politics is not a joke. Not only power but also money and status are at stake. Politics in Zagreb is a high-stakes affair. One roll of the dice can make a huge difference, and the people of Zagreb know it.

Notorious .Zagreb has a reputation---notoriety---throughout Croatia. It is that city where those things happen that do not occur in any other Croatian city or town.

Many suicides, for example. Also enormous profits and beautiful people and statues found nowhere else in Croatia.

Documented .Zagreb happenings are faithfully recorded on television, in magazines, on the radio, in the theatre---and in the newspapers and wire services. The archives in Zagreb are by far the biggest in Croatia.

Distinctive. Zagreb sports, fashion, and entertainments cannot be found anywhere else in Croatia. Zagreb has everything that is lacking in the other Croatian cities and towns---including an extensive mass-transit system.

Famous .Zagreb is well-known for many people, places and events. All the major government officials and politicians are connected with Zagreb---for example, the Croatian minister of science, education and sport.

The cathedral in Zagreb is far more splendid than other Roman Catholic churches---including the one in Dubrovnik---and gets major renovation projects. **The** only Croatian 18-hole championship-standard golf course is in Zagreb.

The Madhouse **Theatre Company performs** annually in Zagreb but not in any other Croatian city. The Cest **is d'Best** yearly street festival takes place only in Zagreb and nowhere else in Croatia.

International. Zagreb has all the foreign embassies---including the American. The capital city has the only major airport in Croatia where airplanes arrive and depart daily for the other important airports of Europe, including Frankfurt in Germany. Zagreb has most of the Croatian speakers of foreign languages, including English.

Impromptu. People and events in Zagreb are more spontaneous than elsewhere in Croatia. The people tend to be impulsive. (Somebody in Zagreb who has never met you before will invite you to dinner.)Such events seem to be unplanned.

Biggest. With population of one million, the capital city has more people than any other place in Croatia.(This is not true of

Washington, another national capital because it Is not the largest city in the USA)

Many people now live in the suburbs of Zagreb which can be reached by car, taxi and a network of suburban. The land-area of Zagreb is compact for a city with such a large population and seems small but nevertheless it is the biggest in Croatia.

High-profile. The tallest buildings in Croatia are to be found in Zagreb .It also has the tallest smoke-stacks and a higher mountain than other big cities in Croatia.

Zagreb is the only Croatian city included in daily international weather reports on television and in the international press.

Zagreb is featured in such publications as *National Geographic*. Resorts such as Dubrovnik and Split are mentioned although they also attract large numbers of tourists from Europe and elsewhere but only in the summer. Zagreb is attracting tourists year-round.

Atmospheric. Culture in Zagreb is far superior to in the rest of Croatia. So is fashion and sport. So is cuisine and entertainment .The atmosphere is also more military and political. There is much more shopping in Zagreb than anywhere else in Croatia---for cars, clothing, friends, spouses, etc.

Moody. Zagreb has moods that come and go. Optimism and pessimism. Religiosity and secularism. Regionalism, nationalism and internationalism. Loyalty and rejection. Acceptance and rebellion. Self and family.

The emotional climate changes quickly and all the time.

In conclusion, Zagreb goes through transitions day to day, month to month, and year to year.

POREC

We arrived at the all-season Hotel Neptun which is next to the harbor - on Wednesday, May 14th. They have a free ferry to the nearest beach island of Saint Nicola but we elected not to go because the weather was cool. It was also too early for the nudist camps to be flourishing. We did nothing exceptional except tour the town's center, took some photos and had a leisurely dinner so we were well- rested for the boat trip to Venice the next morning **on *Prince of Venice*. The speed of the boat averaged 26 knots.**

JOHN RIM'S COMMENTS ON POREC TOWNSHIP

To understand Porec, think of this old saying.

When in Rome, do as the Romans do.

Remember, however, that Porec was a tale of two cities. Rome and Venice.

The Romans---long ago---discovered all of Istra, a large area that includes Porec.

They found some people there, on hillsides, but killed the men and enslaved the women and children.

To reach Istra, the Romans marched overland around the northern reaches of the Adriatic Sea. A long road to Porec.

They also came by ship from ancient Venice which lies to the north and east of Rome. Traveling by ship saved time. It was a shortcut.

The Romans developed the entire area of present-day Istra County.

They also moved south and east, as far as they could easily travel, and reached Dubrovnik---which the Romans developed to their liking. Everywhere the Romans went, they built ports, permanent roads, aqueducts for water, and houses in the Roman style, called Mediterranean style. They built coliseums for entertainments and temples for the Roman religion.

Later, Christian churches were added. The earliest churches were organized secretly, in defiance of the pagan Roman religion. After Rome officially adopted Christianity and encouraged the Vatican to be located nearby Rome, the secret church groups in Porec came out into the open.

Later dwellings were constructed in the Venetian style after Venice became independent and created the Republic of Venice. This Christian republic not only swallowed up Porec but also the rest of Istra,, all the way to the larger port city of Pula on the Adriatic – Dubrovnik, too.

VENICE

John planned this part of the trip especially for Hope who was very patient throughout the trip with my family and book matters. I also believe that the others enjoyed this tranquil and quaint city, its unusual food and its beauty. We particularly enjoyed the gondola tour of the city through its many waterways. I was impressed that there were no automobiles or trucks to pollute the air yet literally millions of residents and tourists survive in this city. They do have one potential pollution problem with drainage.

There are 60,000 residents and 20 million tourists who visit each year.

I got lost once when I had to detach from the group to try to purchase another portable camera. I was amazed at the amount of twisting passageways and thousands of alleys. I did get to the group in time to catch the boat back. I missed the tour guide's lecture but I think I saw more of the city. The people, like me, were on the go so there was little opportunity to interact as I did in Croatia where people were very friendly and helpful. If they did not speak English, they would try to find someone to help you.

JOHN RIM'S COMMENTS ON VENICE

Venice became a sea power just as Rome had been a land power. The Venetians became famous as sailors and navigated far and wide. Porec was their backyard as they voyaged to Africa and even Asia and the Americas.

The Venetians paralleled the China travels of Marco Polo, who went by land but most Venetians went by sea.

Although the Roman Empire eventually disintegrated and the **Republic of** Venice disappeared, the stamp of Rome on Porec was indelible. Even to this day, the city of, too, leaves its mark on Porec.

Both the Romans and the Venetians saw in Porec the potential for a vacationland. That concept remains to the present day.

Present-day Porec is micro-managed by a development company--founded in West Germany during 1953---that calls itself Riviera Holding. It owns and operates Riviera Hotels and Resorts as well as Riviera Tours. **There** is a subsidiary in Zagreb called *Porec*.

235

The Germans could not get a foothold on the French Riviera so they settled for another Riviera in _Croatia_ instead. They own hotels, campsites and nudist camps---and the waterfront north and south of Porec.

The Neptun Hotel on the Marshal *Tito Promenade*t along he sea owes its name to the Roman Temple of Neptune that was built in Porec long ago. The ruins of that temple can still be seen in Porec.

What lies in the future for Porec?

It continues to be like a set of twins.

In the ancient past, it was both Roman and Venetian.

In the distant future, it will become international but also Croatian.

RETURN TO ZAGREB THE THIRD TIME

We learned that Don left for home the very next day, May 15th, after we left for Istra. The note he left with the hotel said that the medication which Hope left with him helped some but he still felt bad. He may also have been homesick. He made several back-home calls to his wife and children.

The next morning, May 20th John, Hope, Sergei and I took a cab to the airport for the next phase of our trip – Estonia. We took flight 819 to Prague on Czech Airlines and switched to flight 876 to Tallinn, Estonia which left 21:15 on May 20th. Because of our late arrival, we stayed at the Ulemiste Hotel near the airport.

ESTONIA: NOT MY ROOTS

The four of us arrived at the Tallinn airport in Estonia's capital late Wednesday night, May 21st and stayed overnight at the contemporary Ulemiste Hotel.

The cab driver to the hotel gave me my first Estonian experience. At that time of night---rather early morning---he expected a large cab fare instead of a **quick trip the nearest hotel for our** group of passengers with suitcases and accessories. The .cabbie was furious because of his bad luck.

The next morning we had an excellent Scandinavian breakfast, followed by a tour of Tallinn that began with the passenger port---the harbor zone. We saw high-speed catamarans that connect Tallinn with Helsinki **and** overnight deluxe cruise ferries equipped with many bed-rooms, dining-rooms, cafes, dance halls and music halls---as well as space for numerous trucks, buses, sports utility vehicles and passenger cars.

Near the harbor we saw indoor and outdoor markets---in the vicinity of Kat Street---with many kinds of souvenirs. I struck up a 25-minute conversation with one of the sales-people for my introduction to life in Estonia today.

We walked from the port to the central Tallinn commercial district by way of Old Town, the modest Hanseatic legacy---with several tall churches--surrounded on all sides by rather new construction of high-rise office buildings, hotels and apartment-houses, nearby and on the horizon.

At one entrance to Old Town, which is encircled by formidable stone walls and gates, we encountered "Fat Magaret," a tower of large circumference used first of all as a fortification, with cannon overlooking the harbor--later converted to a prison---and in recent years, a four-story-high maritime museum which we inspected at length. At its base was a bronze plaque expressing gratitude to the British Royal Navy for its defense of Tallinn in 1918-1920.

We had a mid-morning snack at The Three Sisters Cafe in Old Town, followed by our inspection of a French bakery named Bonaparte. Then, in search of an inexpensive and disposable camera, we fell into a souvenir shop---head-first. The worried shop owner administered *first aid* to a bruised forehead.

To comfort ourselves after our fall, we had something to drink in a traditional Russian restaurant adjacent to the Tallinn city hall. We postponed a full lunch for another hour and another place.

Next we inspected a large McDonald's restaurant in Old Town, and saw that it was popular as a hang-out for teen-agers and young adults---but we decided to skip the hamburgers and French fries.

After looking at the main post office, and a new hotel called *Tallink*---and also Best Eastern---we located a genuine restaurant in the basement of a building called Estonia House. The service was good, and the food---filling.

The best for us was a conversation with the restaurant owner, an expatriate from the USA with many talents---including painting of murals, portraits and landscapes. This man has come to Estonia, the land of his ancestors, as adjutant to a high-ranking U.S. Army officer who briefly served as head of the Estonian armed forces in the early 1990s. The restaurant owner had recently made a visit to Estonian troops serving with NATO.

He was the embodiment of an artist-cum-warrior---and also a businessman with two restaurants, one successful and the other not so (as he admitted.) Another of his ventures, a publication called *Global Estonian,* was under-capitalized---but it was his risky walk on a political-rope which led to magazine's death.

It was our intention to return to Tallinn for another look---which we did several days later---but this first contact with Tallinn was now about to end. We set out on a long walk along Tartu Boulevard, toward the main bus station, for us a rendez-vous where we re-connected with the Popovs mother and son, Hope and Sergei. There followed a 150 minute car ride to the northeastern tip of Estonia---Narva---on the present-day border with Russia.

On the route to Narva, John highlighted various historical sites along the northern coast, including the-abandoned uranium processing facility in the once-secret town of Sillamae.

We did not go to Paldiski, 35 kilometers west of Tallinn, but John talked about it as we traveled along a recently-modernized expressway. .Around 1944, the Soviet navy built a submarine base in the port of Paldiski that included two fixed nuclear submarine reactors in training center. The reactor facility was dismantled in August of 1994 but remained under Russian Navy until September 1995---four years after the latest resurrection of Estonia's independence from Russia.(In other words, the Russians were in no hurry to leave.)

On occasions between 1700 and the present day, Estonians declared themselves independent of Russia. Genuine independence had been declared around 1918 and there was much fighting between Estonians and Russians in 1919 .Independence was disrupted again for a long period---two generations---from 1940 to 1991, but, has now resumed.

In recent years Estonia joined the European Union and the North Atlantic Treaty Organization (NATO)to buttress its independence from Russia. Presently a pair of NATO fighter aircraft regularly patrols the Russo-Estonian border, in the skies above the River Narva which constitutes the international boundary.

In the city of Narva, right on the border with Russia, , John and I stayed at Sergei Popov's apartment on Street of Heroes while Sergei was catching up with friends and assisting his mother, Nadezhda (Hope in English) Popova. We home-visited Hope's apartment---on Pushkin Street---and her two Dachshund dogs called Rickover and Angel---and recently re-named Grishenka and Grushenka.

Apartment buildings in Narva were generally three or five stories high, of concrete block construction, Russian-style. Newer buildings were faced with brick .There was also the occasional wooden house.

We used buses and cabs for transportation. **The** bus network was reasonably-priced, with generous senior discounts.

Narva offers an unobstructed view of neighboring Russia, including the Russian *Johnstown* (Ivangorod) and its obsolete stone-walled fortress.

Narva has an obsolete stone-walled fortress of its own. A pair of fortresses, on opposite sides of the same river, makes for an unusual sight.

The big city of St. Petersburg, Russia's former capital and the birth-place of prime minister Vladimir Putin, is **only** 50 miles from Narva---which continues to be a melting pot(for nations, peoples and culture, old and new) and is now the easternmost city in the European Union.

Some of the areas and sites we visited:

<u>Narva's high-rise fortress and museum of history</u>. The fort was built by the Danes in the 1370s on the west bank of the river

Narva. This stronghold was continuously improved by subsequent German, Swedish and Russian owners.

Heavily damaged during World War II, Narva Castle (fortress) was restored during the Soviet period to its pre-war glory.

A controversial Lenin statue was later moved from former Lenin Square to a corner within the fortress walls, less than 100 yards distant.

The present-day museum does provide excellent coverage of various periods---Danish, German, Swedish, and Russian---in the city's history.

We took pictures of :

1. the vehicle-and-pedestrian bridge across river Narva

2. high-rise Narva fortress *plus* the surrounding network of ten smaller forts

3. the Russian fortress in *Ivangorod*(Johnstown) the river

4 the .so-called Dark Garden, a bluff with views of the river, fortifications and Johnstown

5. sandy beach along the river and lagoon

6. <u>Krenholm textile complex</u> .Designed by a British industrial architect. Once this Narva group of factories and warehouses was the largest textile plant in Europe. John purchased---and gave me as a souvenir---one of their high-quality towels to bring back to the USA. Today the owners of Krenholm live in Sweden. (Many Estonian enterprises ,banks and tele-communication companies, enjoy Swedish ownership.)

BACK TO TALLINN

Ulemiste Shopping Mall, adjacent to Ulemiste Airport in Tallinn, turned out to be the most swank upscale center we saw in Estonia. (Narva shopping malls did not compare---but not for want of trying.) We apparently were not dressed well-enough to attract the attention of Ulemiste Mall sales clerks or else they were not interested in selling low-profit wares such as disposable cameras. The women clerks did seem to be more competent..

On our second tour of Tallinn, at the very end of the trip, we explored parts of Tallinn, Estonia's capital---situated near the south coast of the Gulf of Finland.

1. **Cathedral Hill** was---and still is---the seat of central authority.

Until 1877this seat of government was considered to be a separate town---in German, *Dom zu Reval*, meaning the residence of the German aristocracy, civilian and military, who served **the Russian tsar.**

After five centuries of landownership, 20,000 remaining Baltic Germans finally abandoned Estonia around 1938 when Adolf Hitler invited them "to come home."

Three years later, the German Wehrmacht became the military occupation force in Tallinn---and the rest of Estonia.

But only until **1944...at which time** the Red Army, commanded by Josef Jugash-vili(Stalin)what remained of the Hitlerite armed forces in **Estonia**---then called the Republic of Estonia by some, and the Estonian Soviet Socialist Republic by others.

Today the former Dom zu Reval---now named *Tompeaa*-in Estonian--is the seat of the' government, and also is home to many embassies and official residences. We toured the walls and various bastions of"Castrum Danorum," and inspected the Russian Orthodox *Alexander Nevsky* Cathedral that was built during the period of Russian Empire. We were not able to go inside Toompea castle because the parliament was in session.

2.**Old Town** is the old Hanseatic city where medieval trade grew. It united with Cathedral Hill relatively recently---in the late 1800s. Old Town combined with Cathedral Hill(Toompea) became one united UNESCO World Cultural Heritage site in 1997.

We read about Church dedicated to the Norwegian Saint Olav. Between the years 1549 and 1626, the high Gothic spire made it the tallest building in the world! Originally a Norwegian (Roman Catholic) Church, the services are now Baptist.

We toured *Niguliste,* an old (German) church, near Town Hall Square.

3.**The Estonian town** lies south of Cathedral Hill and Old Town. The place where Estonians first settled, they were practically in the countryside. **In** Tallinn, Estonian women and men were long in the minority---until the 1850s, when they at last outnumbered the local Baltic Germans in the Estonian capital.

A new museum got our attention. It is on the border between Estonian town and Cathedral Hill.. Named Museum of Occupations, it features many black-and-white documentary films (" newsreels") that portray Estonian history as it unfolded between the 1930s and the 1980s. Two occupations by foreigners are in the films: the German military combined with the Secret Security Police (*Gestapo*) occupation during the Second World War, and the two Russian occupations just before and immediately after the German one.

The museum publishes handbooks and guide-books in English, cataloging the exhibits that include military uniforms, medals, official documents---and articles of everyday life such as a telephone booth, a row boat, suitcases, and prison doors, monumental statues of the previous political elite and personal diaries and correspondence. There is a cafe and small auditorium as well.

4.The Suburbs. Built on low-lying hills and plateaus surrounding the port of Tallinn, the suburbs mostly came into existence during the 20th century. We visited Lasnamae, where John lived when he first Estonia at the end of the year 2000. His first tours of Estonia took place earlier---in 1998---so he has now been connected to Estonia for a decade.

John's mother-in-law resides today on Kivila Street in Lasnamae, in the neighborhood called **Mustakivi (Blackstone)** .Of Greek ancestry, she long ago lived in Gruzia (Georgia) on the Black Sea, in the vicinity of Sukhumi, capital of Abkhasia---which declared its independence in September of this year, **2008.** She moved to Estonia decades ago and expects to be buried there next to her husband.

In a different neighborhood near the central bus station, we visited a military cemetery bordering on the suburbs.

Our attention was riveted on a tall bronze statue---sometimes called *The Liberator*---depicting a uniformed (unknown) soldier from the Second World War who lived and died in Estonia the conflict. Much has been written about this statue, which is also the most talked-about war memorial in Estonia. At that moment, we were the only visitors.

We want to return briefly to the liveliest person we met in Estonia---Viido Polikarpus.

We had lunch in his Estonia-House Restaurant, across the street from the Ministry of Foreign Affairs. He is he cosmopolitan, painter, writer, photographer and entrepreneur.

He recounted his life history over lunch..

His parents and he crossed the Baltic Sea from Estonia to Sweden when he was little---they fled northwest as the Red Army was approaching Tallinn from the east. The family emigrated to the USA and settled in New Jersey.

Viido Polikarpus entered Officers Candidate School (OCS) and earned a Green Beret in the Special Forces, an elite fighting unit, at Fort Benning, Georgia.

He was also a participant in the book project *Down Town* that was authored by Tappan Wright King. **Viido** then became editor and publisher of a new magazine The *Global Estonian*---in English.

In 1990, when Estonia moved toward independence from Russia , the Estonian Government offered a high-ranking U.S. Army officer the chance to train young recruits for the Estonian armed forces. He in turn asked Viido to be his assistant. They both arrived in Estonia in 1991.

Later Viido was a visitor to Estonian troops serving in Afghanistan with the NATO forces there. He permanently left the armed forces to begin his latest venture – Estonian House Restaurant---with its two locations. One location is now closed, and for sale.

HISTORICAL DATES

1285Estonia becomes the northern-most member of Hanseatic League, a mercantile and military alliance of German-dominated cities in Northern Europe

1346The **Danes,** who had captured Tallinn earlier**, sell** the city and other parts of northern Estonia to the Germanic **"Teutonic Knights." Tallinn ("Danish city")** become a crossroad of trade between Western Europe, Northern Europe and Russia... Population of 8,000, a town now well-fortified with imposing walls and 66 defense towers

1710**Swedish** troops in Tallinn...Capitulate to Imperial Russia

February 24, 1918.Independence Manifesto is proclaimed--- followed by Imperial **German** occupation, and then war of independence **Russia.**

February 2, 1920Soviet Russia acknowledges the independence of the **Estonian Republic** permanently---but later it turns out this was temporary.

1940Estonian Republic occupied by the **Soviet Union**(Union of Soviet Socialist Republics or USSR)and is re-named Estonian Soviet Socialist Republic

1941-1944EstonianSocialist Republic is occupied by Nazi **Germany** and re-named Ostland

1944Ostland (Estonia) occupied by USSR---again---and gets name Estonian Soviet Socialist Republic once more

1980Summer Olympics are held in Moscow---but Olympic yacht races are held at Pirita, a suburban village north-east of Tallinn in the Estonian Soviet Socialist Republic, temporarily part of the Soviet Union---but the USA refuses to extend diplomatic recognition to the Estonian SSR.(Instead, Washington recognizes an Estonian government-in-exile, meaning a government temporarily outside the borders of Estonia.)

August 20, 1991independent democratic capitalist Estonian republic is re-established, as the Communist Party in Russia is going to be disbanded(temporarily)after the complete collapse of the Soviet Union in August 1991.

2004The Republic of Estonia becomes a member of the European Union

2004The Republic of Estonia becomes a member of the North Atlantic Treaty Organization(NATO) of which the United States of America is also a member

August 20, 2011To be the 20th anniversary of re-establishment of Estonian independence

----

Postscript : *Amnesty International* expressed concern(2006)that the language policy of Estonia may violate the human rights of the Russian-speaking minority in Estonia who chose **not** to return to Russia although they were invited by the authorities in Moscow.

This sentiment is echoed by the Russian Federation---capital, Moscow---which alleges that there is discrimination against the Russian-speaking minority in Narva, Tallinn and some other cities in Estonia.

Some Russian speakers decide to become Estonian citizens. Others try but fail to meet the requirements. Yet others are not interested in Estonian citizenship but wish to reside in Estonia if they get permission to stay.

Most of them get permission to stay and are given residence permits but without citizenship. The Estonian Government actively tries to promote the use of the Estonian language, especially in all schools.

John Rim is trying to persuade the Estonians to organize some NATO schools (for teen-agers)and to promote the use of the English language for future dealings with" the West, "some of the islands of Europe (Great Britain, Ireland, Gibraltar, Malta)and also the USA---as well as other nations where the English language is popular and is in use, including Finland, Sweden, Norway, Denmark, Iceland and some others.

I left Tallinn for Prague on Czech Republic Airlines Flight 877 at 0529 and arrived in Prague, the Czech capital, at 0630 local time.

I left Prague11 a.m. local time for John F. Kennedy International airport in New York, and arrived at quarter past two (New York time) the afternoon of the same day.

It's a small world.

BACK TO THE USA

I was fortunate to have my friend Don Vercheck and his friend Nancy Campbell pick me up at Kennedy International airport. However, when I arrived home, I found a catastrophic condition in my office: the computer was empty. The only operating program was Mozilla Fire Fox which replaced an existing Microsoft program. All my emails, all my files, all my email addresses, all my investments software, my book, my book photos etc were gone even though I had a Mentor back-up unit and several thumbs drives available. As a result of this, I temporarily lost a dear bridge and computer friend. We however soon reunited and had a laugh over this.

In addition to the computer problem, my cash flow was eliminated because the contract with Raymond James ended. This did not stop some long-term clients who became millionaires with my help from calling me for opinions and advice during the market turmoil. I could not join another firm because my Series Seven license expired. Raymond James would not continue to sponsor me as a licensed broker after retirement even though I was continuously managing millions of clients' dollars during these three years. I, however, reluctantly agreed to overlook a few select portfolios that agree in principle to the strategy of the old *Super 25* Program outlined earlier. Integrity pays dividends.

Now I faced several months of computer reconstruction with the other computer consultant. Fortunately my part-time typist gave me her hard and disc copy of the book and photos. By September, things were just about normal. I did need an innovative strategy to get my brain functioning again and stop the aging process. Quoting an old Chinese Proverb *Learning is far more precious than gold.*

I think the Croatian and Estonian trip—in combination with my daily yoga exercise-helped me to manage and recover quickly. I also believe that some of the medications to improve memory were definitely effective. I finally had my cataracts removed after another auto accident even though two ophthalmologists said they still were not sufficiently ripe. (I was told by the Mayo Clinic a year ago to take them out.) The two ophthalmologists thought my poor vision was due to side effects of my two brain surgeries. That may be true but my vision improved.

I suggest international travelers consider services like Travelocity over direct reservations. One does receive lower rates with better accommodations and breakfast.

My two long time role models were Benjamin Franklin and Alexander Hamilton. The former who forged ahead with his 13 virtues and his ideas. Alexander Hamilton who kept climbing from a homeless beginning to a Revolutionary War standout. Both were tremendous leaders.

HEALTH/EXERCISE
AND MEDITATION

Guard the health both of body and of soul. Greek proverb

WAYS TO COUNTERACT MEDICAL
PROBLEMS – 1994 AGE 62

This was a period of marginal health for me. In June of 1994, I went to the Mayo Clinic, Scottsdale, Arizona for a complete medical check-up. I heard from Brother Ed that "the needs of the patients come first at the clinic." This clinic was founded by William J. Mayo, his brother Charles and their father William Worrall Mayo. Their mission was "to provide the best care to every patient every day thorough integrated clinical practice, education and research. The best interest of the patient is the only interest to be considered, and in order that the sick may have the benefit of advancing knowledge, a union of forces is necessary."

I needed consultation for my imbalance and blurred vision as well as headaches and memory deficits. Fortunately I only had a mild cover over a portion of the retina in the right eye.

My intellectual function was not typical for dementia or memory deficit. Simply applying artificial tears or eye drops for dry eyes during the day and an eye ointment when I went to bed, a

251

series of balance and eye exercises, and reduction of drug intake were useful. One simple eye exercise was consciously blinking repeatedly while reading or looking at a computer screen to help spread my own tears evenly. During any free time at the clinic, I toured the country side and visited with my brother and his wife Eva for family connection and intimacy.

EYE EXERCISES

Some of the eye exercises that proved to be effective are:

GAZE STABILIZATION

(Do not wear glasses while doing eye exercises. As eyes get stronger, order weaker lenses.)

Hold a finger approximately 12 inches from your nose. Focus on your finger. Turn your head quickly from side to side while continuing to focus on your finger. It is important to maintaining eye contact with your finger. Complete this exercise 2 times per day for about 40 seconds.

Read a large print book out loud while turning your head from side to side.

Standing erect, toss a small ball in the air focusing on the ball and catching it. It is important that the focus be on the ball while it is in the air.

Blink gently one hundred times; then squeeze your eyes tightly 3 times.

Close the eyelids and press the eyeballs gently into the socket with the heel of each hand; hold to a count of 10. Repeat.

EYE PUPIL EXERCISE

While in a totally dark room, turn light on and off for at least 3 minutes. Follow this procedure: Turn light on for one second, then turn off for 5 or 6 seconds (darkness), next turn light on and off twice, QUICKLY. Repeat 6 or 8 times or 3 minutes. This exercise enables the pupil to function in both light and darkness. It helps overcome fuzzy vision.

VESTIBULAR EXERCISES FOR BALANCE

Stand in a doorway:

Stand with your feet together with your eyes open. Then try turning your head from side to side.

Stand with your feet together with your eyes closed.

Stand with one foot partially in front of the other with your eyes open. With your eyes open, turn your head from side to side.

Stand with one foot in front of the other with your eyes open, while turning your head from side to side. Also do this with your eyes closed.

Stand on one foot, eyes open. Eyes closed.

Place foam/pillow in a corner or next to a wall with a sturdy chair placed in front of you. Remove your shoes when standing on the foam. Do not touch the wall or the chair except as you need to in order to maintain your balance. Stand on the foam/pillow:

With your eyes open.

With your eyes closed.

With your eyes open, turning your head from side to side.

With your eyes closed, turning your head from side to side.

Follow a randomly waved object with your eyes only.

March in place on the foam with the eyes open while turning your head from side to side.

TIPS TO EASE TENSION-REDUCE STRESS

Attitude is an important key. The way you feel & think affect your attitude. Work on your attitude.

Change the way you think. Concentrate on something else to break the chain of thought that is producing stress.

Think positively. Some underlying emotions promoting stress are anxiety, insecurity & fear. A few things to keep in mind:

You can only do one thing at a time.

 All that needs to be accomplished will be accomplished.

You have achieved before & there is no reason why you won't achieve again.

Take a mental vacation. Reflect on an enjoyable place you would like to be. Visualize your self on the beach in the Bahamas. Create the mental image in detail. The imaging is relaxing, therefore relieves stress.

PUT YOUR ATTENTION ON DOING ONE TASK AT A TIME – Breathe, Relax & Focus; Thinking about all the things that need to be accomplished is overwhelming & immobilizing…

Count to ten – SLOWLY…

Look away to relax your eyes…

Take several deep breaths – SLOWLY…

Belly breathing defeats anxiety & nervousness

When experiencing stress, your pulse races & you start breathing quickly

Force yourself to breathe slowly as if the stress is gone, whether it is or isn't…

Move around…

Listen to a relaxation tape…

Listen to music that is soothing & enjoyable…

Exercise

Think pleasant thoughts & talk to yourself…

LOWER BACK EXERCISE PROGRAM

My back-injury incurred losses of muscle strength and joint motion. Many factors contributed to these losses in addition to the injury itself, such as:

Lack of good physical exercise throughout life, thus creating weak muscles and an imbalance between the flexor and extensor muscles (muscles needed to bend or stand erect).

With some injuries, the presence of defect in the bones of the spine contributes to a less healthy back. These defects may be present at birth or develop later in life.

Weak back muscles which are indicated by a history of multiple episodes of back pain. This is a signal that the spine is poorly supported. The vertebrae, discs, ligaments and muscles are being subjected to increased wear and tear, and damage.

With some injuries, the body's natural protective measure muscle spasm and guarding of the injured area in order to promote healing. While these measures are normal and necessary to healing, they do add to further muscle imbalance, weakness and loss of joint motion.

The following exercises were successful in alleviating my lower back pain. These should be done at least three times a week for best results.

Lie on stomach and allow all muscles to relax completely.

Press-up on hands. In very slow motion, tilt head backward. Push hands against floor and begin to raise trunk. Spine must be curved.

Standing back bends. Stand in a relaxed posture, spine straight. Very slowly and gently bend backward several inches. Keep arms high; look upward. Hold without motion for a count of ten.

Double knee to chest.

Single knee to chest.

Hamstring stretch.

Pelvic tilt.

¼ sit-ups.

Upper body and/or leg extension

I had a choice to live in continued misery and pain but I choose not to allow misery and pain to control my life. I worked every day in seeking the return of a strong, usable, healthier, functioning back and a return to a state of wellness and living.

I recommend that your back rehabilitation program should be carried out under the guidance of your physician.

BRAIN TUMOR REMOVED—1997 AGE 65

In 1997, Dr. Robert Duckrow, UCON Medical Center suggested that I have a brain lesion removed --excision of right frontal cortical oligodendroglioma). I became sold on the idea when he suggested that it also might resolve my impotency problem. We tried the psychiatrist a few times (not successful).

 The operation was done at Yale New Haven Hospital by Dr. Spencer on 9/2/1997. The post hospital stay was at New Haven Medical Center and ten days of loving care was given to me by my sister-in-law Judy at Brother Bernard's home. I recovered rather quickly and returned to work in about seven weeks.

CORONARY ARTERY BYPASS—1999

The heart is the hidden treasure of man. Hebrew proverb

In 1999, I had a two-vessel coronary artery bypass at the suggestion of Dr Michael Blum of Yale. Dr. S. Jack Landau of New Haven was my earlier cardiologist. In 1985 I underwent a cardiac catherization by Rene Langou at the suggestion of Dr. Landau. It was determined that I had coronary disease with two lesions in the left anterior descending. One was 30% obstructed and the other not clearly defined so I was treated medically. It is just possible that subsequent and perhaps the current complaints were gastro esophagus reflux rather that heart- related disease.

The two-vessel coronary bypass was done by Dr. Sabert Harsham at Yale Hospital on 4/27/1999 based on the results of a prior catherization. The post five day hospital stay was at New Haven Medical Hotel. I again stayed for two weeks at my brother's

Bernard home in Waterford CT under the care of my sister-in-law, Judy Pisacich.

The recovery period may have been shorter than three months because of the superb rehab program at the Hoffman Heart and Vascular Institute of Connecticut at St. Francis Hospital in Hartford --- and walking my black cocker spaniel dog, Quake, at least twice a day. This strengthens my calves and ankles as well as restoring stability and balance.

One result of this most painful and longest recovery period was low blood pressure.

HEART & VASCULAR EXERCISE

Some of the exercises we did at St Francis' Heart and Vascular Institute, Hartford, included:

WARM-UP

Bending over and backward 10-15 times

Bending knees down & up 10-15 times

Bending to each side 10-15 times

Reach up high with right & then left hand 10-15 times

Lean to the right & to left 10-15 times

Bend right & then left calf 10-15 seconds

BICEP CURL WITH DUMBBELLS

This tones your biceps and helps in carrying and lifting. Stand with your feet shoulder-width apart. For resistances hold two dumbbells between the weights of 2 to 5 pounds without pain. Flex your elbow and inhale slowly until your hand reaches shoulder level. Hold, and then lower your arm slowly while exhaling slowly. After 10-15 times, roll shoulders clockwise and counterclockwise 3-4 times. This tones your biceps and helps in carrying and lifting

LATERAL RAISE

Stand in a lunge position with the hands holding two dumbbells on the thigh of the legs. Point your elbows as high as you can toward the ceiling, making your upper arm parallel to the ground. Slowly extend your arm until it is straight as it will go. Pause for a second, then lower back to starting position. Repeat 10 times for one set. Rest for one or two minutes by rolling shoulders clockwise and counterclockwise 3-4 times. Then complete a second set of 10 repetitions.

OVERHEAD PRESS

Stand with feet-shoulder-width apart. With a dumbbell in each hand, raise your hands, palms facing forward, until the dumbbells are level with your shoulders and parallel to the floor. To a count of two, slowly push the dumbbells up over your head until your arms are fully extended-but don't lock your elbows. Pause. Then, to a count of two, slowly lower the dumbbells back to shoulder level, bringing your elbows down close to your sides.

Repeat 10 times for one set. Rest for one or two minutes. Then complete a second set of 10 repetitions.

Make sure you:

Keep your wrists straight.

Don't lock your elbows.

Don't let the dumbbells move too far in front or behind your body.

Breathe throughout the exercise. Breathe in through the nose while raising the arms and exhale while lowering the dumbbells.

TRICEPS EXTENSION

Stand in a lunge position with the hands on the thighs of your legs.

Grab two dumbbells. Point your elbows as high as you can toward the ceiling, making your upper arm parallel to the ground.

Slowly extend your arms until they are straight as they will go --- but do not change the position of your elbow. Pause for a second, and then lower your back to starting position.

Repeat ten times for one set. Rest for a minute or two. Then complete a second set of 10 repetitions.

IMPORTANT: Your upper arm and elbows should not move at all during the entire set.

WALL PUSH-UP

Find a wall that is clear of any objects. Stand a little farther than arm's length from the wall.

Facing the wall, lean your body forward and place your palms flat against the wall at about shoulder height and shoulder-width apart.

To a count of four, bend your elbows as you lower your upper body toward the wall in a slow, controlled motion, keeping your feet planted.

Pause - Then to a count of two, slowly push yourself back until your arms are straight. Do not lock your elbows.

Repeat 10 times for one set. Rest for one or two minutes. Then complete a second set of 10 repetitions.

SQUATS

Stand with feet slightly more than shoulder-width apart. Extend your arms out so they are parallel to the ground and lean forward a little at the hips.

Making sure that your knees NEVER come forward past your toes, lower yourself in a *slow, controlled motion,* until you reach a near-sitting position.

Pause Then to a count two, slowly rise back up to a standing position. Keep your knees over your ankles and your back straight.

Repeat 10 times for one set. Rest for a few minutes. Then complete a second set of 10 repetitions.

Note. Placing your weight more on your heels than on the balls or toes of your feet can keep your knees from moving forward past your toes. It will also help to use the muscles of your hips more during the rise to a standing position.

STEP-UPS

Stand alongside the handrail at the bottom of a staircase. With your flat and toes facing forward, put your right foot on the first step.

Holding the handrail for balance, to a count of two, straightens your right leg to lift up your left leg slowly until it reaches the first step. As you're lifting yourself up, make sure that your right knee stay straight and does not move forward past your ankle. Let your left foot tap the first step near your right foot.

Pause. Then, use your right leg to support your weight. To a count of two, slowly lower your left foot back to the floor.

Repeat 10 times with the right leg and 10 times with the left leg for one set. Rest for one or two minutes. Then complete a second set of 10 repetitions with each leg.

Make sure you don't let your back leg do the work, and don't let momentum do the work.

COOL DOWN

Bend knees down & up 20-30 seconds

Right & left leg extended 15 seconds each

Bend right & left calf 10-15 seconds each

Standing tall roll shoulders clock & counterclockwise 10-15 seconds each.

Standing tall inhale through nose & exhale through mouth – 5 breaths.

PHOTO GALLERY

A picture is a poem wanting (i.e. lacking) words. Latin proverb

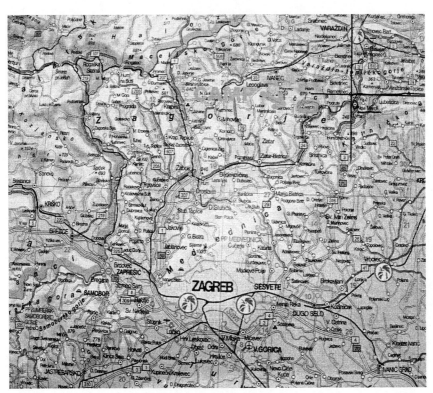

Remetinec area of Croatia

Inside Holy Rosemary Crown Church (Kraljice Svete Krunice) – John Rim, Father Pavlek, Matt Perry, Donald Langenfeld

Outside Holy Rosemary Crown Church (Kraljice Svete Krunice)

Visiting family grave sites back of church

Pisacich Coat of Arms 1628

Plot of land where Mom was born

Matt Perry, Fabijan Pisacich, Ivan and Dubravka Cindori

Mom & Katherine Pisacich 1924

Friend Carol Dorman 1940

Dad Pisacich 1929

Mom Pisacich 1929

West Mifflin Home 1954

Blast Furnaces Carnegie Steel Duquesne

Waynesburg College Graduation
1953

Anna Pisacich 1960

St Anne's Sunday School Class 1952

Shigo Family Reunion 1961

Matt & Mary Ann Perry, Cleveland 1962

Contempo's Eye Make-up Line 1968

McCleary's Ft Lauderdale 1985

Peter Perry Cromwell 1992

John Rim & Matt Perry 1992

Bates Family after Dorothy's Memorial Service 2003

Dorothy & Joel Blum 2006

Logan Utah Family Reunion 2007

MY FOURTEEN LIVES:
A SUMMARY

Men at some time are masters of their fates. Shakespeare

There was a change in my destiny after each of the thirteen episodes. Fortune is not on the side of the faint-hearted but rather on the side of the bold.   Good as well as bad are necessary to make one capable.

LIFE 1: DECEMBER 1952 –
CONCUSSIONS THAT AFFECTED MY LIFE

*Those having torches will pass them
on to others.* Greek proverb

At age 10, I flipped over the handlebars of my bicycle during a race. At the age of 20, I was knocked out running down steps to the supply store for some equipment needed in a laboratory experiment at Waynesburg College's Chemistry Lab. I suffered a concussion that damaged frontal lobes inside my skull. I had a seizure in 1953, and another one soon after, in the Navy. The threat of another seizure was always on my mind until the operation in September of 1997.

LIFE 2: MARCH 1954 – MY FIRST JOB
A BUMMER BUT A MENTOR CAME

To know how to suggest is the art of
teaching. American proverb

In Elizabeth, New Jersey, I met Alfred Drucker, a chemist who was transferred from Brazil by Reichhold Chemical Corporation. Alfred introduced me to Dr. John Skeen, Research Director of Nuodex Corporation after I indicated dissatisfaction with my first professional employment, at International Printing Company. He hired me as supervisor of two older chemists who were veterans of the Korean War and were employed by Nuodex in this relatively new department. Dr. Skeen soon became my mentor.

My work at Nuodex resulted in publication of two articles in *Plastics Technology* journal with my chemical engineering professor at Brooklyn Polytechnic College as co-author. I immediately became an authority on poly-vinyl-chloride. This is how I received an offer from Geigy Chemical Corporation. Mr. Drucker also helped me get my Geigy ultra-violet light absorber product approved by their cost- conscious Reichhold Chemical. Corporation My product was considered more effective as an absorber and did not add color to the finished product.

LIFE 3: APRIL 1957 – BIG MISTAKE
AT MY BEST CORPORATE JOB

Be not arrogant when fortune smiles, or
dejected when she frowns. Ausonius

When I joined Geigy Chemical Corporation in Ardsley, N.Y., I used poor judgment by not going to the corporation's headquarters in Basel, Switzerland, for six months of management training. I was afraid that I could have a seizure on such a trip.

However, I met Ms. Lenny Rosenboom in the company cafeteria. Company policy was against our dating but later she introduced me to some of the old rich and powerful in Bronxville, New York.

LIFE 4: MAY 1962 – MY BEST PLANNED VENTURE—FEAR TAKES OVER

It is a bad plan that admits of no modification. Publius Syrus

I backed out of a licensing venture called Specialty Chemical Corporation— because one of my partners objected to the recruitment of another well-qualified partner-to-be. I had been able to round up an excellent team of professional talent, a very cooperative licensor, and good financial backing but…

LIFE 5: JANUARY 1965 – NEW FRIEND VANISHES - FOR 30 YEARS

A friend, a single soul dwelling in two bodies. Greek proverb

I met Dr. John Rimberg as a project director for my first motivational research study on behalf of Sears Roebuck & Co in the 1960's. He invested in Contempo Cosmetics when its future was uncertain, to help with the cash flow. Then he vanished until I needed him to edit this book.

LIFE 6: SEPTEMBER 1968 –COULD NOT FIND THE PERSON WE NEEDED FOR NEW VENTURE

Do not think too far ahead lest you fall close by. Arabic proverb

I signed an exclusive licensing agreement with Gala Cosmetics Ltd. for the U.S and Canadian distribution and manufacturing rights. It was my intent to stay with DeSoto Chemical Corporation (Des Plaines, Illinois) and work part-time at Contempo Cosmetics. This way, we would have sufficient cash-flow to pay for a senior sales person. My wife Mary Ann was to be president and the senior sales person was to work with her. The search was unsuccessful.

LIFE 7: JANUARY 1971 – FAILURES AT WORK AND AT HOME

There is no faith in women, horses or swords. Persian proverb

The demise of Contempo Cosmetics, separation from my wife, divorce and lack of work during this 1971 recession caused me to lose confidence in myself. Yoga, meditating and MENSA friends helped me recover quickly. The Sear's attorney was right – pay yourself the back salary owed, and file for bankruptcy. I would not have additional friends but I would get a fresh start. Perhaps even enough self- confidence to start another venture because I was flooded with ideas at that time.

LIFE 8: JUNE 1980 – BRAIN TUMOR REMOVED

I would rather be healthy than rich. Latin proverb

I had a left suboccipital craniotomy with total excision of the left acoustic neuroma. – approx 4 cm. . The condition was overlooked for five years while the four-centimeter tumor was growing.

I had a rendezvous with death during the operation, and again while I was in intensive care. I am sure the prayers, meditation and positive feelings of my friends of various religions, creeds and diverse paths contributed greatly to my miraculous recovery.

However, I did not receive immediate rehabilitation to help recover lost sensation.

Deafness in one ear (loss of cranial nerves VII and VIII) created a great deal of physical and psychological hardship for the next 30 years. Beginning in 1990, there were signs of personality changes. I became less interested in money, and more in research. I became more introverted and conscious of my hearing handicap, and how mean –spirited people can be.

LIFE 9: MARCH 1983 JOINED SMITH BARNEY, NEW HAVEN, CT

Good management is better than good income. English proverb

I developed success in the new profession, the financial industry, with a branch office of Smith Barney. Most of my clients became lasting friends even when they moved thousands of miles away.

Much of my success can be attributed to the manager, Richard Pignone. He was one step ahead of me intellectually and he was very secure in himself. I had complete use of the office facilities without haggling.

My high sale/close ratio and consistent production made me Number One or Number Two in those trying times. I was willing to invest part of my production dollars in staff. I became dissatisfied and left and left for Drexel Burnham. He went to AG Edwards a year later.

LIFE 10: MAY 94-WHAT IS HAPPENING TO MY EYES?

Guard the health both of body and soul. Greek proverb

At two physical examination in Mayo Clinic they recommended exercises to help my imbalance that was caused by the acoustic neuroma operation. At first my vision problem may have been simply dry eyes caused by a lack of normal tears. . Eye exercises were suggested to help strengthen my eye muscles, weakened by the acoustic neuroma operation. The Mayo Clinic reminded me that I had a membrane over the retina in my right eye and that I had cataracts.

LIFE 11: SEPTEMBER 1997 – REMOVAL OF FRONTAL LOBE TUMOR BUT NO FOLLOW-UP

*Life consists not merely in existing but
in enjoying health.* (Martius)

A right frontal oligo-dene-groglioma resection diminished the possibility of having another seizure. No follow-up therapy to recover lost sensation, complex thought, perception and motor skills.

LIFE 12: APRIL 1999 CORONARY -ARTERY BYPASS

*Have you wealth or have you none; if you lose
heart, all is gone.* American proverb

Post-bypass graft surgery created another problem, hypotension. The systolic blood pressure would be as low as 45 standing. A steroid, helped increase blood pressure.

The cardiology rehabilitation program at the Hoffman Heart and Vascular Institute of Connecticut at St Francis Hospital in Hartford accelerated my recovery of physical skills.

LIFE 13: JANUARY 2007 REOCCURRENCE OF HEALTH PROBLEMS

Joy and Temperance and Repose/Slam the door in the doctor's nose.
Longfellow

The body began to give me new problems in early 2007. I was hospitalized several times for chest pains. On April 30th, my body went haywire: Bleeding, loss of consciousness for 24 hours, fatigue and low blood pressure. Since there was no logical explanation, I thought that the disease was Old Age. It can be more feared than death. Nothing hinders cure so much as frequent changes of medicine. Diet and regular physical workout are more important than the miracle drugs and good physicians.

LIFE 14: BACK TO NORMAL

Time to look back and march forward:

At 4, I was born poor and the United States of America was in a Great Depression. We ate what we grew and cultivated. We walked to where we where going. We were healthy.

At 14: I needed money and worked after school. One job exposed me to greed. I thought it was stealing.

At 24: I did what I learned early on: how to make money.

At 34: I thought I could never have enough money so I went into business for myself.

At 44: I began to admire people who manifested more greed than I did.

At 54: A turning point in my soul: I occasionally lived less lavishly—and felt moved to help a close relative who could not manage by herself. After the unexpected demise of Michael Milken and Drexel

Burnham, I finally decided to accept responsibility for the care of my sister Anna who is mentally-challenged, so to speak. My sister Katherine and my brother Edward, has been doing **everything** – without much time from me—for many years.

I had been too busy making more money. I was living alone, and felt free to do as I pleased. In reality, money had been controlling me for decades even though I believed I was captain of my soul.

At last, I brought my sister to a nursing home in Cromwell where I lived.

I learned from her example, about love and caring—topics virtually absent from any of my textbooks, lectures, technical schooling or business environments. Love and caring had also been absent from my vacant soul. Anna died soon after I accepted responsibility for her care.

Only after her death did I realize how this straight-shooting woman—with an IQ of 72 but also a so-called photographic memory for names, faces and thoughts—was unconditionally loved and respected by so many people in all social strata.

To me, this sister of mine was amazing. Anna proved to be a better role model than the rich and famous—and the politicos. She had nothing to give to others but her own self, which she did. Bog time.

At 64: I still respected money—but greed was making me uncomfortable. Greed in the financial services industry spread and grew. "Wall Street genius" invented more ways to hypnotize investors and customers into yielding their money to a thousands of very greedy people.

As sophisticated "shell games emerged, government oversight shriveled. The new billionaires showed their gratitude by doing favors and bank-rolling increasingly-expensive political campaigns for high public offices. Money-mania and power-mania strolled hand in hand. (The 85-year old senator from Alaska—a convicted felon—was but one example.)

I finally was willing to recognize the disparity in wages among different segments of the labor force—and the steady decline of the middle class as the few wealthy among us grew even richer. Disparities had existed for some years but "there is none so blind as he who will not see."

At 74: I appreciated good health but passionately disliked naked greed. The tight-fisted money-chasers are no longer suitable role models. Warren Buffett became the new role model.

Warren Buffet occupied a grey area for me: He could be merely "the richest man in the world" or he can be a true leader of men.

Meanwhile, I began to learn how greed can be tamed by good laws and genuine American leaders—from George Washington to Andrew Jackson to Abraham Lincoln, and two presidents Roosevelt…and…

My health is good. I can see more clearly what life is all about. Now may be the right time to attack greed head on.

I could write an important book with built-in audience appeal. A book on an important theme: charity. (Giving both time and money.)

Andrew Carnegie said that a rich man should give away his wealth during his lifetime and die without a penny to his name. Carnegie paid for many, many public libraries while he still lived. (About three-thousand.)

John D, Rockefeller complained about the difficulty of distributing his wealth during his lifetime because it was such a large sum—but he tried. (So did J.P. Morgan.)

Warren Buffett has pledged to give most of his $62 billion dollar fortune to charity **upon his death**. He has chosen to help others **after his life is over** when he is no longer around to supervise and correct. Better, he could try to accomplish what Andrew Carnegie, John D. Rockefeller and J.P. Morgan tried. They did not want to perfect a business that would run sublimely for 30 years after the death of the founder. (They were not that naïve **about the future**.

The timing could not be better.

Warren Buffet can make a difference today at the highest level, the international economy. The money-lenders had taken over the temple. \they vied to be "top dog" but they proved to be sons of bitches.

Buffet, working hand-in-hand with Bill Gates, could offset those tight-fisted money chasers by setting an example. Bill Gates is now giving 100% of his **time** to foundation work.

How is Warren Buffet spending his time? Making money? (Again?)

I am ready for the book tour. To listen to others---and share my timely ideas. I will also try to make money promoting this book to help the following four non-profit institutions in this economic crisis. The book profits will be divided equally among these institutions: Waynesburg University... Connecticut Rivers Council of Boy Scouts of America... North Carolina High School Studies Foundation... and Rainbow Foundation Sihtasutus.

FINANCIAL DOCUMENTS

1. AT&T BREAK-UP 12/15/1984

1000 shares of AT&T on 12/15/1984 would cost $58,625 .Early 2007 those 1000 shares were worth $363,674.08 consisting of the following shares:

AT&T Incorporated	6074
Avaya Incorporated	108
Comcast Corporation Class A	678
Idearc	70.7
NCR Corporation Common	62
Qwest Communications International Incorporated	709
Verizon Communications, Inc. Common	1414
Vodafone Group PLC Sponsored ADR	875
cashed out partial shares	$68.08

AT&T (CUSIP 001957109)

5/29/59   3 for 1 split

6/22/64   2 for 1 split

4/16/99   3 for 2 split

ex: 2/16/84 record date 12/30/83

For each 10 shares of American Telephone and Telegraph, holders received 1 new share.

Holders with less than 10 shares will not receive any shares of the regional companies, but will receive cash for fractions. Holders owning 500 or more shares will receive certificates for whole shares and cash for fractions. Holders with 10-499 shares received certificates for whole shares and cash for fractions and may consolidate their holding in any one or more of the divested companies.

THE FOLLOWING ARE THE 7 COMPANIES DISTRIBUTED FROM AT&T:

TRANSFER AGENT: BOSTON EQUISERVE (800) 348-8288

AMERICAN INFORMATION TECHNOLOGIES   CUSIP: 026804104 (AITOLD)

3 FOR 2   1/26/87

2 FOR 1   1/24/89

1991 Named changed to <u>AMERITECH CORP NEW CUSIP: 030954101 (AIT)</u>

2 FOR 1   1/21/94

2 FOR 1   1/27/98

Agent Bank- Equiserve/First Chicago Trust of New York (800) 351-7221

10-8-99 Merged into SBC Communications, Inc. (CUSIP 78387G103) received 1.316 new shares for every old.

<u>**BELL ATLANTIC   CUSIP: 077853109   (BEL)**</u>

2 FOR 1   4/18/86

2 FOR 1   5/2/90

2 FOR 1   6/30/98

6/30/00 - 1 for 1 name change to Verizon Communications, Inc. New Cusip 92343V104

Agent Bank- Boston Equiserve   (800) 631-2355

Verizon Communications CUSIP: 92343V104 (VZ)

11/17/06 – Spin-off to Idearc   CUSIP 451663108.   0.05 shares of Idearc for each share of Verizon.

BELLSOUTH CUSIP: 079860102 (BLS)

3 FOR 1   5/23/84

3 FOR 2   2/24/87

2 FOR 1   11/8/95

2 FOR 1   12/28/98

Agent Bank - Chase Mellon Investor Services (800) 631-6001

STOCK MERGER EFF. 12/29/06. RECVD 1.325 NEW FOR 1 OLD SHARE.

NEW CUSIP 00206R102 AT&T INCORPORATED

NYNEX CORP   CUSIP: 670768100 (NYN)

2 FOR 1   5/1/86

2 FOR 1   9/18/93

8/15/97 Merged with Bell Atlantic (CUSIP 077853109) .768 new for each old

Agent Bank - Boston Equiserve   (617) 575-3170

PACIFIC TELESIS   CUSIP: 694890104 (PAC)

2 FOR 1   6/10/86

2 FOR 1   3/25/87

4/6/94 - Spun off Air Touch Communications on a 1 for 1 basis

4/1/97 - Merged with SBC Communications (CUSIP 78387G103) @ .73145 new for each old.

Agent Bank- Equiserve/First Chicago Trust of New York (800) 351-7221

SOUTHWESTERN BELL   CUSIP: 845333103 (SBC)

3 FOR 1   5/26/87

2 FOR 1   5/25/93

4/28/95 Named changed to SBC Communications, new CUSIP 78387G103.

2 for 1 3/20/98

Agent Bank - Equiserve/First Chicago Trust of New York (800) 351-7221

NAME CHANGE EFF. 11/18/05. RECVD 1 NEW FOR EACH OLD SHARE.

NEW CUSIP 00206R102 AT & T INC

U.S. WEST CUSIP: 912889102 (USW)

2 FOR 1   5/29/86

2 FOR 1   5/3/90

Spin Off 11/1/95 1 US West Media Group for each 1 US West.

 6-15-98 US WEST MEDIA CHANGED NAME TO MEDIAONE GROUP INC. & SPUN-OFF US WEST @ .02731

6-30-00 U.S. WEST merged with QWEST COMMUNICATIONS INTERNATIONAL INC @ 1.72932 new for each old. NEW CUSIP 749121109

Agent Bank- Bank of New York (800)524-4458

7/21/00

MEDIAONE GROUP INC. (CUSIP 58440J104)

CASH & STOCK MERGER EFF 7/21/00

REC 0.95 NEW, $30.85 PER SHARE AND A TOP-UP PAYMENT OF $5.42 FOR EACH OLD

NEW CUSIP 001957109 AT&T CORPORATION

Agent Bank – Equiserve/Boston Division (781) 575-3170

10/1/96

SPIN OFF OF LUCENT TECHNOLOGIES (CUSIP 549463107)

Received 0.324084 LUCENT FOR EACH SHARE OF AT&T

2 FOR 1 split 4/2/98

2 FOR 1 split 4/5/99

Agent Bank – Bank of New York (800) 524-4458

5/31/02 - Spin off of Agere Systems Inc Class A (CUSIP 00845V100) @ .01078 and Agere Systems Inc Class B (CUSIP 00845V209) @ .26456 per each share of Lucent.

Agent Bank – Bank of New York (800) 524-4458

5/27/05_AGERE CLASS A & CLASS B, reverse split 1 new for 10 old shares.

NEW CUSIP 00845V308 AGERE SYSTEMS INC NEW

1/2/97

SPIN OFF OF NCR CORP (CUSIP 62886E108)

.0625 NCR CORP. FOR EACH SHARE OF AT&T

Agent Bank – Chase Mellon Investor Ser (800) 526-0801

5/17/99 1 for 10 reverse split followed by a 10 for 1 forward split. All certificates of 9 shares or less dated on or prior to 5/17/99 were cashed out at $42.30 per share.

10/02/00

SPIN OFF OF AVAYA INC (CUSIP 053499109)

Received 0.08334 AVAYA INC., for each share of Lucent.

Agent Bank – Bank of New York (800) 524-4458

6/30/99

AIRTOUCH COMMUNICATIONS (CUSIP   00949T100)

CASH & STOCK MERGER. REC $9.00 & .50 NEW FOR EACH OLD

NEW CUSIP 92857T107 VODAFONE AIRTOUCH PUBLIC LTD. 5 for 1 forward split, ex-date 10/4/99.

7/31/00 - Name change, 1 for 1 to Vodafone Group PLC ADR. New CUSIP

92857W100.

Agent Bank – Bank of New York (800) 524-4458

7/09/01

SPIN OFF OF AT&T WIRELESS SERVICES INC (CUSIP 00209A106)

CUSIP (00209A106) RECEIVED 0.32180 AT&T WIRELESS SERVICES INC., FOR EACH SHARE OF AT&T.

Agent Bank – Chase Mellon Investor Services (800) 756-3353

10/26/04 cash merger with Cingular Wireless at $15.00 per share. Agent Bank is Mellon Investor Services. Phone 800-777-3674

11/19/02

SPIN OFF OF COMCAST CORP CLASS A (CUSIP 20030N101)

Received 0.3235 COMCAST CORP NEW CLASS A for each share of AT&T.

Agent Bank – Equiserve/Boston Division (781) 575-2965.

11/19/02

AT&T CORP (CUSIP 001957109)

REVERSE SPLIT EFFECTIVE 11/19/02, 1 new for 5 old shares. NEW CUSIP 001957505 - AT & T CORP- NEW

Agent Bank - BOSTON EQUISERVE (800) 348-8288

11/18/05

AT&T CORP (CUSIP 001957505)

Stock merger into SBC Corporation. Each old share was exchanged into .77942 new. New CUSIP 00206R102 – AT&T INCORPORATED.

Transfer Agent – Computershare Investor Services (800) 245-7630

11/18/05

SBC COMMUNICATIONS INC (CUSIP 78387G103)

Name changed 1 for 1 into AT&T INCORPORATED. NEW CUSIP 00206R102

Transfer Agent – Computershare Investor Services (800) 245-7630

12/29/06

BELLSOUTH CORPORATION (CUSIP 079860102)

Stock Merger into AT&T Incorporated. Each old share was exchanged into 1.325 new.

New CUSIP 00206R102 – AT&T INCORPORATED.

Transfer Agent – Computershare Investor Services (800) 245-7630

2. COMPUTATIONAL FORMULAS USED IN THE SUPER 25 PROGRAM ---

As of 20 April 1997. This supersedes the document of the same name from 14 April 1996.

Terminology:

This Year -- The company FY ending in 1997?

Last year -- The company FY before that

Next Year -- The Company FY after this year

I just process the data... I leave to you (MVP) the problem of figuring out how to enter the available data in the proper slot.

<u>Manual Inputs:</u>

All EPS values (as decimal dollars)

All dividends (as decimal dollars)

Next 5 years growth rate [Z] (as a decimal fraction)

Adjustments including Value Line timeliness [L] and safety[N] and Zacks'

"Analysts' Evaluation" [M].

(a variety of administrative data is also manually input but is not germane to the computations and is not listed here.)

The CURRENT PRICE [K] may be manually input or may be obtained automatically by a data base download.

<u>Computations:</u>

[O] Value Price = P/E Ratio * Current Price [On = AEn * Kn]

[P] % Difference=Value Price-Current Price as % of Value Price

[Pn=100*(On-Kn)/On]

[U] Div. Yield = This Yr.(1997) Dividend / Current Price

[Un = AZn/Kn]

[V] Average EPS growth rate - Past 10 years = Average of the computed growth rates from 86-87 to 95-96 [@SUM(BNn.. BWn)/10]

[W] Same but the last 5 years, 91-92 to 95-96.[@SUM(BSn.. BWn)/5]

[X] Current EPS growth rate, 96-97 [BXn]

[Y] Predicted EPS growth rate next year 97-98 [BYn]

[Z] Manually input predicted next 5 years annual EPS growth

[AA] Combined Growth EPS Growth Rate = Average of the previous 5 items [AAn=@SUM(Vn..Zn)/5]

Effective weightings:

Next 5 years	20%		Year -5	6%
Next year	20%		Year -6	2%
This year	20%		Year -7	2%
Last year	6%		Year -8	2%
Year -2	6%		Year -9	2%
Year -3	6%		Year-10	2%
Year -4	6%		earlier years	0

[AC] Value P/E Ratio = Div. Yield (%) + Adjustment + Combined Growth Rate (%) [ACn=AAn+(ABn+Un)*100]

[AD] Actual P/E Ratio = Current Price/This year's (1997) estimated EPS.   [ADn=Kn/ATn]

[AE] Ratio = Value P/E / Actual P/E [AEn=ACn/ADn]

[BL]	84- 85	[BCn/BBn-1]
[BM]	85- 86	[BDn/BCn-1]

[BN]	86- 87	[BEn/BDn-1]
[BO]	88- 89	etc.

[BP]	last	89- 90	
[BQ]	10	90- 91	
[BR]		91- 92	[ANn/BHn-1]

[BS]	last	92- 93	[AOn/ANn-1]
[BT]	5	93- 94	[APn/AOn-1]
	last		

[BU]	3 years	93- 94	[APn/AQn-1]
[BV]		94- 95	[ARn/AQn-1]
[BW]	last year	95- 96	[ASn/ARn-1]

[BX]	this year	96- 97	[ATn/ASn-1]
[BY]	next year	97- 98	[BYn=@IF(AUn>0,
[BZ]	next 5 years	[Zn]	+AUn/ATn-1,BZn)]

[CA] Min 91-97+   [CAn=@MIN(BSn..BZn)]

[CB] Min 86-97+   [CBn=@MIN(BNn..BZn)]

[CC] Min Avg 91-97+   [CCn=@MIN(Wn..Zn)]

[CD] Min Avg 86-97+   [CDn=@MIN(Vn..Zn)]

[CE] Threshold= Hurdle Rate - Yield [CEn=$CE$1-Un]

Hurdle Rate is a manually input decimal fraction at CE1

Growth Premium Rate is the same at CM1

EVALUATION:

A   The EPS Growth Rate for this year, next year, the next 5 years, and EACH of the last 10 years is equal to or greater than the threshold rate.

A-   The EPS Growth Rate for this year, next year, the next 5 years, and the AVERAGE growth rate for the last 10 years is equal to or greater than the threshold rate, and there were NO EPS decreases during the evaluation period.

B   The EPS Growth Rate for this year, next year, the next 5 years, and EACH of the last 5 years is equal to or greater than the threshold rate.

B-   The EPS Growth Rate for this year, next year, the next 5 years, and the AVERAGE growth rate for the last 5 years is equal to or greater than the threshold rate, and there were NO EPS decreases during the evaluation period.

Z   The EPS Growth Rate for this year, next year, the next 5 years, and EACH of the last 3 years is equal to or greater than the threshold rate.

D   None of the preceding evaluation criteria are met. The default condition.

E   (EMERGING GROWTH) The EPS Growth Rate for this year, next year, the next 5 years, and each of the last 3 years is equal to or greater than the threshold rate PLUS the growth premium rate.

0   Manually input to override an automatic evaluation. Usually used when data is so erratic as to produce ridiculous results which need to be supressed in further processing.

EVALUATION COMPUTATIONS:

[CF] A   [CFn=@IF(CBn>=CEn,"A","-")]

[CG] A-   [CGn=@IF(CDn>=CEn#AND#CBn>=0,"A-","-")]

[CH] B   [CHn=@IF(CAn>=CEn,"B","-")]

[CI] B-   [CIn=@IF(CCn>=CEn#AND#CAn>=0,"B-","-")]

[CJ] Z   [CJn=@IF(@MIN(BUn..BZn)>=CEn,"Z","-")]

[CK] D   [CKn=@IF(@MIN(BUn..BZn)<CEn,"D","-")]

[CL] E   [CJn=@IF(@MIN(BUn..BZn)>=CEn+$CM$1,"E","-")]

The assumed order of precedence of these categories (except E) is the order given above. Note the inclusions. Anything rated an "A" will also meet the criteria for A-, B, B- and Z; Any A- will be a B-; Any B will be B- and Z, etc. Only Z and D are mutually exclusive--everything not a Z will show as a D. "E" is a standalone situation and amounts to a subset of Z.

CAUTION AND WARNING

THE LOGIC AND THE FORMULAS THAT IMPLEMENT IT WERE DEVELOPED TO DEAL WITH CONTINUOUSLY INCREASING EARNINGS. THAT IS, THE EPS GROWTH RATE IS ALWAYS A POSITIVE NUMBER. DECREASING EARNINGS PRODUCE NEGATIVE EPS GROWTH RATES WHICH IN TURN LEAD TO SOME <u>STRANGE</u> RESULTS. BE CAREFUL.

NOTE ON AUTOMATIC INPUTS

As of this writing (4/20/97), the model is structured so that a variety of inputs may be loaded directly from Zacks' Investment Research "Investment Wizard" monthly data base. These include:

Current FY estimated EPS [AT]

Next FY estimated EPS   [AU]

Estimated EPS growth rate--next 3-5 years [Z]

Current Price   [K]

Zacks' Analysts' Evaluation [M]

The data requirements and operating procedures for this operation are documented separately.

GASTRONOMIC DELIGHTS FROM MY FAMILY AND FRIENDS

During the Depression, our family generally had a work and meal routine every day. Also, we basically were forced to be vegetarian and we walked everywhere because that was what we could afford. This probably reduced the medical expenses as well. Only later did we start eating meat and sweets. Grapes were also available in abundance for about a month or so after Dad made wine. Dad would always purchase apples by the bushel when he had a fruit cellar in our West Mifflin home.

The work and meal routine was as follows:

Monday: Wash Day.

The main meal was "Gra" (Navy Beans and Sauerkraut with "Sgunc" (corn meal mush)

Tuesday: Ironing Day.

The main meal was home made vegetable soup seasoned with lard or butter when we had cows. The side dish was cheese strudel that was made from our curds.

Wednesday: Dust-up, Baking and Cleaning Day

The main meal was mashed potatoes with our curds (sour milk)

Thursday: Wash Windows and Clothes Patch-up

The main meal was beef soup with large noodles. Mother usually baked a busy day cake (Yellow sweet cake).

Friday: Sewing and Clothes Patch-up Day

The main meal was home made soup with potatoes, square noodles seasoned with butter. She also made cheese cake with buckwheat flour or corn bread with cheese in it.

Saturday: Cleaning and Bath Day. Also finish up on clothes patching. In the summer, mother was busy making hay.

The main meal was barley or bean/barley soup. In the summer time she made fresh vegetable or potato soup. Later mom and Sister Kate would make enough pies and cake for dad, three growing boys, my two sisters and mother for all of the following week.

Sunday: Rest Day

The main meal was chicken soup and chicken

Later, we almost always had pancakes or French toast and sausage for breakfast.

When we killed a cow because it no longer milked, mother canned the beef for special occasion use. We also had smoked ham, kabassi or bacon when we butchered a pig. If a racing bird of mine would land on a house roof at least several times during daily flight practice, they would land in the stew pot especially if it was not fit for breeding i.e. poor race track record.. On occasion, I would also donate a rabbit or two for a different and festive meal. Late summer dad would make wine and sauerkraut for canning. Mom would can tomatoes, tomato juice, corn, string beans, peaches, pears and plums for the winter.

FAVORITE FAMILY AND FRIENDS RECIPES

The following recipes are simple dishes from family and friends from the Old Country. An irony is some of these peasant meals are now very popular with the best connoisseurs. They also prefer the produce, meat, dairy that are purchased from small agricultural farms. One secret for their good food flavor lies in their gentile, slow cooking, as opposed to fast grilling technique.

A popular dish when we grew up in West Mifflin was Smetana (heavy sour cream) poured over low-fat cottage cheese made at home, sprinkled with salt, paprika and chopped onions, scallion, garlic, radish and/or horseradish and served with recently baked, dense yellow corn bread.

Some of the olive oils from Croatia are offered in prestigious wine boutiques. The olive trees that date back to the Roman Empire receive special attention and care. Washing the olives in the sea also makes their olive oil even more special.

Ground red paprika, hot or sweet, is the main condiment of Dad's and Mom's birth place. This area is also a botanical garden for mushrooms in its forests, along side rivers and in the meadows.

I also included favorite recipes from my close friends and relatives in America. Some of the cuisines described below should thrill your palates while others are quite simple and nutritious and can cure your ill's more than pills. Some of the recipes include packaged foods for shortcuts for a quick meal for the people who get home from work. There is something for All Social Occasions.- for those that would like to start making a meal from scratch and to those that need to make it quick . Remember, if you eat it for supper, you can't have it in the morning and that a food meal ought to begin with hunger. Enjoy!

BREADS

STICKY ROLLS

From Judy Pisacich

This was always a hit. The only problem is that some of us would indulge rather heavily and leave no room for the main meal. The roll recipe makes 20 rolls, so number of servings depends on how many rolls each person consumes. Some of the men (excluding Bernie) in the family have been known to indulge rather heavily! I make the rolls for Easter dinner and other times throughout the year by special request

  1/3 cup firmly packed brown sugar
  ¼ cup margarine
  2 teaspoons honey
  1/3 cup chopped pecans
  2 cans Pillsbury refrigerated Quick Crescent Dinner Rolls
  2 tablespoons margarine, melted
  ¼ cup firmly packed brown sugar
  1 teaspoon cinnamon

Preheat oven to 400 degrees. In small saucepan, combine first 3 ingredients; bring to boil. Spread in increased 13x9-inch pan. Sprinkle with pecans; set aside. Separate 1 can crescent dough into 4 rectangles. Lay rectangles end to end to form 1 long rectangle; firmly press perforations to seal. Brush rectangle with melted butter. Combine brown sugar and cinnamon; sprinkle over dough. Separate second can of crescent dough into 4 rectangles. Place end to end over first dough rectangle; seal edges and perforations. Cut filled rectangle crosswise into 20 strips. Twist each strip 2 times. Place twists in prepared pan. Bake 15 to 20 minutes or until golden brown. Invert immediately to remove from pan.

CHOCOLATE CHIP PUMPKIN BREAD

a chocolate delicacy from Sarah Pisacich

2
2pumpkin
1/2oil
1/2-free chocolate pudding
4egg whites
1 ½-purpose white flour
1 ½ cups whole wheat flour
2cinnamon
1 ¼
1teaspoonsoda
1chocolate chips
Cooking spray

Preheat oven to 350°. Combine first 5 ingredients in a large bowl, stirring well with a whisk. Lightly spoon flour into dry measuring cups; level with a knife. Combine flour, cinnamon, salt, and baking soda in a medium bowl, stirring well with a whisk. Add flour mixture to pumpkin mixture, stirring just until moist. Stir in chocolate chips.

Spoon batter into 2 (8 x 4-inch) loaf pans coated with cooking spray. Bake at 350° for 1 hour and 15 minutes or until a wooden pick inserted in the center comes out clean. Cool 10 minutes in pans on a wire rack, and remove from pans. Cool completely on wire rack. Yield: 32 servings (serving size: 1 slice) NUTRITION PER SERVING:

CALORIES 152(30% from fat); FAT 5g (sat 1.2g,mono 2.5g,poly 1.1g); PROTEIN 2g; CHOLESTEROL 0.0mg; CALCIUM 10mg; SODIUM 137mg; FIBER 1.1g; IRON 1mg; CARBOHYDRATE 26.5g

ONION FOCACCIA CROSTINI-BREAD

From Albert Bates

1 cup olive or local cold-pressed oil, divided
2 large yellow onions. Chopped or sliced
1 ½ tsp sea salt, divided
Pinch freshly ground black pepper
1 tbsp dry yeast
1 tbsp sugar or equivalent sweetener
I cup warm water (about 110 degree F)
3 Tbsp kosher salt
3 ½ cups of all-purpose flour
2 cloves garlic, minced
12 ounces hard cheese or vegan cheese, thinly sliced

Add 3 Tbsp oil to a large pan over medium heat. When hot, add onions, ½ tsp sea salt, and pepper. Sauté until brown but not burnt, about 15 minutes, stirring often. Cool to room temperature, Stir together yeast, sweetener, 2 Thsp oil, water, and cooled onions and stand 2 minutes to dissolve yeast. Add kosher salt and flour. Mix until dough comes away from sides of bowl. Grease a clean bowl with 1 tsp oil. Add dough and turn to coat. Cover and place until doubled in size, about 1 ½ hours, Grease a large baking sheet with 2 tsp oil. Turn dough out onto sheet. Punch down and press dough out to fill the pan. Brush with oil. Sprinkle with remaining salt and pepper. Lightly cover and let rest for 1 hour. Preheat oven to 350 degree F. Bake for 30 minutes or until golden.

Sprinkle the focaccia with garlic, cheese and any remaining oil. Raise oven temperature to 400 degree F and broil about 3 inches from flame until cheese to seethe and soften, 3 to 4 minutes. Cut the focaccia into diagonal crostini and serve hot. Serves 6.

Substitutions:

Use baguette crusty whole-wheat or multigrain bread, fougasse or baked pizza crust.

Use crumbled tofu with nutritional yeast in place of cheese.

Add sun-dried tomatoes, olives, pickled peppers.

APPETIZERS

CRABMEAT ON ENGLISH MUFFIN

from Matt Perry—ideal for cocktails on a cold day.

I have two receipts. I'll give you one and tell you the differences on the other:

    1 cans crabmeat
    1 sticks butter- melted
    Dash tobacco, Worcestershire sauce, salt & pepper
    1 tsp sour cream
    1 cup shredded sharp cheddar cheese
    6 English muffins
    Broil 5 min
    Cut in quarters

The other formula used 1 jar of old English cheese spread and tablespoon of mayonnaise lieu sour cream as well as dash of garlic salt. I also put garlic salt in the above formula as well after spreading on English muffin, you can freeze. Bake @400 F for 10 minutes

KIELBASA

From Eva Pisacich— a big hit at a party

2-3 lb. kielbasa, cut diagonally into 3" chunks
Sauce - 20 oz. can crush pineapple
½ cup brown sugar
12 oz. bottle of Heinz chili sauce

Mix sauce ingredients and pour over kielbasa in a 2 qt. Pyrex dish. Bake uncovered at 325 degrees for 1 hour 15 minutes; turn to baste. Bake 10-15 minutes longer.

PEAR ANTIPASTO

From Albert Bates

3 ripe Anjou, Comice or local pears
1/3 cup fresh lemon or other citrus juice
3-4 ounces local hard or vegan cheese, unsliced or graded
1 Tbsp balsamic vinegar

Halves and core the pears, leaving their skins intact. Pare each half into thin slivers. Spray with lemon juice to keep them from turning brown. Place 4 or 5 slices of pears and ½ ounce of cheese on each salad plate. Moisten cheese with a few drops of balsamic vinegar and serve. Serves 6.

SOUPS

BEANS & SAUERKRAUT

From Katherine Teresa Gorscak

Wash and soak 1/2 pound Pinto beans over night.. Drain and wash again. Put into bigger pot. Add 1 chopped onion plus 3 cup hot water. Simmer until beans are soft. Add washed small can sauerkraut. Cook another 30-40 minutes.

In a frying pan place 4 tablespoons oil. Heat up, and then add 3 to 4 tablespoons flour. Let flour get to light brown color. Add flour mixture to cooked beans & sauerkraut which has been seasoned to taste.

Let the soup thicken for another 10-15 minutes. If too thick add a bit of hot water. If you have a ham bone it will make it taste better.

POTATO SOUP SUPREME

From Eva Pisacich — delicious

Cook slowly for 5 min:

    1 cup finely diced onion
    1 tablespoon melted butter

Add:

    2 cups finely diced potatoes
    1 ½ cups water (may use 1 can chicken broth - add water to
        make 1 ½ cups)

Cover and boil 15 min or until potatoes are tender (do not drain potatoes)

Add:

> 1 can (10 ½ oz) Campbell's Chicken Rice soup
> ½ teaspoon salt
> 1/8 teaspoon pepper
> 2 cups evaporated milk (do not substitute canned milk)

Heat thoroughly, but do not boil.

SPLIT PEA SOUP

> From Albert Bates—a quick body warmer on a cold day.

> 2 cups dried split peas
> 2 carrots, finely chopped
> 1 large onion, chopped
> 10 cups water or soup stock
> Salt and Pepper to taste
> Optional spices: bay leaf, red pepper, garlic powder, thyme tarragon, marjoram, ground cloves, or allspice.

Combine split peas, carrot, onion, and water in large pan. Cover and bring to boil. Simmer 30 minutes or until all vegetables are tender. Season to taste. Serves ten.

SALADS

CAULIFLOWER SALAD

> From Eva Pisacich
> 1 head lettuce
> 1 head cauliflower
> 1 small onion, finely sliced
> 1 lb bacon, fried and crumbled

2mayonnaise (or less) spread over top
1/3 cup Parmesan cheese, sprinkled over top
¼ cup sugar, sprinkled over top

Spread mayonnaise to end and sides. Refrigerate overnight - must be covered tightly. Toss when ready to serve

To keep fresh, toss only what will be served (use 3 qt. oblong Pyrex dish).

PINEAPPLE-BEET WOK HAY COLE SLAW SALAD

From Albert Bates

2 Tbsp vegetable oil
1 ½ tbsp minced fresh ginger
2 large cloves, garlic, minced
1 medium red onion, thinly sliced
2 bunches watercress, steamed, washed, and drained
¼ cup fresh basil, coarsely chopped
Pinch sea salt and freshly ground black pepper
½ head green cabbage (about 5 cups), shredded
1 cup cooked beets, diced and cooled, or 15-ounce can of diced beets, drained
1 cup or 15- ounce can of pineapple tidbits
2 Tbsp vinegar (or to taste)

Make the wok hot enough by flicking a bead of water into the pan, Id it vaporizes in a second or two, it is hot enough. Quickly turn off the heat, swill in the oil. And then turn the heat to high. This prevents the oil from smoking. Swirl in ginger and garlic and quickly add onion, watercress, basil, salt and pepper. Stir-fry until watercress wilts. Turn into a bowl and toss with the cabbage, beets, pineapple, and vinegar. Serve at room temperature. Serves 6.

Wash the wok with hot water and a soft sponge. Dry over low heat for 1-2 minutes. This keeps the wok cured, unlikely to rust, and ready to use.

SIDE DISHES

PANCAKES

From Sahara Pisacich

1 egg
1 c flour
1 c milk (more if the batter is too thick)
2 tbls of vegetable oil
1 tbls of sugar
3 tsp of baking powder
½ tsp of salt

For whole wheat pancakes, substitute the flour with whole wheat flour and the sugar with brown sugar.

Beat all ingredients until batter is smooth. Cook on frying pan.

CORN PUDDING

From Roni Waltzer — great as a side dish to the main course.

1 can whole kernel corn
1 can cream style corn
3/4,and cooled
1/2 cup sugar
1/2 cup flour
4 eggs, lightly beaten
1/4 cup evaporated milk

Combine all ingredients (eggs last) and pour into a greased casserole dish. Bake one hour at 375 degrees until golden brown on top. Let stand a few minutes before serving.

SWEET POTATO AND CARROT PUREE

From Judith Pisacich

4 large sweet potatoes (about 2 lbs)
1 lb of carrots
2 1/2 cups water
1 Tablespoon granulated sugar
6 Tablespoons butter
1/2 cup milk
salt and freshly ground black pepper to taste
1/2 teaspoon ground nutmeg

1) Scrub potatoes and cut a small, deep slit in the top of each. Set on the center rack of preheated 350 oven and bake for about an hour or until potatoes are tender when pierced.

2) Peel and trim carrots and cut in 1 inch lengths. Put in saucepan and add water, sugar and 2 Tablespoons of butter, salt and pepper to taste. Set over medium heat, bring to a boil and cook uncovered until water has nearly evaporated and carrots begin to sizzle in the butter, about 30 min. The carrots should be tender. If not, add a little more water and cook until done.

3 Scrape out the flesh of sweet potatoes and combine with drained carrots in the bowl of a food processor fitted with steel blade. Add remaining butter (4 tablespoons) and 1/2 cup milk and process until very smooth.

4) Add nutmeg and a dash of pepper if more is needed. Stir or process to blend.

5) To reheat transfer to ovenproof serving dish and cover with foil. Heat in 350 preheated oven for about 25 minutes or until hot. This is an easy dish to make ahead and reheat.

ENTREES-VEGETARIAN

BROCCOLI CASSEROLE

From Judy Pisacich – my favorite casserole. Nice way to serve guest broccoli even in the colder months.

1-10oa package thawed frozen chopped broccoli
1 can of cream of mushroom soup
¼ coup of grated cheddar cheese
¼ cup milk
¼ cup mayonnaise
1 beaten egg

Mix ingredients together, put in casserole. Sprinkle ¼ cup of bread crumbs on top. Bake at 350 degrees for 45 minutes.

EGGPLANT TOMATO CASSEROLE

From Phyllis Klaben

1 large eggplant about 1 1/2 lb
1 1/2 tsp salt
2 eggs beaten
2 tbs. melted butter
Fresh ground pepper
2 to 3 tbls chopped onion
1 tsp crushed oregano
1/2 cup dry breadcrumbs
2 large tomatoes sliced thin

2 oz Cheddar cheese grated and 1/4 cup grated Parmesan cheese

Peel and slice eggplant. Put the slices in a pan with the salt and about an inch of boiling water and cover tightly. Cook about 10 Minutes and drain. Mash the eggplant and mix in the eggs, melted butter, pepper, onion, oregano and breadcrumbs. Butter a shallow 1 to 1 1/2 quart baking dish. Cover the bottom with half the tomato slices. Spoon in all of the eggplant mixture and spread evenly.

Arrange the rest of the tomato slices on top. Mix together the Cheeses and sprinkle over the top layer of tomatoes. Add a sprinkle of paprika and bake at 375 degrees for about 45 minutes. Serves 6.

ENTREES – NONVEGETARIAN

STUFFED CABBAGE

From Katherine Teresa Gorscak. (This was my favorite dish. I always wanted it when I visited home in Pittsburgh.)

2 heads of cabbage
1 lb ground beef
1 lb smoked ham, chopped
¼ c smoked bacon, chopped
2 thsp flour
1 cup uncooked rice
2 tsp paprika
1 onion, chopped
1 egg
2 thsp oil
1 lb smoked ham hocks or pork rib
Salt and pepper to taste

Fry bacon in its own fat. Add onion and sauté five minutes. Remove from heat and drain excess fat. Allow to cool slightly, combine with ground beef, chopped ham, rice, 1 teaspoon paprika, salt and pepper, remove large outer leaves of the cabbage, place filling in each leaf and roll up from center to outer edge. Tuck sides into center to hold roll together.

Cut remaining cabbage into strips. Add another half pound of sauerkraut if desired. Place half the sauerkraut in the bottom of large pot. Arrange cabbage rolls over sauerkraut. Add smoked ribs or ham hocks. Cover with remaining sauerkraut. Heat oil and brown floor in it. Add a teaspoon paprika and water to make a thick roux. Cook for 5 minutes. Pour roux over cabbage rolls. Add water to cover cabbage and simmer over low heat for ½ to 2 hours until rice is fully cooked. Do not stir cabbage rolls while cooking. Instead, shake pot occasionally to prevent sticking. Transfer to warm serving dish.

DALMATIAN POT ROAST

From Katherine Teresa Gorscak

This would have been nice to know when I was younger and entertaining a female friends. Eat well, drink well – and do your duty well.

5 lb beef-top round
10 oz smoked bacon
20 oz onions
8 oz parsley
5 oz carrots
4 cloves garlic
10 oz pealed tomato
10 oz fresh celery
8 prunes

3 quarts dry red wine
2 tsp mustard
10 oz olive oil
Bay leaf, rosemary, thyme
Salt and pepper to taste

Wash and drain meet. Cut bacon into match-like sticks, Chop onion and garlic. Cut vegetables into small strips. Pierce beef with sharp knife and place garlic into and around meat. Place beef into large pan, cover with wine. Add chopped onion, thyme, bay leaf, rosemary, pepper, and cubed celery to meat. Cover pan and refrigerate for 12 hours.

Heat oil and place beef (only) into pan with oil. Brown meat briskly and remove from pan. Add contents from marinade into oil and fry briskly. Add browned meat, peeled tomatoes, prunes, and remaining items into pan. Mix and cook for 2-3 hours from a higher to lower temperature during cooking time. Remove meat and slice. Strain juice from pan and use as sauce.

THE CHICKEN CACCIATORE

From Judy Pisacich—this is an "A La Pisacich" meal.

1 small chicken
1/3 cup olive oil
1 large onion, diced
1 medium green pepper, diced
2 garlic cloves, minced
1 28-oz. can diced tomatoes
2 8-oz. cans tomato sauce
½ cup red cooking wine
Salt, pepper, sugar
½ teaspoon allspice, ½ teaspoon thyme, 2 bay leaves

Stew chicken and remove meat from bones. In Dutch oven, sauté onion, green pepper, and garlic until tender, about 5 minutes. Add tomatoes with their liquid, remaining ingredients, and chicken; heat to boiling. Reduce heat - cover and simmer 40 minutes. Recipe will serve 4-6 (using 1 lb. of spaghetti).

PORK CHOPS O'BRIEN

from Eva Pisacich

6 pork loin chops (1/2" thick)
1 tablespoon cooking oil
1 can (10 ¾ oz.) condensed Cream of Celery soup, undiluted
½ cup milk
½ cup sour cream
¼ teaspoon pepper
1 cup (4 oz.) shredded cheddar cheese, divided
1 can (2.8 oz) French-fried onions, divided
1 pkg. (24 oz.) frozen O'Brien hash brown potatoes, thawed (with onion and green pepper)
½ teaspoon salt (sprinkled on top of chops)

In a skillet over medium high heat, brown pork chops in oil, set aside. Combine the soup, milk, sour cream, pepper, ½ cup cheese and ½ cup onions, fold in potatoes. Spread in a greased 13 x 9 x 2 in. baking dish. Arrange chops on top, sprinkle with salt. Cover and bake at 350 for 40-45 min until pork is tender. Uncover, sprinkle with remaining cheese and onions. Return to the oven for 5-10 min or until cheese melts. servings.

BARBECUE

VEGGIE TURKEY BURGER

From Karen Purcell

This slowly but surely became very popular at our cookouts. A very tasty diversion from hamburgers and hot dogs. You can eat these measurably and defy the mediciners.

1 egg white
¼ cup bread crumbs
¼ cup shredded carrots
¼ cup finely chopped onion
¼ cup finely chopped green pepper
Salt & pepper
2 T parmesan cheese
1 lb ground turkey

Combine egg white and bread crumbs. Stir in veggies, salt and pepper. Add cheese and turkey meat. Mix with hands. Makes 5 turkey burgers

SARMA (STUFFED CABBAGE)

From Jan Czepiel

1 Large head cabbage
Large pot of boiling water
1 pound ground pork
3/4 pound ground beef
1/4 pound bacon, chopped very fine
1 onion chopped and browned in oil or lard
1 cup cooked rice
1 t. salt

1/2 t. pepper
1 whole egg
1 pound sauerkraut

Remove pot of water from heat. Place the head of cabbage in the water. Let stand for one hour. Meanwhile prepare meat mixture. Mix meat with rice, seasonings, onion and egg. Remove the head of cabbage from the salt water and remove leaves one at a time. If the center stalk of the leaf is too big, trim it down. Put 2 heaping T. of meat mixture in core end of cabbage leaf. Roll up and tuck cabbage ends in. Place sarma in Dutch oven. Put a layer of sauerkraut on top and then another layer of sarmas. Continue until all sarmas are used. Add water to cover. Place one pound of spare ribs on top. If any cabbage was left over, cut in pieces and place on top of ribs. Add a few chopped tomatoes if desired. Cook for 2

2 pound sauerkraut, drained
1/2 t. caraway seeds [optional]
1 can kidney or red beans
4 smoked ham hocks
2 quarts of water

Boil meat for 1/2 hour. Add sauerkraut, beans, onion and seasonings; simmer for 1 1/2 hours or until meat is very tender. Thicken with the following.

Melt 3 T. lard or oil in a large skillet. Stir in 3 T. flour, simmer until mixture browns. Add some of the sauerkraut juice slowly, mixing until smooth. Pour into soup and bring back to boil for 10 minutes. Take ham hocks and spare ribs out before serving soup and place along side.

PASTRIES/DESERTS

EASY STRUDEL

From Katherine Teresa Gorscak

Dough:
2 Cups Flour
1/2 Cup Oleomargarine
2 Tablespoons Vinegar
1/4 Cup Ice Water
3 Egg yolks

Cut oleo into flour as for pie crust. Add egg yolks, vinegar, and water mixture. Mix well, cover and refrigerate over night or 3 hours. Divide dough into 3 parts. Roll out on floured cloth or board 10 in x 15 in

Cheese Filling:
3 lb Ricotta Cheese
1/2 pint sour cream
1/2 cup sugar
4 egg yolks

Mix ricotta cheese and sour cream. Continue to mix egg yolks and sugar. If needed add 1/4 to 1/3 cup uncooked farina to make thicker. Spread on one end of dough about 3 inches wide and roll until all of the dough is used up (3 Rolls). Bake at 350º for 40 to 45 minutes

LADY LOCKS

From Katherine Gorscak

High cholesterol and lots of calories but a favorite at high holidays and special occasions. Makes about 50 or 60 4-inch locks.

Sift together:
3 Cups Flour
¼ Teaspoon SALT
2 Tablespoon Sugar

Beat 3 egg yolks plus 1 cup ice water. Mix into flour mixture. Beat well the above mixtures. Divide dough into 3 parts. Roll each part out. Divide Crisco into 9 parts. Spread Crisco over rolled dough. Fold dough into half and again into half. Then place on floured aluminum foil. Refrigerate 1 or 2 hours. Roll dough out the second time and spread Crisco over the entire dough. Do the same as the first time. Roll out 3rd time and spread Crisco. Fold again and place in aluminum foil. Refrigerate. Roll out ¼ inch thick. Cut into strips about 5 inches long. Wrap around lady lock forms. Bake on cookie sheet at 450 degree until slightly brown. Take off forms when cool.

Filling:
2 cup milk
8 tablespoon corn starch

Cook in saucepan. Let cool. Beat well 2 cup sugar. 2 cup Crisco and 2 teaspoon vanilla.

Add corn starch mixture to the Crisco, sugar and vanilla mixture. Beat well for about 5 minutes and add 4 tablespoon marshmallow cream and beat well. Set in refrigerator (can be made a day ahead). Fill

Lady Locks with a pastry bags.

POTICA (CROATIAN NUT ROLL)

From Janet Catherine Czepiel and Katherine Gorscak

A must for festive occasions and entertaining special guests. The rolls can also be filled with prunes, apples or hazelnuts.

8 Cups sifted flour
1½ cup Luke- warm milk
1/2 cup Luke Warm water
2 package dry yeast
¾ cup sugar
1/3 tsp salt
4 egg yolks
½ cup butter

FILLING

Make the walnut filling the night before so it will be cool when the dough is ready to spread. Mix milk, salt, butter and sugar. Heat slightly until butter melts and sugar is dissolved. Add nuts, and then to stretch mixture, you can fold in beaten egg whites.

The rolls can also be filled with almost anything including prunes, apples, hazelnuts, etc.

2 lbs ground walnuts
2 cups sugar
½ cups butter
4 egg whites beaten
1 pint half and half
2 tsp Vanilla

Back to making the dough, Stir yeast into luke warm water, set aside until dissolved. Mix butter, sugar and salt. Add egg yolks, yeast mixture and 2 cup flour. Mix thoroughly. Add remaining flour and turn dough out on a floured surface. Knead until smooth, elastic and does not stick to surface. Place in greased bowl and let rise 1 hour or until in bulk. After it has risen, divide into 4 equal parts. Do not knead. Roll each piece to about 1/8 inch thick.

Place dough on large floured cloth, roll out and stretch until almost paper thin. Spread with walnut filling. Lift edge of cloth and let dough roll up like a jelly roll. Put in a well greased pan. Let rise for 11/2 hours until light as bread. Bake in 250*oven, 1 hour covered and 1 hour uncovered until golden brown. For the last 15 minutes, the heat may be turned up to 275*.

DEVONSHIRE CREAM

From Eva Pisacich
Try it – You'll like it.

1 package Knox Gelatin (heated until gelatin dissolves); cool
¾ cup water; add to gelatin
1 cup sour cream, add to gelatin

Heat the water in microwave until hot, no need to boil gelatin, mix until dissolved.

Beat together until sugar dissolves:

1 cup heavy cream
½ cup sugar
1 teaspoon vanilla

Mix heavy cream with gelatin and sour cream mixture. into mold or bowl.

Doesn't take long to gel, so you don't need a lot of time ahead. Use on cream puffs or scones, serve on fruit.

SOFT CHOCOLATE CHIP COOKIES

From Sarah's mother, Mrs. Williams – a chocolate delicacy

¾ cup brown sugar
¾ cup white sugar
1 cup shortening
2 eggs
One teaspoon baking soda dissolved in 2 teaspoons of hot water
One teaspoon salt
2¼ cup flour
1 teaspoon vanilla
1 cup of walnuts
1 bag of chocolate chips

Beat eggs, and then add sugar and shortening. Add salt and vanilla, then mix. Mix in dissolved baking soda. Add flour and mix. Add chips & nuts and mix. Place heaping teaspoon size portions on baking sheet. Bake at 350 degrees about 10 minutes. Eat while they are still warm.

DUMPCAKE

Phyllis's friend

I can apple/cherry pie filling
1 (20 oz.) can crushed pineapple
½ c chopped walnuts (optional)
½ c coconuts (optional)
1 box yellow cake mix
1 stick butter

Mix first four ingredients to 9x13 inch pan. Sprinkle dry cake mix over fruit and nut mixture. Silver stick of butter and lay out systematically corner to corner. Bake at 350 degrees for 45 minutes or until golden brow

AMERICAN EQUIVALENT
TO CROATIAN FIRST NAMES

NAME	GENDER	AMERICAN EQUIVALENT
Anna	F	Anna
Ante	F	Anthony...very popular on the Dalmatian
Anica	F	Anna...a nickname like "little Annie"
Antonija	F	Antonia
Antun	M	Anthony...popular around Zagreb
Anita	F	as in English
Ana	F	Ann/Anna
Bosko	M	short for Bozidar, also Bozo, which is Theodore
Bara	F	Barbara
Blaz	M	Blaise
Dejan	M	no English equivalent, but more common among Serbs than Croats
Darko	M	Darius
Dora	F	same as in English
Evic	F	Eve, or "little Evie"...the "ica" o a a nickname of sort.

Fabijan	M	Fabian
Filip	M	Philip
Franciska	F	Frances, female
Franjo	M	Francis/Frank, male
Ivan	M	John, Proper form
Ivanka	F	Joanne/Joanna/Janet…a feminine form of John
Ivica	M	male nickname for Ivan, which means John or Johnny
Ivo	M	another form of Ivan, John
Janica	F	derivative of Jana, another way to say Anna/Ana
Josip	M	Joseph
Joza	M	nickname for Joseph
Jurek	M	nickname for Juro, which means George
Jelena	F	Helen
Jelica	F	nickname for Helen
Karolina	F	Carolina
Katica	F	Nickname for Katherine/Katarina… like Kathy
Klaudija	F	Claudia
Krunoslav	M	no English equivalent of which I am aware,
Ksenija	F	Xenia
Klara	F	Clara
Katarina	F	Katherine
Ljubica	F	nickname for Ljuba which can be either English

Lovro	M	Lawrence
Luka	M	Luke
Ljuba	F	same as Ljubica
Mara	F	same as Maura in English
Marica	F	nickname "little Mary"
Marija	F	Mary
Marijana	F	Mary Anne
Marijo	M	Mario
Mario	M	same as above
Mato	M	Matthew
Mihael	M	Michael
Mirko	M	no English equivalent, means "peace maker"
Miro	M	same as Mirko
Miroslav	M	no English equivalent but it means "peaceful Slav"
Manda	F	same as in English, Amanda
Mihaela	F	feminine form of Michael, Michaelina
Nevenka	F	no English equivalent
Nada	F	Hope
Pavao	M	Paul
Senka	F	no English equivalent
Snjezana	F	means "snowy"
Tihomir	M	no English version, means "quiet peace"
Tomislav	M	Thomas
Tamara	F	same as in English
Terezija	F	Theresa

Valent	M	Valentine
Valentin	M	Valentine
Viktorija	F	Victoria
Vlado	M	short for Vladimir, no English equivalent
Vera	F	same as in English
Zdenka	F	no English version
Zeljko	M	no English version
Zvonimir	M	no English version but this name means something close to "bell of peace"…this is the name of the first Croatian King

POSTFACE (EPILOGUE)

This book is the only child of Matthew Perry, artist. It is his creative gift to the ages.

At the outset, there was structure: *The Fourteen Lives of Matt Perry*. This was a product of Matt Perry's logical style. It gave the book itself a semblance of organization.

The remainder—the bulk of the book– is chaotic as is life itself. It holds a mirror to the real world of Matt Perry.

The great strength of this work is the rare combination of a powerful memory for detail and a professional honesty about the hits and misses, the rights and the wrongs, the successes and the failures over a life-time—a span of more than 75 years.

John Rim
10/13/2008

Printed in the United States
134616LV00004B/2/P